ACCLAIM FOR

TRUMPNATION

A revealing attempt to separate Trump the reality from Trump the reality show." —*USA Today*

"Highly entertaining." —*New York Times*

"Never having met O'Brien...I don't presume to know whether he's having fun yet. But I doubt that I'm alone among members of the Fourth Estate in experiencing a twinge of envy." —*New Yorker*

"At the start of his career in hype and carnival barking, the press fawned over Trump; he made great copy. It's refreshing that reality has finally crept into the coverage." —*Village Voice*

"An engrossing romp...hilarious...peppered with wit and irony...the perfect base to Trump's acidic persona...an instructive tongue-in-cheek primer for would-be Trumps." —*Publishers Weekly*

"Sarcastic at times, hilarious and irreverent at others, the book demystifies the star of *The Apprentice* as the poor man's rich man and portrays him as a potty-mouthed P. T. Barnum with a bad comb-over." —*Palm Beach Post*

"Entertaining...gets down and dirty...a myth-busting biography." —*Kirkus Reviews*

"Somewhere there is another country, far beyond the pale, known as Bad Taste, and Trump has devoted his life to racing through it and staking as many private claims as possible, pausing only to yodel back to the homeland songs of himself."
—Michael Lewis, author of *Liar's Poker* and *Moneyball*

TrumpNation
The Art of Being The Donald

By

TIMOTHY L. O'BRIEN

GRAND CENTRAL
PUBLISHING

NEW YORK   BOSTON

Grand Central Publishing
Hachette Book Group
1290 Avenue of the Americas, New York, NY 10104
grandcentralpublishing.com
twitter.com/grandcentralpub

Originally published in hardcover and ebook by Warner Business Books in
October 2005
First Trade Paperback Edition: June 2016

Grand Central Publishing is a division of Hachette Book Group, Inc. The Grand
Central Publishing name and logo is a trademark of Hachette Book Group, Inc.

The publisher is not responsible for websites (or their content) that are not
owned by the publisher.

The Hachette Speakers Bureau provides a wide range of authors for speaking events. To
find out more, go to www.hachettespeakersbureau.com or call (866) 376-6591.

The Library of Congress has cataloged the hardcover as follows:
O'Brien, Timothy L.
    TrumpNation : the art of being The Donald / Timothy L. O'Brien.—1st ed.
        p.   cm.
    Includes bibliographical references and index.
    ISBN 0-446-57854-1
    1. Trump, Donald, 1946–   2. Businessmen—United States—
Biography.   3. Real estate developers—United States—Biography.
I. Title: Trump Nation.   II. Title.
HC102.5.T78O34   2005
333.73'15'092—dc22

2005015536

ISBN: 978-0-446-69617-3

Printed in the United States of America

RRD-C

10   9   8   7   6   5   4   3   2   1

For my children, Cooper, Jeffrey, and Greta

CONTENTS

*By the way, I can be more presidential than anybody.
I can be more presidential, if I want to be, I can be more
presidential than anybody . . . I would say more presidential,
and I've said this a couple of times, more presidential
than anybody other than the great Abe Lincoln.
He was very presidential, right?*
—DONALD TRUMP,
March 8, 2016

Donald Trump tapped me on my arm as we flew to Los Angeles on his jet and between bites of Oreos confided a little something: "Clint Eastwood is the greatest star ever," he told me. "All those Sergio Leone Westerns. Nobody was cooler."

This wasn't entirely true, I suspected. Deep down inside, Donald has always believed that *he's* the greatest star who has ever existed.

Once upon a time—long before *The Apprentice* and the golf courses and the TRUMP-branded-underwear-vodka-mattresses-steaks-wine-and-who-knows-what-else and the questionable online education venture and the choreographed wrestling farces and the phallic skyscrapers and the sprawling casinos and the boxing matches and the magazine covers and the beauty pageants and the fisticuffs with City Hall and the serial bankruptcies and the bungled real estate deals and the yacht and the airline and the shady, thuggish business partners and the three marriages and the football team and the 2016 presidential race and the size of his Trump junk and the litany of DOPES! and LOSERS! and the guerilla takeover of GOP debates and the flagrant race-baiting and the Great Wall of Mexico and the proposals for deporting eleven million people and the 6.6 million Facebook friends and the seven million Twitter followers and the brawls at political rallies and the flip-flopping on abortion and the punishments for abortions and the nuclear weapons for Japan and South Korea and the white supremacists and Megyn Kelly's menstrual cycle and John McCain's war record and Hillary Clinton getting schlonged and Barack Obama's birth certificate and Mitt Romney's kneeling—Donald set his sights on Hollywood.

When Donald was eighteen he wanted to be a movie producer. He told me that he'd considered attending the University of Southern California to study filmmaking after he graduated from military school in 1964 (several years later he even produced an ill-fated Broadway show, *Paris Is Out*). Inevitably, perhaps, he was drawn instead into his wealthy father's real estate business. Still, Donald's fascination with movies never wavered.

While we watched *Sunset Boulevard* together on yet another flight aboard his jet, Donald leaned in over my shoulder during one of the film's iconic scenes: Gloria Swanson as the silent film star Norma Desmond, bemoaning the arrival of the talkies. "Oh, those idiot producers. Those imbeciles! Haven't they got any eyes? Have they forgotten what a star looks like?" Desmond says. "I'll show them. I'll be up there again! So help me!"

"Is this an incredible scene or what?" whispered Donald, who understands the manic energy needed to constantly challenge and bat down anyone who doubts your star power. "Just incredible."

The vaudeville showman and the superstar are central to Donald's cinematic sense of himself and propel him forward in life, business, politics, and everywhere else. Whether he's bragging to the media about a handful of expensive buildings, firing anxious young entrepreneurs as a reality TV titan, or body-slamming Jeb Bush in pursuit of the White House, Donald doesn't care that deeply about the buildings, the TV show, or the presidency, really. Each of those things is just a prop that he uses to embroider *The Donald Show* with ever more attention.

Donald's need to occupy center stage, enveloped in the warm glow of the spotlight, gazed at, listened to, and retweeted by millions, explains the zany, bespoke cartwheels he keeps turning for all of us. And the guy Donald thinks we—the voters, the viewers, the critics, the fans, the readers, the dumbfounded masses—see when he goes all Sergio Leone on the world? Clint Eastwood, squinting, flipping his poncho over his shoulder to expose his six-shooter, the badass dueling his way through *The Good, the Bad, and the Ugly*. That's who Donald projects whenever he narrows his eyes and scowls for the cameras. Somewhere in the world there is an old, burdened mirror that the Hollywood aspirant has gazed into time after time to practice his Eastwood pose, late at night when no one else can see him.

Donald Trump on *The Apprentice. Photo © NBC.*

Although Clint Eastwood looms large in Donald's imagination, his favorite movie is *Citizen Kane*, and he feels a special connection to that film's director and star as well.

"I loved Orson Welles. He was totally fucked up. He was a total mess. But think of his wives. Think of his hits," Donald told me. "He was like this great genius that after twenty-six, never did it. He became totally impossible. He thought everybody was a moron, everybody was this, everybody was that; if he had a budget he'd exceed it by twenty times and destroy everything. He became impossible. I loved that."

What's not to love about somebody like that?

Somebody like that, channeling Welles, might have launched his signature and never-to-be-replicated-again creation, Trump Tower, when he was only thirty-seven, a tyro who had seemingly lapped his father and dispensed with a history built entirely on his dad's financial support, who was on the cusp of bringing a bunch of banks along on a mammoth and misbegotten shopping spree, who was still the bright and shiny young face of the new New York. It would be easy for somebody like that to look back on his business career today and think of Trump Tower as a high point, his own *Citizen Kane*, and to wonder if the human shingle who survived that mess was the business titan he had wanted to become when he first began his march out of Queens.

But somebody ultimately humbled by those past glories would have to be a little more introspective, less gleeful, more grounded, less effervescent, more disciplined, less unyoked and more rational than somebody who could waltz from his induction in the World Wrestling Entertainment's Hall of Fame and into a landmark presidential bid that had him spinning the Republican Party from his finger like a yo-yo. He'd have to be somebody other than the presidential candidate who, in lieu of releasing his tax returns as proof that some portion of his self-proclaimed billions consisted of real dollars, released a letter from a doctor noting that his "physical strength and stamina are extraordinary" and that he had a good chance of being "the healthiest individual ever elected to the presidency."

There's much to ponder as Mr. Id's candidacy steamrolls past his competitors in this 2016 election season—and as he continues to court his base of frightened, angry, and economically displaced voters on Twitter and Facebook with the same fearmongering and social media savvy that made Father Charles Coughlin a radio sensation during the Great Depression and Joe McCarthy a star chamber draw on TV during the Cold War.

Will Donald's vivid ignorance about foreign affairs make him a little trigger-happy if he comes into possession of the nuclear launch codes? Will his Jurassic grasp of the global economy make him a less than ideal steward of immigration policy and trade agreements? Will his bro-hemian distaste for certain women and his plantation owner's approach to "us" versus "them" leave large swaths of voters disenchanted or disenfranchised? Will Donald's almost pathologic tendency to make up a lot of stuff all of the time catch up with him, or will a significant portion of the media continue interviewing him unarmed with basic facts about his track record?

Maybe Donald knows from experience that many of those harder questions may not get asked.

"One thing I've learned about the press is that they're always hungry for a good story, and the more sensational the better," Donald wrote in his first auto-hagiography, *The Art of the Deal*. "The point is that if you are a little different, or a little outrageous, or if you do things that are bold or controversial, the press is going to write about you."

In the spirit of full disclosure, I used to be a writer Donald cultivated. Today, well, not so much. In recent months he has called me "a whack job, a total nut job." He's also described me in multiple Twitter posts as a "real loser," a "really stupid talking head," "dopey," and a "dumb guy with no clue."

Donald's distaste took on its most public form in the shape of a $5 billion libel lawsuit he filed against me and my publisher a decade ago after publication of the biography you're now holding in your hands.

I first met Donald in 1996 when I was writing a book about gambling, *Bad Bet*. I spent a lot of time with him several years later as a *New York Times* reporter. This book you're reading, *Trump-Nation*, required even more time together, and Donald and I talked in depth about his life and times in the various moon palaces he calls home, as well as in his office, his car, his plane, and other Trumpalicious venues.

In the end, Donald wasn't happy with the portrait you'll encounter in the following pages of this book—particularly a few pages that tried to pin down the real parameters of the Trump fortune. That exercise prompted Donald to take me to court on the proposition that my skepticism about his wealth had damaged his ability to be the world's most famous dealmaker. Donald also recently told the *Washington Post* that he simply filed the lawsuit to try to make my life "miserable," so maybe there was something else motivating him.

As my lawyers tried to separate fact from fiction during the suit, Donald slowed things down by initially refusing to hand over unredacted versions of his tax returns and other financial documents we had requested as proof of his riches (the court ultimately required him to provide the documents, but all of that good stuff was sealed, alas). Although Donald had given me estimates of his wealth at the time that ranged from $1.7 billion to $6 billion, sources close to him said his fortune then might have been closer to $150 million to $250 million. Donald had little use for those lower estimates.

"You can go ahead and speak to guys who have four-hundred-pound wives at home who are jealous of me," he offered, "but the guys who really know me know I'm a great builder."

Donald's lawsuit was eventually tossed out of court. During Donald's deposition in the case, my lawyers questioned him about a Deutsche Bank assessment that pegged his fortune at around $788 million. He said the bank's estimate was "ridiculous."

Have you "always been completely truthful in your public statements about your net worth?" my attorneys also asked Donald. "I try," he responded, before advising that he tallied his wealth based on his "attitudes" and "feelings." Later in the deposition, Donald advised that "even my own feelings affect my value to myself."

So here we are now, as a nation, forced to figure out daily how all of us can help the likely Republican presidential nominee explore how his own feelings affect his value to himself.

This little adventure in group therapy is unlikely to end

anytime soon. Sure, some part of it might end, but not all of it, not ever, not when it involves my pal Donald, the Energizer Bunny of the American pop culture landscape.

When Donald launched his presidential bid in the summer of 2015, he wasn't taken very seriously. (He didn't really help himself by boasting during his announcement that he was worth $8.7 billion before proclaiming *just one month later* that his riches had magically grown to $10 billion.)

Sometime during all of that I was invited on TV to discuss the Trump candidacy, and I was asked a version of the question that was in vogue in mid-2015: "Where's the exit ramp for Trump?"

My response was that I thought the whole notion of an exit ramp was sort of a silly, uninformed question, because from Donald's perspective he could afford to hang around for as long as he wanted—and he also wasn't likely to willingly disappear, given that he had only just begun to bathe in a liquid rush of national attention that, for him, was like stumbling onto the Fountain of Youth. Donald was (and still is) running his campaign on a financial shoestring. (Despite assuring the *New York Times* that he had $1 billion in cash on hand to spend when needed, I'll believe he has that kind of cash, or other liquid assets, or marketable securities or whatever sitting around Trump Tower when he starts dumping buckets of it from his window onto Fifth Avenue.)

Donald got to stand in the middle of every presidential debate stage he inhabited, broadcasters were climbing over one another to interview him, and he was having the time of his life. Exit ramps? He wasn't going anywhere. He was running a skeleton campaign on the cheap, which would certainly allow him to hang around until the Iowa caucuses the following February, I said.

Iowa came and went, of course, and media chatter about exit ramps has given way in the spring of 2016 to handwringing about the ugly racial and demographic realities underpinning part of the Trump Phenomenon, a Republican Party at war with itself, and talk about a contested GOP convention in Cleveland in July. Whoosh.

So what might you see hanging alongside Donald's and Clint Eastwood's portraits during a future tour of the Trump White House? An oversized oil painting of Auric Goldfinger, the wealthy, portly Bond villain bent on global domination and control of the world's gold supply.

"I thought Goldfinger was just a great character," Donald told me. "To me he was the best of all the characters. Semibelievable."

As his presidential prospects have grown more concrete, Donald's sense of the kind of megapresident he will be has grown apace. Despite a dearth of foreign policy expertise and advisers whose own bona fides are equally elusive, he tweeted that "I alone can solve" the horrific problems that Islamic terrorism presented. On the domestic front, he reassured all of us, also via Twitter, that "if I win, all of the bad things happening in the U.S. will be rapidly reversed."

Even if Donald isn't his party's nominee, or even if he's the nominee and then he gets throttled in the general election, he's still not going away. In part that's because he's gotten a real taste of a favorite drug he's dipped into in the past but has never fully experienced until now: full-on, nonstop international attention. Donald has been busily and successfully building his audience as the author, producer, director, and star of his own, one-man tragicomedy, *The Man Who Would Be President*, and he's reveling in every minute of it. Addicts don't easily break those kinds of habits.

But there's another reason we'll also have to brace ourselves for Donald surfing ubiquitously around our airwaves and the Internet for the foreseeable future. He has won the allegiance of a voting bloc that mainstream political, media, and business institutions overlooked for the better part of a decade: working-class, postindustrial Americans thrown to the ground by the forces of economic globalization and the long, uprooting arm of the 2008 financial crisis. Donald, the reality TV star become a reality presidential contender, has brutally and ham-handedly funneled those voters' fears about immigrant labor and overseas threats into a tight, albeit relatively small, coalition. He is also likely to remain those voters' standard bearer and spokesman for quite some time (so get ready for a Trump talk show on Fox if Donald doesn't snare the White House).

In the meantime, I'll leave you with this book, so you can acquaint yourself more deeply with what it's like to live in *TrumpNation*.

TRUMPNATION

I am the American Dream, supersized version.
—Donald Trump

*"All right," said the Cat; and this time it vanished
quite slowly, beginning with the end of the tail,
and ending with the grin, which remained
some time after the rest of it had gone.*
—Lewis Carroll,
Alice's Adventures in Wonderland

SMOOTH OPERATOR

OUNTING A DAIS ON THE THIRD FLOOR OF MACY'S FLAGSHIP STORE on Herald Square in Manhattan—up past jewelry, cosmetics, and accessories; manicures, pedicures, and activewear—Donald John Trump is in his element.

Several women in black cocktail dresses with plunging necklines are hawking gold-hued, skyscraper-shaped boxes containing Donald's new signature line of men's cologne, Donald Trump: The Fragrance. Macy's touts each little vial of $60 magic as "the uncompromising men's fragrance. Persuasive, commanding, determined. A passion for power. Inspired by the man who demands the best—and achieves it." Estée Lauder, Donald's partner in the fragrance venture, discloses that the cologne's recipe includes a secret "exotic plant" that generates a "green effect with woody undertones, rounded out with peppery accents" and "citrus notes with hints of mint, cucumber and black basil." Topping off all of these scents are "earthy, herbaceous and spicy notes."

When the cologne's marketing campaign launched several weeks earlier, Donald noted in a press release that his partnership with Estée Lauder was "huge." An Estée Lauder executive was slightly more explicit about the Trump scent. "We are confident that men of all ages want to experience part of Trump's passion for taste and luxury," she said. "People want to know him on every level."[1]

And here, on the same New York street corner where Macy's has successfully corralled the middle class for more than a hundred years, shoppers are, indeed, getting a chance to know Donald on every level.

Sade's 1980s standard, "Smooth Operator," pipes away in the background on the sound system. About a hundred people gather amid the shoe racks and the men's suits on Macy's third floor to observe Donald in action. Although the onlookers surround the dais where the fifty-eight-year-old mogul stands, they, too, are surrounded by every manner of Trump paraphernalia. Copies of Donald's new book, *Think Like a Billionaire,* are in full supply, its jacket flap inviting readers in: "It's not good enough to want it. You've got to know how to get it. Real estate titan, bestselling author, and TV star Donald J. Trump is the man to teach you the billionaire mind-set—how to think about money, career skills, and life."

Boxed sets of Trump: The Game are also stacked about, advising potential buyers that "It takes Brains to make millions. It takes Trump to make billions." Another panel of the box, in a nod toward Donald's hit reality show, *The Apprentice,* chirps, "I'm Back and You're Fired!" Standing bolt upright atop some of the same stands holding the books, the games, and the cologne are foot-high dolls wearing bold red ties and blue suits that stoically try to approximate a rather inimitable hairdo. Donald J. Trump 12″ Talking Dolls. "Says 17 Phrases: 'I have no choice but to tell you you're fired.' Plus More!" Press a button on its back and Trump Doll says: "Have an ego. There's nothing wrong with ego."

Donald's main attraction this evening, however, is not his books, his cologne, or his talking dolls—or the bottled water, online business school, Atlantic City casinos, or Manhattan buildings that also bear his name. Instead he is launching yet another branded product, this time a line of men's suits called the Donald J. Trump Signature Collection. Breast pocket inserts in each suit say that the frocks represent "the ultimate achievement in clothing manufacturing" and carry Donald's own seal of approval: "I searched the world to procure the finest imported fabrics. Expert tailors have crafted suits to my rigid specifications. The result is a garment worthy of the Trump name."

Rodney Bullock, a thirty-nine-year-old fashion design student, stands among those at Macy's who are craning their necks for a glimpse of Donald. Bullock says he might consider buying one of the suits.

"He's in the public eye. That's attractive in itself," Bullock observes of Donald. "He's about money. He has a name. He means money. I want to go after that look. People are all here because they want to see the man who's on TV firing people. They want to see if he really exists. Living in a city with millions of people and we're all starstruck. That's what it boils down to."[2]

Gary Brody, co-president of Marcraft, the company that makes the Trump Suits, offers his own interpretation of Donald's bright-tie-dark-suit clothing mojo. "We really wanted to emulate his style. I call it neoclassical. It's power dressing."[3]

Bo Dietl, a private investigator and former NYPD detective who is a fixture on Don Imus's morning radio show and regularly holds court at a legendary East Harlem eatery called Rao's, peels a Trump Suit off a rack. Dietl, who has been a friend of Donald for about twenty years and says he is a partner in the Trump Suits venture, helps one customer, an ex-cop wearing a gray sweatshirt, squeeze into a suit coat.

"Kids are going to wear these suits because they want to be like Donald Trump," says Dietl, who swears casually, frequently, and passionately. "I think Trump will be for Macy's like Martha Stewart is for Kmart and shit. Donald represents success and people want to buy his suits because they think that success will rub off on them."[4]

Donald, as all of his advocates and aficionados here at Macy's know, has tapped into the pinwheeled, deep-pool hankerings of every last John and Jane, every Juan and Juanita, who ever wanted to be somebody in America.

"Donald is a brand," adds Brody. "He really is the face of New York."

Up on the dais, carrying a microphone and accompanied by four male models wearing his new suits, Donald chats up the ratings success of *The Apprentice*, compliments Macy's owners for doing business with him, praises a beautiful woman standing in the crowd directly in front of him, and then sits down like Santa Claus to accommodate signature seekers. Unable to sit still, he jumps to his feet and then does something he claims to detest: Although Donald is a lifelong germ-freak ("I feel much better after I thoroughly wash my hands, which I do as often as possible . . . there is no way, after shaking someone's hand, that I would eat bread. Even walking down the street, as people rush up to shake my hand, I often wonder to myself, why? Why risk catching a cold?"[5]), he begins avidly pumping hands and taking pictures with every shopper who approaches him.

"I think the brand is huge," Donald later tells me about the Trumpification of all that he surveys. "What is it about me that gets Larry King his highest ratings? When sweeps week comes I get a call from every television personality begging me to be on their show.

"If you don't win you can't get away with it. And I win, I win, I always win. In the end I always win, whether it's in golf, whether it's in tennis, whether it's in life, I just always win. And I tell people I always win, because I do.

"I guess to a certain extent it is all about winning when you think about it, and it's about style. It's probably about winning with style.

"A lot of people build a brand and they study it very carefully and every move is calculated. My moves are not calculated. My moves are totally uncalculated. I've got a brand, sometimes despite me. And it's a hot brand."[6]

I HAD WANDERED OVER TO THE MACY'S EVENT ON A DECEMBER EVENING AT the end of 2004 because Donald had invited me. Why he invited me I wasn't entirely sure, other than that he often liked to call and invite me to things, or to complain about how unfairly I treated him in stories I wrote, or to tell me he had seen a story of mine he liked and that I seemed to treat others much more fairly than I treated him. On the *Today* show one morning he told Katie Couric that he thought I was "a total whack job." Not long after that he invited me to fly with him on his jet to see a ballroom renovation at his Palm Beach estate.

On another occasion, after a colleague and I wrote a story about his looming casino bankruptcy, he called to remind me that I'd tried to "extort" an autographed copy of one of his books, *How to Get Rich,* from him for my mother. When I told him that was un-likely since my mom had been dead for about a decade, Donald didn't miss a beat. He immediately began speaking glowingly of his private golf course in Westchester, New York, and suggested that we play a round there together sometime soon.

On still another occasion, when he called me at *The New York Times* from George Steinbrenner's box at Yankee Stadium during the World Series, I mentioned that the cell phone number he was using looked different.

"That's because I'm borrowing someone else's phone," he said.

"That way you don't have to pay for the call, right?" I replied.

"You know me well," he chuckled.

And when I told him about this book he invited me to the Trump Suits premiere, accelerating into high-octane promospeak without blinking. It will be the biggest, the best, the very, the unique, in the whole world, very, very, very, very special, gotta come, it's really amazing, and when you think about it, stupendous, it's another example of how I, and you may not believe this but, really, really fantastic, and it's quite something because, people tell me that it's never been done, just all over the world, the entire world, and really, really something, so unbelievably successful, and I mean really big, like the new golf course I'm building in, and the new building I own in, fantastic, a new standard, and I mean, nobody's seen anything so fabulous, the sheer quality of, so you've really got to be there, man. Okay, man? Are you coming?

A month later Donald would still be talking up Trump Suits. Walking through Trump Tower's lobby on the way to his limousine one evening, he paused by a glass display case containing bottles of Donald Trump: The Fragrance. "You know the suits, the suits are—okay you're gonna kill me for this, I know it," he said, grinning. "But they're best sellers; the best-selling suits in the history of Macy's. They sold like thirty-five in the first week. It's incredible."[7]

Rolling through Manhattan in his limousine, Donald confided that he was nervous about his pending marriage to Slovenian model Melania Knauss, which was just ten days away. "It's all in the hunt and once you get it, it loses some of its energy," he said. "I think competitive, successful men feel that way about women. Don't you agree? Really, don't you agree?"

Gamblers were also uncertain about Donald's third trip to the altar, but being romantics they kept hope alive. The day before the wedding, BetWWTS, a Caribbean bookmaking operation, laid favorable odds that the marriage would last through 2005.

"As has been seen recently with the likes of Brad Pitt and Jennifer Aniston, celebrity marriages are always a good bet to end a bit prematurely and the divorce rate among superstar couples is simply astronomical," said Stuart Doyle, BetWWTS's senior bookie. "While several celebrities can only manage a few months of blissful marriage, history has shown that Trump's past relationships have extended a few years. Despite being an overwhelming favorite to make it through the rest of the year together, there's always a chance that 'The Donald' could tell wife number three 'You're Fired!' at any given moment."[8]

By the time we boarded Donald's private jet—a lushly appointed 727 with gold-hued sinks and gold-fabric seat coverings where he recommended we sit for a lengthy interview on his way to Los Angeles—he told me that he believed his union with Melania would endure. Boxing promoter Don King was also optimistic, later memorializing Donald and Melania's wedding as a "spontaneous combustion of love."[9]

Donald also knew that something special distinguished his union with Melania from his previous marriage to Marla Maples. Marla, he told me, bored him. "I was bored when she was walking down the aisle," Donald said of his wedding with Marla. "I kept thinking: *What the hell am I doing here?* I was so deep into my business stuff I couldn't think of anything else."

Donald said his nuptials with Melania were overdue, that he and his wife-to-be were in sync, and that he was ready to commit. "We've lived together for five years, I owe that to her now," he told me. "I guess we'll know in two years if I'm divorced again." And was he ready to have more children? "Sure, when you're rich you can have as many kids as you want. Being rich makes it easier to have kids."

On board his plane Donald was the consummate host, inviting me to enjoy the view from the cockpit, fetching sandwiches and sodas, asking for advice about the *The Apprentice*, trading gossip about business honchos from Michael Eisner to Harvey Weinstein, Bill Gates, and Richard Branson. Donald was relaxed, funny, courteous, eager to help.

About ninety minutes into the interview, he cut things short. "I need a break . . . have you ever seen *Pulp Fiction*? Do you like it? Let's watch it!" We moved into the plane's central cabin, where he raised the lid on a chest of his favorite movies (his top two are *Citizen Kane* and *Gone with the Wind*). Donald pulled out *Bloodsport*, a 1988 kickboxing movie starring Jean-Claude Van Damme. That, too, was one of his favorites. "It's a little bloody, but it's really fantastic. It's one of those movies you tell your kids not to watch and then you sit down and watch it yourself and you're hooked. It's a great movie. I love it." We elected to watch *Pulp Fiction*.

As *Pulp Fiction* rolled, Donald pulled several bags of potato chips and a sack of Oreos from a cupboard and set them on the table to snack on during the film. He stretched out his legs, began popping Oreos, and smiled—delighting in the dialogue booming from speakers somewhere above our heads, somewhere tens of thousands of feet above the Midwest. "Sam Jackson should have gotten the Oscar for this, not Travolta," Donald mused. "My favorite part is when Sam has his gun out in the diner and he tells the guy to tell his girlfriend to shut up: 'Tell that bitch to be cool! Say: "Bitch be cool!"' I love those lines."

A little bit later Donald tapped me on the arm, sharing a random thought. "Clint Eastwood is the greatest star ever," he said. "All those Sergio Leone Westerns. Nobody was cooler."

DONALD IS, OF COURSE, UBIQUITOUS. HIS GILDED NAME GLEAMS FROM THE facades of skyscrapers and casinos financed with other people's money; his face is plastered on the sides of buses, on the roofs of taxicabs, and across highway billboards; he dispenses wisdom in a string of best sellers, in an eponymous magazine, in radio commentaries, and in countless television appearances; he is a huckster for credit cards, telephones, ice cream, and women's clothing, and, in addition to his suits, he sells branded cuff links, ties, socks, watches, eyewear, and lounge attire. *The Apprentice* attracts millions and millions of viewers each time it airs on television and has spawned a Caribbean cruise where travelers get to mix it up with the *Apprentice* cast. Networks are considering a new soap opera called *Trump Tower* in which *Dynasty*-like conflicts are thrashed out in a well-known Manhattan skyscraper. Thanks to Donald, homemaking doyenne Martha Stewart, fresh from a prison stint for financial improprieties, is about to star in an *Apprentice* knock-off of her very own. Donald is also considering adapting *The Apprentice* as a Broadway musical, and he now has his own star on the Hollywood Walk of Fame. *Access Hollywood* ranked him third on its list of 2004's top ten celebrities, just behind Britney Spears and Beyoncé and ahead of Michael Jackson, Tom Cruise, and Jessica Simpson.

Donald promotes himself by playing tic-tac-toe with live chickens and by frolicking with admirable, self-deprecating élan in a bright yellow polyester suit on *Saturday Night Live*. D. J. Trump has emerged as the P. T. Barnum of the modern business world and he is—ultimately and irretrievably—ours.

Donald does it all. He builds, he borrows, he buys, he collapses, he sells, he loves publicly, he schemes privately, he brags, he tele-advises, he pitches, he cashes in, he loses and loses and he still bounces back. Able to leap tall buildings in a single bound, the self-described billionaire remains somehow elusive—even, he proclaims, to himself.

"If you asked Babe Ruth how he hit home runs, he was unable to tell you," Donald told me in an interview for *The New York Times*. "I do things by instinct."[10]

But throughout all of Donald's ministrations to the American public and to would-be entrepreneurs longing to strike it rich, something's been missing. For about twenty years he's been offering reams of advice in books and interviews about the art of the deal, about surviving at the top, about the art of the comeback, about how to get rich, and about how to think like a billionaire. Yet somehow it all rings hollow. And this is why: Donald knows that if he revealed everything and if everyone followed his advice and actually became billionaires *there would be no money left*. That's right: *There would be no money left*. That would be bad for the economy.

But I think it might be interesting to see what would happen if everybody in America struck it rich. So this book is a field guide to TrumpNation. It is a cookbook of sorts meant for all those who want to make it really, really, really, big and become very, very, very rich.

Each chapter will include challenging but instructive TrumpQuizzes that are secret keys to becoming a billionaire, just like Donald. These quizzes can't be found in any of Donald's own books. That's because he knows that if you were able to unlock the recipe behind all of his highly classified but surefire moneymaking strategies, soon *there would be no money left.*

Your answers to all of *TrumpNation's* TrumpQuizzes should be mailed by the end of the year to: Donald Trump, c/o The Trump Organization, 26th Floor, 725 Fifth Avenue, New York, NY, 10022. Donald will tabulate the results in an ultraprivate, ultrasecure, windowless room in Trump Tower. The reader who has the most correct answers, besides having the secret tools needed to become as fabulously wealthy as Donald, will also get one hundred free passes to the finale of Season Twelve of *The Apprentice* and a copy of *How to Get Rich* signed by my mom.

Now then, let's get started.

TrumpQuiz #1

To become a megabillionaire like Donald, you should:

1) Spend $500 and wear a navy, pin-striped Donald J. Trump Signature Collection suit.
2) Spend $550 and wear a gray, pin-striped Donald J. Trump Signature Collection suit, with a vest.
3) Memorize all the correct moves in Trump: The Game.
4) Watch Clint Eastwood movies.
5) Eat lots of Oreos.
6) Just pretend.
7) Read this book.

CHAPTER ONE

TRUMPTV

The original idea of The Apprentice *came to me while
I was in the Amazon jungle making* Survivor: Amazon,
watching a bunch of ants devour a carcass.
—MARK BURNETT[1]

I N 1948 ALLEN FUNT, A GOOD-HUMORED BALD GUY WITH A VOYEUR'S
love of the absurd, produced a new TV program for American
airwaves. It was called *Candid Microphone*, and every Sunday
night at eight o'clock on ABC it dished up foibles, embarrass-
ments, unlikely scenarios, and gaffes that featured real people responding to unreal setups. A year later the program was renamed
Candid Camera. It was America's first reality TV show.

Funt's crew secretly filmed unwitting people walking into the
middle of bizarre, often hilarious, and relatively harmless situations—a visitor to an old-fashioned Automat would try to buy a
sandwich from a hostile vending machine that talked back; a com-
pact car would suck down oceans of fuel in front of a puzzled gas
station attendant; a bowling ball would return to a confused
bowler with its finger holes missing; dogs tried to pee on moving
fire hydrants.[2]

Candid Camera was unscripted, unrehearsed television, and the only actors were those helping to orchestrate the gags. The show bounced around various networks until finally hitting it big during a seven-year run on CBS in the 1960s. After unknowing participants had been duped, Funt clued in the human guinea pigs with a catchphrase that landed in the popular lexicon: "Smile, you're on *Candid Camera!*" Funt never pushed his stunts to the point of outright humiliation; *Candid Camera*'s premise, and its relatively kitschy innocence, hinged on people laughing at themselves. The show's high jinks made it a prime-time hit, and it thrived for decades after its debut in syndication, specials, and remakes.

However popular *Candid Camera* may have been, though, it represented a genre—with the exception of a few popular shows like *COPS, Real World,* and *America's Funniest Home Videos*—that lay dormant on American prime-time television until the late 1990s. Then, stung by a loss of viewers and watercooler buzz to more innovative, more targeted, and more creatively unshackled cable operators, network television programmers revisited reality. The show that ushered in the new era in network programming debuted in the summer of 2000 on CBS, and it became a ratings powerhouse known as *Survivor*. By stranding contestants in punishing locales and pitting them against one another, *Survivor* attracted about fifty-one million viewers to its first-season finale and spawned a host of sequels and knockoffs including *The Bachelor, American Idol, Fear Factor,* and *The Osbournes*. Although as voyeuristic as any of its predecessors, *Survivor*'s emotional traction was a far cry from the mild sandbox play of *Candid Camera*. It was meant to be provocative, Darwinian, and as riveting as a catty soap opera or a gripping serial novel; *The Most Dangerous Game* on steroids, unfolding weekly in your den, bedroom, and dorm. And *Survivor* was the brainchild of a former British paratrooper, skydiver, scuba diver, Beverly Hills nanny, and used-clothing salesman named Mark Burnett.

Burnett's unusual pedigree included dangerous firefights he was involved in during the British invasion of the Falkland Islands when he was only eighteen years old. "Real stuff," Burnett told *The*

New York Times's television reporter, Bill Carter. "Horrific. But on the other hand, in a sick way, exciting."[3]

After knocking about through a series of jobs in Los Angeles, Burnett's enthusiasm for the hair-raising and the physically challenging coalesced into his first successful TV pitch, *Eco-Challenge*, an outdoor competition show first broadcast in 1995—a show Burnett, who had no television experience, landed on the tube through sheer persistence and that became famous for the episode in which a leech squirmed into one contestant's urethra.[4]

About four years of relentless door knocking, and ample inspiration from British reality shows that were already hits, also preceded *Survivor*'s sale to CBS in 2000. But after Burnett launched *Survivor* into the ratings stratosphere, he had his pick of prime time openings waiting to be filled. His slate would come to include *Combat Missions*, a show featuring former army and navy commandos rescuing hostages; *Destination Space*, an astronaut bake-off in which the winner gets catapulted, like a commando, aboard a rocket to a space station; *The Restaurant*, a behind-the-scenes look at the kitchen and business of a Manhattan bistro, where the chef-owner was a culinary commando; *The Contender*, a reality boxing show co-produced by movie commando and pugilist Sylvester Stallone; and a scripted comedy called, inevitably, *Commando Nanny*.

But the most popular show Burnett produced other than *Survivor* was *The Apprentice*, and the cult status it immediately achieved when it first aired in early 2004 illustrated Burnett's ability to stir up viewers' anxieties—whether about being torn up in the jungle or torn up in the workplace. *The Apprentice* also showed that Burnett, a British immigrant who was the son of factory workers, had a grasp of the personalities that held sway in the American imagination, a sensibility that came straight out of his own experience.

"I came here with nothing, with maybe a hundred bucks in my pocket and had to get a job," Burnett recalled. "And these wealthy people who had made their money themselves, I worked for. It did show me what could be achieved in America, what's possible if you have some vision to take big risks. And I always wanted to do a show that was about entrepreneurialism. It led on, quite frankly, to *The Apprentice*, where a bunch of people, I wasn't sure how many at the time, would vie to be the apprentice of a master of industry. I knew clearly there was only one master who was colorful enough, charismatic enough, who is really a billionaire, was Trump.

"But also, what an intimidating guy to interview with and I thought: 'How about a 13-week televised job interview to be Trump's apprentice, six-figure salary, and be president of one of his companies.' It just clicked."[5]

Burnett, a showman who donned a brown felt Akubra, à la Indiana Jones, reveled in the Trumpster zeitgeist. During his long-gone days of scrambling for a buck selling T-shirts on Venice Beach, Burnett devoured a little tome called *The Art of the Deal*, and he credited its author, Donald, with inspiring his own business ventures.[6]

"He's a regular guy who speaks his mind, who goes against the establishment all the time," Burnett said of Donald. "He's sued New York how many times, and won? This is a brilliant businessman that stands for what is great about our country, what makes America the best country in the world.

"He loves business and loves to orate about business. He always tells me: 'You know where the real jungle is? Manhattan, New York City. That's my jungle and that's the real jungle, Burnett. There's more snakes here and more things that can kill ya here than any jungle in the world.' "[7]

Burnett and Donald met face-to-face for the first time in early 2002, after Burnett asked Donald if he could use the Wollman Skating Rink in Central Park to stage a *Survivor* episode. A year later, with visions of the "Sorcerer's Apprentice" episode from the Disney film *Fantasia* in his head, Burnett decided to pitch Donald on the idea of doing a reality television show together. In early 2003, after preparing spreadsheets and schedules outlining what would become *The Apprentice*, Burnett phoned Donald from his car on his way into Manhattan from the airport. He asked Donald if he had time for a meeting the following week. Donald suggested he come over right away. About forty-five minutes after Burnett arrived at Trump Tower, the two men agreed to try to sell a reality show together to the networks.

Burnett pitched *The Apprentice* to the four major networks and wound up with CBS and NBC as final bidders. Jeff Zucker, a thirty-eight-year-old programming whiz who began his career overseeing a revival of the *Today* show before being given responsibility for all of NBC's television holdings, led the negotiations for the network. Desperate to find a replacement show for *Friends* to anchor the lucrative Thursday-night lineup he and NBC had built around the sitcom, Zucker reeled in *The Apprentice*.

Donald said that ABC missed out on *The Apprentice* because the network tried to get the show cheaply. "What happened is, instead of saying, *Yes, we want to do it*, they started to chisel. Instead of offering the $2 million a show that was necessary to do because of production value—that Mark really wanted and I knew nothing about because I am not in that world, he said you need like $2 million a show—they said, 'We'll give you $1.7 million.' Mark then went to the other networks; they all wanted it. He went to NBC and Jeff Zucker actually locked the group in the room until they signed it.

"They locked the door. They took out a pencil or a pen, made the changes in pencil and a pen. I don't even think there were even lawyers. Like the old days when I used to do real estate deals in Brooklyn. You would be afraid you would lose the deal so you would sit a guy in a room and say, 'Cross off that word.' "[8]

Burnett said that he and his partner had to do a little bit of convincing to get the broadcasting executives to play ball.

"All of the networks wondered if anyone outside New York really cared about Trump and would it work, but I had a track record and I stuck by my guns," Burnett told me. "I believed in the format and I don't think they understood how well Trump would telegraph across the screen—and how his take-no-prisoners approach appealed to people all over the world. So they bought it."[9]

For his part, Zucker said he was determined to snare *The Apprentice* from the get-go, and, like Donald, said that he locked Burnett in a room at NBC and wouldn't let him leave the negotiating table until they had a deal. Zucker also had no doubts about Donald's broader appeal beyond New York.

"I'm a New Yorker, I come from New York, I was aware of Donald and all of the publicity he attracts, and that he was a character, and I knew immediately that I wanted to do the show," Zucker told me. "I was not worried about how well it would play outside of New York. I knew that Donald was universal. He's the quintessential made-in-America story: He's been up, he's been down, he's been back up again."[10]

Although Donald was the inspiration for *The Apprentice*, Burnett was its architect. He brought Donald aboard as executive producer and split international licensing rights and ownership of *The Apprentice* brand with him. Donald made $50,000 an episode to showcase his one-of-a-kind, carnivalesque traits: the High Plains Drifter glower, the eyebrows that wandered around his forehead like fuzzy Slinkies, the bicycle-helmet hairdo, the toughest-guy-in-the-bar swagger, the Day-Glo silk ties, and, above all, his unfailing, spot-on assessments of contestants' strengths and weaknesses—and an unflinching willingness to say exactly what every viewer was already thinking about the ambitious, conniving, befuddled, and aspiring apprentices. Donald, as ringmaster and court jester, was channeling America.

Around all of this, Burnett had a very specific, opéra bouffe narrative in mind. "The philosophy of *Survivor* is to build a world and destroy exactly what you've built for personal gain, and *The Apprentice* is a kingdom: I've taken a castle and a throne, and the king (Trump) is saying, 'Off with your head,'" Burnett noted. Contestants, he added, are "so drawn to the horror of being excluded, of being killed, it's magnetic. What's really interesting about these types of shows is they're unpredictable, but in a very familiar setting."[11]

At the time that Burnett hoisted Donald into *The Apprentice*'s firmament, Donald was, more or less, a down-on-his-luck real estate promoter with a failing casino company whose mantra and appetites appeared to be stuck in a Reagan-era time warp. The Cheshire Cat of the business world, Donald had watched many of the assets he assembled a decade earlier evaporate around him until all that was left was a mesmeric, well-known name. He had morphed into "Trump," the human marquee. But *The Apprentice* rescued him from all of that.

Season One of *The Apprentice* kicked off in bravura, tele-novella fashion with Donald—in his limo! in his chopper!—reintroducing himself to America.

"New York, my city, where the wheels of the global economy never stop turning, a concrete metropolis of unparalleled strength and purpose that drives the business world," he said in the show's introduction as the camera raced across the Hudson River and then swooped and nose-dived around Manhattan's granite-and-glass canyons. "If you're not careful, it can chew you up and spit you out. But if you work hard you can really hit it big. And I mean really big.

"My name is Donald Trump and I'm the largest real estate developer in New York. I own buildings all over the place, model agencies, the Miss Universe Pageant, jetliners, golf courses, casinos, and private resorts like Mar-a-Lago, one of the most spectacular estates anywhere in the world," he added. "But it wasn't always so easy. About thirteen years ago I was in serious trouble. I was billions of dollars in debt. But I fought back and won—big league. I used my brain. I used my negotiating skills. And I worked it all out. Now my company is bigger than it ever was and stronger than it ever was and I'm having more fun than I ever had.

"I've mastered the art of the deal and I've turned the name *Trump* into the highest-quality brand. And as the master I want to pass my knowledge along to somebody else. I'm looking for [pregnant pause] . . . The Apprentice."[12] Cue Olympian music as Donald's helicopter banked steeply, tipping its rotors in a salute to the Big Apple.

Donald's *Apprentice* intro was laced with a number of howlers. By most reasonable measures, for example, Donald was not remotely close to being the largest real estate developer in New York, and his loose collection of cash-poor assets did not approximate the value of what he was juggling at the top of his game in the late 1980s. But *The Apprentice* presented our hero at full, rat-a-tat tilt, and he exploited the opportunity with singular gusto. The show also managed to lend Donald a patina of corporate grandiosity. *The Apprentice*'s woody, dark Fortune 500 boardroom, for example, bore little resemblance to the Trump Organization's actual office space on the twenty-sixth floor of Trump Tower. The real thing was a tad run-down and worn, surprisingly vacant, ornamented with Lucite chandeliers, maroon-velvet chairs, cushy pod furniture, and other decor that smacked of a JFK Airport lounge, circa 1970. The Trump Organization's boardroom on *The Apprentice*, on the other hand, was all shadow, anxiety, and financial power, an inner sanctum where final reckonings occurred.

As *The Apprentice* rolled out its contestants, instantly handicapping them proved irresistible. Troy seemed to be a rube, an unwary lamb quick to the slaughter. Bill had the look and voice of a Chicago Bears fan. How could he win? Kristi was statuesque, well spoken, and aggressive. Maybe. Omarosa was statuesque, well spoken, and aggressive. Maybe. Kwame was smooth, smart, handsome. A shoe-in. And Sam. Gee, Sam looked very wired and springy. Interesting. Amy was polished and confident and blond. Possibly. Nick had a husky voice matched with a Baby Huey face. No way. There was a Rainbow Coalition on the show that included two African Americans, an Asian American woman, college grads, someone who had been in a soft-core porn film, somebody who never made it past high school, women, men, lots of Type A's, and lots of possibilities for conflict and very non-PC infighting. And almost all the instant handicapping (at least mine) proved to be shallow, superficial, and wrong.

Even Donald admitted to having unfounded doubts about the star power of some of his contestants, especially Omarosa Manigault

Stallworth, an African American woman who bared her self-absorption, claws, and accusations of racism to great effect.

"I didn't think she had it. But she was great casting," Donald said of Stallworth. "We didn't know she was the Wicked Witch until the audience found she was the Wicked Witch. We had an idea but you never know how it is going to be picked up."[13]

For some of the contestants, getting on the show was an epiphany. Troy McClain, a thirty-four-year-old with a nascent real estate lending business who emerged as one of the savviest contestants in Season One, grew up in Idaho being encouraged to think small. "I was told if I was anything above a gas station attendant that was doing good," he told me. "But I wanted to get out of that."[14]

After reading *The Art of the Deal* in high school, McClain wrote in his yearbook that he planned to make it his mission to meet Donald one day. When his wife later encouraged him to respond to the first casting call for *The Apprentice* in early 2003, he heeded her advice. He was hardly alone. There were about 215,000 others who wanted a shot with Donald and all of them sent ten-minute audition tapes, along with fairly elaborate personal and job histories, to Burnett's team. McClain made a subsequent cut to a group of eleven thousand who went through face-to-face interviews. In July 2003 he survived another cut to a smaller group of fifty contestants who were flown to Santa Monica and sequestered in a hotel for another ten days' worth of interviews. At the end of that session, McClain was told he was in the final group of sixteen contestants who would get to be on the show; the producers gave him two weeks to tie up loose ends at home before shooting began in New York in September.

Shooting lasted seven weeks, from September to November, and during that time the contestants shared an eight-bedroom, one-bathroom abode and were kept away from outside media. When *The Apprentice* aired the following January it became so popular (the first-season finale would draw twenty-eight million viewers) that NBC executives would later introduce Donald to advertisers as the man who saved their network.

"I just wanted to meet Trump," said Nick Warnock, a twenty-eight-year-old copier salesman who made the Season One cut. "I had read about him all the time and heard about him all the time growing up in Bayonne, New Jersey. He was the people's millionaire to us and he seemed to be somebody who just enjoyed life.

"I was in it for a few laughs and an experience with the Trumpster. I never knew the show was going to be the big monster that it became. None of us knew that."[15]

The first task Donald assigned the apprentices, from the floor of the New York Stock Exchange, was to sell lemonade. It seemed an overly mundane task for the cast of mini moguls. But as an insightful student of the American business scene—my nine-year-old son, Jeffrey—pointed out about that task, lemonade stands are great businesses because "kids will beg their moms to get lemonade." (The core principle behind successful marketing to kiddies.) The guys couldn't sell lemonade, Jeffrey also observed, "because they're men." (The core principle behind many problems.) And the women were able to sell glassfuls of lemonade because, Jeffrey said, "they're using sex-o-wality, like giving their phone numbers and kisses on the cheek." (The core principle behind many other problems.)

Donald wound up agreeing with Jeffrey. Taking stock of the men's Episode One demise, Donald pointed out that "the women proved that sex sells." Hardly the stuff of Harvard Business School case studies, but certainly part of *The Apprentice*'s real-world curriculum. To reward the women who won the lemonade duel, Donald gave the group a tour of his fab Trump Tower triplex, a residence that looked as if the high roller's suite at Caesars Palace had been airlifted intact to a perch high above Fifth Avenue. Donald's home was outfitted in sheets of beige-pink marble, mirrored walls, massive chandeliers, an electronically controlled romanesque fountain, and ceiling murals aswarm with Renaissance cherubs. Donald, as good mentor to his thirsty contestants, made it very clear what they could learn from the tour.

"If you're really successful, you'll all live just like this," he promised them.[16]

Jeffrey, watching a DVD of the show at home with me, wasn't sure he wanted to live that way. "It's all richy and everything, but tacky," he said. "It's all gold-ish." But two of the *Apprentice* contestants thought otherwise about Donald's marble nest. Kristi Frank (later fired) described it as "breathtaking," while Tammy Lee (later fired) was beside herself: "Oh my gosh, this is, like, really rich."[17]

For viewers, *The Apprentice*'s payoff, however, was not in seeing the rewards bestowed on winning teams but in witnessing the fate Donald meted out to losers in the boardroom. This was when Donald became unavoidably compelling, as he roasted and toasted the little squibs daring to compete for his favor. And it was from the boardroom that Donald launched his banishment—"You're fired!"—into the larger American vernacular. It was also the venue in which viewers got to see just what a young job hunter might do for a really, really, very, very big job with Donald.

Donald made it clear in that very first boardroom confrontation that hard work alone could never assure anyone of business success. Talent, genetically determined talent, was a prerequisite, and it fell to spring-loaded Sam Solovey to serve as Donald's yes-man on this point.

"You don't believe in the genetic pool?" Donald quizzed Solovey.

"I've got genetic pool big time, Mr. Trump," Solovey responded, his panic rising. "Just like you got from your father, Fred Trump, and your mother, Mary Trump."

Solovey—spooked that the lemonade debacle might end his dream of becoming Donald's apprentice—dropped to the floor outside the boardroom and began crawling around on all fours to relieve his stress. (At this point Jeffrey shouted at the TV: "He's a zombie!") Solovey was spared in Episode One, allowing him to survive into Episode Three and to savor the moment when Donald, once again discarding his fear of germs, deigned to shake his hand.

"That was one of the biggest moments of my life, shaking that man's hand," Solovey panted.[18]

Alas, Donald gave Sam the Man the heave-ho at the end of that very same episode, prompting Solovey to zap Donald with an eerie, Tony Perkins–style staredown that crossed over from thwarted ambition into a whole new realm of restraining straps, ice packs, and long needles—anything at all that might have kept the fired tyro safely at bay. "A lot of people think I'm certifiably insane," Solovey later offered.[19]

Donald—a veteran of military school, Manhattan real estate battles, New York City politics, New Jersey casino shenanigans, proctological media scrutiny, and marriage—had, of course, seen far worse than Solovey.

"I think *The Apprentice* is very, very true to high stakes business," Donald intoned. "I believe that the pressure that you see, that the anxiety, the pain, the joy, the victory, I think it's all true to very high stakes business. And I mean business at the highest level."[20]

Other castoffs were far less postal than Solovey, but equally rattled when the time came for Donald to get rid of them. In Episode Six, Jessie Conners, her eyes as wide as Bambi's, unsuccessfully begged for a reprieve: "Please don't fire me, Mr. Trump." In Episode Eight, Ereka Vetrini, teetering on the brink, also tried to forestall the inevitable: "Don't say it, Mr. Trump."

Jennifer Crisafulli, fired in Episode Four, Season Two, after labeling two griping customers "old Jewish fat ladies," offered the most telling recollection about the sting of Donald's ax: "You don't understand. Your—your—your senses are so heightened, and the moment is so surreal. Let's face it, it's Donald Trump in front of you. You know, live in person, larger than life, saying, 'You're fired,'" Crisafulli said on the *Today* show. "What you don't see is there are little itty-bitty bullets that come flying, invisible bullets, out of his fingers into your chest, and you're like *pu-pu-pu-pu-pu*. And you just, 'Oh.' It was awful. I mean, I got canned last night in front of forty million—twenty—I don't know how many people."[21]

And on *The Apprentice* went, slipping the bonds of predictable business discourse and entering tele-arenas where no-nonsense tycoons like Donald played hardball and a larger corporate fantasyland where every New York minute ticked toward a possible beheading. It was grueling stuff, all those lemonade sales, art openings, casino promotions, flea markets, ad campaigns, charity events, bottled-water sales, and auctions. Court intrigue that snagged a high-spending demographic of college-educated TV viewers and modern Madame Lafarges adored by advertisers, *The Apprentice* sprinted toward its various climaxes. Season One's contestants all became mini celebrities and Oprah Winfrey later presided over a post-season retrospective with Donald and his minions on her TV show, a love-fest briefly disrupted by charges of racism bandied about among the ex-contestants. *The Apprentice*'s plotlines also echoed well beyond the confines of the tube: When Season One contestants had to spend a day wringing money from a competition involving pedicabs, it gave Manhattan pedicabbies a big bounce in their real-world business.[22] A Season Two competition involving Ciao Bella ice cream caused the tiny company's Web site traffic to jump from twelve thousand to one million visitors in one day. Ciao Bella had never advertised on TV before and the day after the show, the thirteen locations selling ice cream featured on *The Apprentice* sold out their entire stock before noon.[23]

Donald sat in judgment during most boardroom showdowns with two other Grand Inquisitors: George Ross, a seventy-six-year-old investor and Brooklyn Law School grad who helped Donald assemble the original Trump Tower and Grand Hyatt sites; and Carolyn Kepcher, thirty-five, who managed two of Donald's golf courses. Ross, a wizened gnome, and Ms. Kepcher, steely and observant, sat at the boardroom table like bookends, calmly offsetting Donald's kinetic, magnetic, drill-sergeant routine as the trio put their stable of contestants through their paces.

"Those [boardroom] sessions were brutal. They went on for two hours and they were just brutal," said Warnock, who was one of the last four aspiring apprentices still in contention by the end of Season One. "I think the appeal of the show is that everyone has struggled in the workplace and everybody can relate to that. It's the ultimate reality show because it's not some thing where people are eating worms. I'd never do that. But everybody's had a job and dealt with a boss."[24]

Only a few weeks into the show, Vegas oddsmakers began taking bets on who would win—as good a measure as any that *The Apprentice* had arrived. Through it all, McClain recalled how surprised he was by some of his competitors' shortcomings as entrepreneurs. "I couldn't believe how much street smarts some of these people lacked," McClain said. "They all talked about their education and their jobs, but they couldn't deliver."[25]

Donald's popularity won him a spot as *Saturday Night Live*'s host and some advice from the comedy show's producer, Lorne Michaels, when Donald quizzed him during rehearsals about the nature of stardom.

"Which is bigger, a television star or a movie star?" Donald asked.

"A television star," Donald recalled Michaels replying. "Because you are on in front of thirty million people, every week, virtually every week. Whereas a movie star, if you do a big movie, a $100 million movie, which is a big movie at $10 a head, that is ten million people once a year or maybe twice a year."

"I never thought of it that way," Donald said.

"But every movie star wants to be a television star and every television star wants to be a movie star," Michaels added.

"You know, Lorne, it won't always be this way," Donald mused. "Someday NBC will call me and say, 'Donald, the ratings are no good and we are going to have to cancel.'"

"No, Donald, there is only one difference," Michaels replied. "They won't even call."

Donald later recounted the conversation with a broad smile, relishing how Michaels ended it: "He looked at me with a face that has seen the world before, and knows television better than anybody. He looks at me, and says: 'No, Donald, there is only one difference. They won't even call.' Which I love. They'll say: 'Fuck him, it's over.' "[26]

And Donald continued to be surprised by the mercurial, flash-in-the-pan nature of tele-stardom.

"I would have never thought that Omarosa was a star," he said to me. "I didn't think she was that attractive. I didn't think she was anything. And she became a star. And Sam—who would have thought a guy who is five foot four with a fresh mouth—and he's crazy—would be a star?"[27]

In the end Bill Rancic (architect of the victorious strategy on *The Apprentice*'s legendary pedicab episode) triumphed in Season One by eclipsing Kwame Jackson, who had been undermined by his rubbery inability to rein in the scheming, self-absorbed, and deceitful Omarosa Manigault Stallworth. Oh, the humanity.

Jeffrey thought Jackson should have been the victor, but Jeffrey, a sentimentalist, is no Donald. And Donald, quite correctly, fired Jackson and anointed Rancic—who was much more decisive and on top of things than Jackson—as Apprentice Numero Uno.

The Apprentice hauled in advertising rates of about $287,000 for each thirty-second commercial spot,[28] helping to pay Rancic's $250,000 salary at the Trump Organization, which NBC, not Donald, footed. (Boosted by Season One's popularity, NBC charged an average of about $431,000 for a thirty-second ad during Season Two, allowing the network to pull in about $106 million in advertising revenue between September and November alone.[29])

As victor, Rancic chose to go to Chicago to help Donald complete a new skyscraper he was building there. At the time, financing for the project was up in the air because Donald's partner, Hollinger International, was swamped in a corporate scandal and withdrew. Donald, whose own cash position was squeezed by ongoing casino woes at his Atlantic City properties, said he was prepared to make up Hollinger's share himself.

Although Rancic wound up glad-handing and speechifying on Donald's behalf and had no substantive management duties in Chicago, he said he reveled in his new job and was unconcerned about the solidity of Donald's finances. "I'm sure it will work out. It always does with Mr. Trump," he told me. "Sometimes I'll spend half a day in Mr. Trump's office and just watch. It's an incredible business experience."[30]

The Apprentice also benefited from the dexterity with which Burnett and his team whittled down hours upon hours of tape to the starkest emotional quotient and then layered bits of artifice on top of the "reality." When Donald punted losers from the boardroom, for example, all offered up their own eulogies as they were shooed away from Trump Tower in a taxi, their final interview filmed in the cab's backseat. Once taping stopped, however, the cabs simply turned right around and took the losers back to a hideout, where they were muffled and muzzled until the show had completed production.[31]

The Apprentice's success helped NBC temporarily bandage some of the wounds *Friends*' departure had inflicted, though post-*Friends* airings of *The Apprentice* during its second season saw viewership slump by millions—suggesting that NBC's tele-yuppies had given Donald more than just a leg up in America's affections. Still, *The Apprentice* was a phenomenon, attracting more than sixteen million viewers to its second-season finale. It also gave Donald renewed luster and the cultural clout of a business guru. And in the galactic sprawl of American tele-culture, this meant that *The Apprentice* quickly became part of oddly earnest dialogues at the country's business schools.

David Urban, a marketing professor at Virginia Commonwealth University in Richmond, maintained an online commentary called "Deconstructing the Trump-ster" that analyzed each episode of Season Two. His penetrating analyses came with "lessons learned" that offered such bromides as: "Don't dump on the consumer," and "When in doubt, don't stick out."[32]

Ivana Ma, an *Apprentice* wannabe, ignored Professor Urban's last dictum in Season Two, Episode Thirteen. Finding herself in doubt about the best way to sell candy bars, Ms. Ma decided to drop her skirt and stick her bottom out. This strategy spurred Professor Urban to uncork some constructive criticism on his Web site: "It was a cheap trick that made Ivana look like a dancer in a strip club," he scolded. "Even worse, she only sold one candy bar with this lame scheme."

Other business school professors decided to directly adopt *The Apprentice* into their students' course work.

"I really started getting into it because students were bringing it up in class," said Matthew Will, a finance professor at the University of Indianapolis who used *The Apprentice* as a teaching tool. "When you talk about business in the classroom [Donald's] name is the one that comes up at the beginning and the end, with some Bill Gates thrown in. He knows how to hit our hot buttons."[33]

Aware that frequent appearances in *The Apprentice*'s boardroom were unhealthy for the unwary or the incompetent, and that you could work with other participants to maneuver unwitting contestants into that space, Season Two combatants turned their bake-off into a catty, clawing *Lord of the Flies* rerun.

Pamela Day—with Wharton, Harvard Business School, investment banking, and a software start-up stamped on her résumé—roared into the second season as an obvious Donald favorite, sprinkling the F-word throughout her on-camera sentences almost as frequently as he did off camera. Day was a tough competitor, and everyone playing against her knew it; they all looked for opportunities to get rid of her, and she spent little time trying to ingratiate herself with any of them. Bam. By Episode Five, Day was toast, set up by her own teammates to take the boardroom hit for the mispriced sponges—yes, sponges—that their team was forced to peddle on a home shopping channel. (Day's pre-season entreaty to the show's producers to make the tasks more complicated than Season One— "I hope we're going to do something a little bit more strategic.

I hope we're going to use our brains a little bit"[34]—apparently fell on deaf ears.)

Day's compadres took their sponge trafficking seriously, however. In a nasty boardroom confrontation, Stacy Rotner (thankfully punted from the show two episodes later) took a moment to warn Donald about the dire perils of ill-considered sponge-ing: "If you want another Enron on your hands, Mr. Trump, here's Pamela." Oh no! Another Enron! The tragic, messy sponge affair led Donald and Kepcher to convey a crucial business lesson to Episode Five participants: You really have to think hard about how much you charge for something.

Of course, any workplace actually run like the operation Donald presided over in Season Two would have devolved into a dysfunctional compost pile. "You don't solve problems by simply firing people," said David Cadden, a management professor at Quinnipiac University in Hamden, Connecticut. "I think the notion that somebody's got to get it from an all-knowing CEO emanates from this glorification of the CEO that we've all embraced over the last decade."[35]

But *The Apprentice*'s incessant shark baiting was exactly what made the show captivating, loopy, outré television. It was deliciously voyeuristic and utterly schizophrenic because it placed aspirants in bush-league, seat-of-your-pants entrepreneurial situations and then rewarded them for maintaining the emotional and psychological facades of good corporate soldiers.

Donald's candor and appeal were integral to *The Apprentice*'s popularity, regardless of the harebrained corners into which the show's plotlines sometimes wandered. Smack dab toward the end of Season One, for instance, Donald had his trainees competing to lure gamblers into Trump Taj Mahal, one of his eponymous Atlantic City haunts, at the very moment that his entire casino operation was lurching toward bankruptcy. No matter. In the end, it always came back to Donald. To be sure, his trainees, all jockeying for the master's attention and a shot at a job with his company, were indispensable parts of the mix—as evidenced when Season Two's cast proved far less appealing than Season One's and the second season became larded with too many shots of Donald in his limo! in his chopper! closing deals on the phone!

Even so, Donald was the glue binding *The Apprentice*'s bloodthirsty, dollar-hungry, nitroglycerin-fueled little world together, and he was well aware of what that meant. When two other high-profile entrepreneurs tried to ape *The Apprentice*'s success by uncorking their own knockoffs on television in the fall of 2004, Donald had little use for them.

"There is something crazy, hot, a phenomenon out there about me but I'm not sure I can define it and I'm not sure I want to," he told me in an interview for *The New York Times* on the eve of Season Two's premiere. "How do you think *The Apprentice* would have done if I wasn't a part of it? There are a lot of imitators now and we'll see how they'll do, but I think they'll crash and burn."[36]

And Donald was right.

Sir Richard Branson, founder of the Virgin Group and owner of recording, airline, and other companies that earned quite a bit more money than the kitten's skein of holdings Donald had woven together, seemed to be a businessman with telegenic brio. A handsome entrepreneur who made a fortune bucking the British establishment, Sir Richard unleashed his show, *The Rebel Billionaire*, on Fox, a TV network owned by Rupert Murdoch, a dour-looking Australian entrepreneur who made his fortune bucking the global establishment.

The Rebel Billionaire (subtitled *Branson's Quest for the Best*) showcased Sir Richard leaping from an airplane, traversing a balance beam connecting two hot-air balloons, and standing on the wings of a soaring biplane as he led a group of entrepreneurs-in-waiting through business school boot camp. Lest the idea be missed, the show was all about risk taking. *The Rebel Billionaire* bombed, failing to draw even a tiny slice of *The Apprentice*'s audience.

After Donald dismissed *The Rebel Billionaire* by saying Sir Richard

had "zero personality," Sir Richard snapped back: "I disagree completely with what Trump stands for and his 10 rules of success. I met
him for dinner once, just the two of us, and he spent the whole
evening telling me how when he was down and out a few years ago
and nearly went bankrupt, people he knew and bankers he dealt
with whom he had thought were friends wouldn't return his calls.
He said he had drawn up a list of 10 of these people and decided to
spend his life trying to destroy them. I told him it was a waste of
energy."[37]

But Sir Richard, fifty-four, also confessed to being something
Donald was most decidedly not: a wallflower. "I used to be relatively shy and I have had to train myself out of it," he admitted. "I
am much more comfortable now in public than I used to be." All
well and good, but wallflowers do not make for compelling hosts
in a medium that rewards the frenetic and dismisses the shy.

Mark Cuban, who purchased the Dallas Mavericks basketball
team for $280 million after parlaying a software start-up and a
perfectly timed dot-com score into what *Forbes* magazine described in 2004 as a $1.3 billion fortune, was not freighted with
Sir Richard's residual shyness. At age forty-five, Cuban was, most
likely, the world's first billionaire to engage in verbose, vast, and
constant blogging. He also had paid his way through college by
teaching disco dancing lessons, relished ripping into NBA officials
and basketball referees from his courtside seat, and bought a $40
million Gulfstream V in an online auction on eBay. Beetle-browed
and as fidgety as a teenager, Cuban preferred communicating with
the media through rapid-fire e-mails and lavished millions of dollars reinvigorating the Mavericks—including recruiting basketball
badboy Dennis Rodman by putting him up in the guest house ad-
jacent to his twenty-four-thousand-square-foot Dallas mansion.[38]
A man the media dubbed "the Cuban Missile Crisis," he also set his
sights on TrumpNation.

In early 2004 Cuban announced that he would star, Donald-like,
in an ABC reality show called *The Benefactor*. Like the hit 1950s TV

show *The Millionaire*, Cuban's program was built around the fantasy of a wealthy patron sprinkling riches on a chosen few. The updated version had contestants performing creative and entrepreneurial tasks that Cuban devised, with the Mavericks owner deciding who made it across the finish line. Cuban planned to fish $1 million out of his own wallet to pay the winner. In the summer of 2004, ABC showed to media critics a promotional clip in which Cuban said it was easier for him to pony up the $1 million than Donald, since Donald's casinos had fallen on hard times. One of Donald's lawyers e-mailed Cuban, threatening to sue him for the remark.[39]

Shortly before Cuban's show debuted, Donald told Jay Leno on *The Tonight Show* that he thought *The Benefactor* would fail. The remarks sent Cuban into a tizzy and he shot back from the electronic ramparts of his "blog maverick" Web site, posting a punctuation-ally challenged note to Donald about how poorly *The Apprentice* would stack up against *The Benefactor*: "The Apprentice's success depended far more on Sam being a goof and Omarosa being a drama queen than anything you did. That's why you kept on bringing them back. The Benefactor's success will depend on how the audience responds to a 2nd grade teacher with satanic like tatoos, a black gay bartender who carries around a picture of Oprah and asks it what Oprah would do, a womens professional football player who wants to kick everyone's ass, a super hot beauty queen, who is far from as innocent as she tries to come across, and 12 others, who are incredibly competitive and realize that for a million dollars, the game is always on."[40]

ABC, aware that viewers were less enamored with these characters than Cuban, pulled the plug on *The Benefactor* shortly into its fall run.

Even after his show was canceled, Cuban kept after Donald. When Donald's casinos nose-dived into bankruptcy in late 2004, Cuban provided hyperlinks to the filings on blog maverick. An entrepreneur scorned, Cuban fired away. "Donald, leave it to you to file bankruptcy and rather than apologizing to shareholders that were wiped out, brag about it being a positive step forward for the company," Cuban wrote in one blog. "Not only are you out of control, you are now out of excuses. You actually have to make this work. You have working capital. You have your self-proclaimed business ability. You have your name on the buildings. Now let's see what you can do Donald. Can you actually make this work?"[41]

Donald was unfazed.

"I don't think either one of them have a television persona. The difference, though, is that Branson thinks he does but he doesn't. And in the Cuban case, it just didn't work. He just doesn't have it for television," Donald said. "If I did Cuban's show, I would have made it successful; if I did Branson's show, it would have been a success. It would have been a success. I say they have no television persona."[42]

The real difference between Donald and Cuban, just like the difference between Donald and Sir Richard, was that Donald was primarily an entertainer who dabbled in business. The other two were primarily businessmen who dabbled, unsuccessfully, in television. On TV, at age fifty-eight, Donald had finally found his métier.

Being in the spotlight was what Donald enjoyed most, what he did best, and, unlike the average businessman, he was willing to do cartwheels to stay there.

"There's something very seductive about being a television star," he said.[43]

Moreover, Donald's *Apprentice* shtick as America's arbiter of business acumen was a singular riff not easily mimicked. Appearing to swim in marble and to live as large as Goldfinger, Donald got suburbanites and city dwellers nationwide to try out for his show, to try to wriggle up next to all of his incandescent star power. Well before this, Donald had even inspired hip-hop artists to memorialize him. One rapper, Raekwon, asked fans to "Guess who's the Black Trump?" Another, Jay-Z, proclaimed himself "the ghetto's answer to Trump."

Donald reveled in his new star status, asserting to me in early

2004 in an interview for *The New York Times* that, "in prime-time television, I'm the highest-paid person."

"You get more than Oprah?" I asked.

"Oprah's not prime time," he retorted.

"You get more than Larry King?"

"Yeah, and Larry King is cable."

More than even the cast of *Friends*? Well, collectively, no, he acknowledged. But individually, yes.[44]

In fact, Donald's $50,000-per-show fee for *The Apprentice*'s debut season did not make him the highest-paid person in prime time. Nor was he anywhere near to clearing the kind of lucre that each *Friends* star took home. But Donald knew what they were making, and he shook the money tree. Before the second season of *The Apprentice* got under way, he told NBC that he wanted $18 million an episode for his future participation. Donald's logic was simple. He was filling very big shoes on Thursday nights: the slot vacated by the six members of the *Friends* cast. The *Friends* stars each made $1.5 million per episode, for a total haul of $9 million per thirty-minute show. As the solo attraction of *The Apprentice*, Donald said, he should be paid $9 million every thirty minutes. Since his show was an hour long, he deserved $18 million a pop.

"That seemed fair," he told *The Wall Street Journal*. "I'm not being totally facetious."[45]

Donald knew he was sitting atop a potential gold mine with *The Apprentice*. The show only cost about $2 million per episode to make, far below the cost of other prime-time fare, and its grosses soared into the multimillions as ad revenue poured in. Donald, never one to patiently develop a business idea or wait around to see what he could rake in, pressed his case. The network ended up paying him "substantially more" than $1.25 million per episode under his new contract, he told me, but he couldn't be specific because the deal was confidential.[46]

This little coin toss with NBC was vintage Donald. Zoom in for the jackpot. Be outrageous in your demands. Keep a straight face.

See what happens. Make a buck as fast as possible. Keep a straight face. Pretend you knew exactly what would happen all along. Keep a straight face.

Yes, it was greedy. Yes, it was tacky. Yes, it was outlandish. It was also funny. It was very funny. Who wouldn't want to be paid $18 million an hour? The least you can do is ask if the opportunity presented itself. So Donald asked.

And every time Donald turned the corporate negotiating process into a theater of the absurd, he rooted himself ever more deeply into the hearts of throngs of Americans—throngs of people everywhere—who dreamed of that moment when they, too, might look across the negotiating table and say, "Hey, give me my $18 million and give it to me now. I just worked a whole hour."

In fact, it was about more than greed. It was love. Those moments when Donald leaped around the corporate merry-go-round like a rabid little kid jacked up on sugar, determined to snatch the brass ring before anybody else got it, were moments when he was authentically passionate. He never really was as passionate about women, hamburgers, Oreos, golf, or the spotlight—all things he relished and adored zeroing in on. But stick a stack of dollars in front of Donald and he sweated.

So if the chance to pounce on a quick deal surfaced, Donald was there. When it became apparent that some business schools had latched on to *The Apprentice*'s verities, Donald decided to open a college of his very own. He applied to the federal government to secure trademark protection for *Trump University*, the name of an institution of higher learning that would offer, according to the application, "on-line courses in the fields of business and real estate."

Although Donald had many vocations throughout his life, teaching was a new calling. His Web site, www.trump.com, promised that Trump University would offer tutelage from Donald and other well-known businesspeople. "In a highly competitive world, the one sure way of being successful is to know everything you can about what you do. . . . And of course you will have the opportunity to learn directly from Donald J. Trump himself. At Trump University you will gain the insight and knowledge you need to get ahead in your career or business," the Web site advised.[47]

Despite the obvious draw of learning from *The Apprentice*'s sorcerer, some folks wondered about Donald's academic credentials.

"It is unclear what position Trump, a graduate of the Wharton School of Finance, will hold at Trump U," wondered editors at The Smoking Gun, who posted Donald's trademark application on their Web site. "Perhaps he can lecture on the importance of having a rich father. Or maybe he could offer a somber Founder's Day reflection on how he actually managed to lose money operating a casino."[48]

The online education industry itself was still working through some kinks. In late 2004 Pennsylvania law enforcement officials sued one online "university" for doling out fake degrees, including a diploma the authorities purchased for a cat named Colby Nolan. After asserting in an application that Colby had experience in babysitting and retail management and paying a $299 fee, the authorities secured an MBA for the cat as well as a bogus transcript with grades and course work.[49]

Despite the fact that some online educators were pumping out cats as graduates, Donald was undeterred and said he intended to be an education pioneer. "Trump University is going to be very big," he told me in early 2005. "It's investment banking and education."[50]

Donald's experimental disposition made him a swashbuckler whom most corporations might not want walking the corridors, and he was perfectly happy not to be a corporate drone. The Trump Organization was a reflection of himself—nimble, engaging, and prone to hype. Although the Trump Organization told *Crain's New York Business* in 2004 that it was the largest privately held company in New York with $10.4 billion in revenue and twenty-two thousand employees—and *Crain's* actually printed those figures[51]—some of *The Apprentice*'s participants wondered, perhaps, if fewer hands were on deck way up there above Fifth Avenue.

Pamela Day, the business maven who met an untimely fate in Season Two, recalled an odd encounter she had with Matt Calamari, the Trump Organization's chief operating officer. Calamari, a hulking, loyal company man with a brush mustache, had worked his way up from being Donald's personal bodyguard into the executive suite—and had earned Donald's undying trust by remaining by the boss's side during the dog days of the early 1990s when Donald's marriage to his first wife, Ivana, was falling apart.

Day said that when *The Apprentice*'s producers told her and other cast members during Season Two that they would get to meet one of Donald's senior executives, she was excited. Up they went to the twenty-sixth floor of Trump Tower, Manhattan at their feet far below. In walked Calamari.

"He said: 'I used to be a security guard and now I'm the COO,'" recalled Day, who underwrote Manhattan real estate deals as an investment banker after graduating from Harvard Business School. "I thought, *What does a real estate company do with a COO?*

"So I said, 'Matt, what do you do here? Is there an org chart?'

"'What's an org chart?'" Day said Calamari responded.

"'Who works here?'" she asked.

Calamari returned with a phone list. Day added that the roster didn't list anyone who was a director of acquisitions, anyone who was a CPA, anyone who was an economist.

"How can a successful company that's this old not have anyone serious doing those jobs?" she asked herself. Deep down inside, she knew the answer to this question. It was because it was Donald's company.

"He's that guy that believes in his own press and drinks his own Kool-Aid and doubles down and then goes bankrupt," she said of Donald. "I didn't associate Trump with financial prudence, though I did associate him with success."[52]

So did most of America. When the final curtain fell on Season Two of *The Apprentice*, the last episode ran for three hours, live, at Lincoln Center—Lincoln Center!—with Donald's face magnified to

Chairman Mao–size proportions on a video screen in Alice Tully Hall. Regis Philbin showed up to help his pal appear presentable in front of 16.9 million people.

Meanwhile *Apprentice* castoffs looked on in dismay, pondering the cruel fates that left them out of the winner's circle.

"I think where the disconnect is, is if you were someone who had really been an entrepreneur you wouldn't be a timid corporate type," said Season One's Solovey, who said he bribed people to let him cut ahead in line during casting calls for *The Apprentice*. "And it's the corporate types who succeed on the show. So you have to ask if the show is about succeeding in corporate America or succeeding as an entrepreneur. I think the show actually rewards corporate behavior, not entrepreneurial behavior."

Solovey also had concern for the great man who shook his hand.

"Donald is going to have trouble going back to his normal life when the show is over because starring in *The Apprentice* is like being on cocaine constantly," said Solovey. "He's going to have a hard time leaving that behind. You can just see it in him. He's got a big ego."[53]

Yes, said Donald, yes I do have an ego. But Donald also had a sense of transition, a sense of the good things that could come with mammoth, ubiquitous celebrity, a sense that maybe he had turned a corner.

"I think that people learned that I'm a nicer person when I did *The Apprentice*. I came across as a nicer person. All I do is fire people all the time and people think I'm a really nice guy," Donald said of his TV exposure. "So it tells you how bad my image must have been prior to making *The Apprentice*."[54]

BEFORE TURNING TO CHAPTER 2 OF *TRUMPNATION*, PLEASE SEE HOW YOU measure up in a new TrumpQuiz. Remember, send your answers to the Trump Organization's Fifth Avenue headquarters. Billions of dollars are at stake. Good luck.

TrumpQuiz #2

To emerge victorious on *The Apprentice,* you should:

1) Let a leech slither up your urethra.
2) Find out before the end of the season whether Donald actually owns any of the projects to which he'll assign you if you win.
3) Grovel.
4) Be extremely innovative and industrious.
5) Pander.
6) When in doubt, don't stick out.
7) Call Donald "Mr. Trump," and mean it.
8) Be smart and be on time.
9) Handle your boardroom grillings like Donald Rumsfeld handles press conferences.
10) Crawl around on all fours whenever necessary.
11) Have a big-time genetic pool.

CHAPTER TWO

TRUMP ROOTS

*My father was the power and the breadwinner, and my mother was
the perfect housewife . . . I was never intimidated by my father,
the way most people were. I stood up to him, and he respected that.
We had a relationship that was almost businesslike.*

—DONALD TRUMP[1]

L IKE SO MANY STRANDS OF A NECKLACE, SOME MORE WORN THAN OTH-
ers and almost all of them marvels of their time, New York
City's bridges have unique identities and their own peculiar
histories. Among the most elegant of them is the Verrazano-
Narrows, a slender, stately crossing that took five years to build and
has a 4,260-foot center span that made it, for a time, the longest
suspension bridge in the world. As a direct link between Staten Island and Brooklyn, and a feeder into Manhattan, its construction
had been pondered and battled over for decades before Robert
Moses, the master planner of post–World War II New York, pressed
the full weight of his public power and finances to the task, plow-
ing through local opposition and upending entire neighborhoods
and traditions to get it built. The Verrazano cost more than $320
million to erect, contained more steel than the Empire State Building, was spun and hung with cable wire lengthy enough to stretch
halfway to the moon, and was anchored by two seventy-story tow-

ers so far apart that the earth's curve had to be considered in their design.[2] But it was built. This was New York.

When the Verrazano officially opened on a rain-swept November afternoon in 1964, Frederick Christ Trump, a successful developer of middle-class housing in Brooklyn and Queens, and his eighteen-year-old son, Donald, attended the dedication ceremony. As Donald would later set the scene, Othmar Ammann, the engineer who designed the Verrazano as well as the George Washington Bridge and was among the most celebrated and well-regarded bridge designers of the twentieth century, stood alone and ignored as the city unveiled his creation.

"The rain was coming down for hours while all these jerks were being introduced and praised," Donald recalled. "But all I'm thinking about is that all these politicians who opposed the bridge are being applauded. Yet, in a corner, just standing there in the rain, is this man, this 85-year-old engineer who came from Sweden and designed this bridge, who poured his heart into it, and nobody even mentioned his name.

"I realized then and there that if you let people treat you how they want, you'll be made a fool," Donald recalled. "I realized then and there something I would never forget: I don't want to be made anybody's sucker."[3]

Ammann—Swiss, not Swedish—was hardly a man ignored or made a fool of in his day.[4] Le Corbusier, for one, had singled out the George Washington Bridge for lavish architectural praise. But Donald's recollection was telling: Someone, somewhere out there was also lying in wait and ready to make a fool of Donald Trump, to get in the way of the things he wanted to do and of the things he wanted to build. For Donald, fighting back and knowing your enemies was more than mere prudence. It was a way of being, even at the tender age of eighteen.

"You know, we live in a vicious world, and oftentimes if you don't say it about yourself, nobody else is going to," Donald told me, pondering Ammann's reticence. "The lesson to me was you might as well tell people how great you are, because nobody else is going to do it."[5]

In a black-and-white *New York Times* photograph of Donald taken about nine years after the Verrazano opened, he is once again standing with his father, but this time the pair are atop a Brooklyn building with Fred's housing project, Trump Village, visible in the background. Just off Ocean Parkway and hard by Coney Island, with the Atlantic Ocean lapping onto the shore and subway trains making aboveground stops, Trump Village was Fred's largest development and a centerpiece of a real estate company that would eventually be valued in the hundreds of millions of dollars. Like most of the developments Fred oversaw, Trump Village was sturdy and efficient, comprising seven nondescript twenty-three-story towers that gave blue-collar workers and the urban middle class a first home or a stopping point on the way to something better.

In the photograph of the Trumps, both men are shot from above and are staring up into the camera with a set of blueprints spread out between them. Neither of them is smiling, and they look every bit the outerborough, first-and-second-generation German builders that they were (Fred and Donald, with a large contingent of Jewish tenants in their buildings, told the press and others for years that the family was originally from Sweden, not Germany[6]). Donald is bundled in an overcoat in the picture, a thick, 1970s tie knotted around his neck, a pile of unkempt, light blond hair spilling around his head. He looks like a kid—no-nonsense, but still a kid—even at twenty-seven. Fred, on the other hand, looks utterly and inexhaustibly formidable. Staring out coolly from beneath a fedora, jaw set, and so in possession of himself that he comfortably sports an outrageous, polka-dot necktie, Fred is all *don't-ever-even-think-of-getting-one-over-on-me* resilience and steel. Shoulder-to-shoulder, father and son occupy a moment that Donald would later recall as a favorite because it was the first time a photograph of him as a businessman ever appeared in a newspaper.[7]

Close to each other their entire lives, Donald and his father were also worlds apart.

By all accounts Fred, who died of Alzheimer's disease in 1999 at the age of ninety-three, was a less flamboyant, less impulsive, and less combative man than his son. Stern, disciplined, devoted to his wife, and quite content to exist far from the spotlight, Fred had pulled himself up by his own bootstraps and had the self-confidence, thick skin, and money to show for it. Despite landing in the middle of high-profile business scandals in the middle of his career, Fred was well regarded within the Brooklyn and Queens nexus of self-made builders, lawyers, vendors, street-smart politicos, and fast-buck boyos who had little use for, or involvement in, the glitter and prices of Manhattan. For the most part they were neighborhood men with deep appetites; ambitious go-getters who divided their time among work, family, and political fund-raisers.

"Fred was dramatically different from Donald," said Jerome Belson, a residential developer and lawyer who was Fred's legal counsel for years. "He was more of a meat-and-potatoes guy. He built one-family houses and six-story buildings that were solid, usual, excellent, and with no particular flair. He was the same as other successful Brooklyn builders of that time. He didn't stand out. He had a superb reputation. You could do it all on a handshake. His word was his bond."[8]

Fred ran his entire business out of a small office in one of his housing projects, at 600 Avenue Z in Brooklyn. Belson, who said he admired both Trumps, recalled that Fred "had a very dry sense of humor and he was all work." Fred was also a survivor. His own father had scratched by as a Seattle boardinghouse owner, then peddled women and booze to Yukon gold miners around the turn of the nineteenth century before finally making a relatively comfortable living investing in Queens real estate. He died when Fred was only thirteen years old.[9] Just two years later Fred and his mother opened a construction business in Queens, with Fred relying on his mother to sign all of the legal papers because he wasn't old enough to do so.[10] Fred started out building one- and two-family homes, financing them on the fly in an era when banks rarely made construction loans to start-up enterprises like his; his earnings supported two siblings and his mother. Armed with a high school education, he spent the following decades patiently expanding his business—building Queens houses in the 1920s and '30s, navy barracks and military apartments during World War II, and large Brooklyn housing blocks for returning soldiers and their families after the war, as well as sniffing out inexpensive properties for sale in foreclosure or bankruptcy—until he ultimately had about twenty-five thousand apartment units under management.

By the time Donald was born on June 14, 1946, Fred was a millionaire. Two years later he began building a mansion for his family in Jamaica Estates, Queens, that over time would expand to nearly two dozen rooms and feature a facade boasting four Georgian columns, each twenty feet high—architectural details that would have appealed to his wife, Mary MacLeod Trump, a Scottish immigrant and homemaker with an affinity for British royal splendor.

"Looking back, I realize now that I got some of my sense of showmanship from my mother," said Donald, whose home decorating impulses as an adult would lean toward Louis XIV on steroids. "She always had a flair for the dramatic and the grand. She was a very traditional housewife, but she also had a sense of the world beyond her. I still remember [her] sitting in front of the television set to watch Queen Elizabeth's coronation and not budging for an entire day. She was just enthralled by the pomp and circumstance, the whole idea of royalty and glamour."[11]

In the mid-1980s Donald, aided and abetted by architectural legend Philip Johnson, contemplated building a sixty-story Manhattan condominium called Trump Castle that featured golden, crenellated turrets on its roof, as well as a moat and a drawbridge. Even Fred, who scoured his construction sites looking for ways to cut costs, sprayed for insects himself to save money, and plucked unused nails from the ground and pocketed them for future use, occasionally indulged in a dose of Anglophilia. Whenever Fred did so, it served a direct business purpose: bestowing a patina of proper British respectability on his middlebrow projects and making them a more appealing sell to prospective tenants and buyers. So some of his apartment houses wound up with names like *Sussex Hall* and *Wexford Hall,* and many of the homes he built had Tudor flourishes.

Fred also embraced flashy public relations early in his career, lofting balloons over Coney Island that contained $50 discount coupons for a $4,990 house, issuing sheafs of press releases extolling the amenities at his projects, billing himself as "Brooklyn's Largest Builder," and maneuvering onto a national best-dressed list alongside Dwight Eisenhower and Winthrop Rockefeller[12]—heady company for a man who lost his father at a young age, never advanced academically beyond high school, and scrambled to make ends meet in his early years.

But Fred eventually started to snare unwanted attention, and a series of public setbacks would make him publicity-averse for the rest of his life.

When Fred began taking aim at New York's booming, post–World War II housing market, most successful builders relied on political connections and large-scale loans if they wanted to make it big. Local politicians helped lay the groundwork by granting zoning variances and land use approvals. They also were conduits to the federal government in Washington, which in turn delivered large mortgage loans, the mother's milk of the building community. As much as Fred was self-made, he never would have become as wealthy as he did without having participated in an innovative public–private construction partnership administered at the time by the Federal Housing Administration. To jump-start efforts to meet a massive and unmet demand for housing, developers submitted building proposals and mortgage applications to the government, the FHA loaned the money, workers got construction jobs, up went apartment complexes and houses, and working-class tenants and buyers got a home. Everybody won. But some, apparently, wanted a little bit more for themselves, and in 1953 Congress launched hearings into possible fraud in the FHA program.

Federal investigators discovered that a former FHA official had approved loans to developers of 285 housing projects that far exceeded construction costs. In exchange for at least $100,000 in kickbacks, the official allowed developers to hang on to about $51 million in excess funds. Fred was subpoenaed to testify before Congress in 1954 about the financing for two of his Brooklyn projects, Shore Haven and Beach Haven. Beach Haven alone included thirty-one buildings (six stories each) and nearly two thousand apartments; it would be Fred's largest development until Trump Village. Although Fred rarely partnered with anyone on his developments, he testified in Washington that he had brought on a brick contractor named William Tomasello as a minority partner in the Beach Haven venture. According to federal investigators, Tomasello had extensive organized-crime ties. According to Fred's testimony in Washington, Tomasello was a ready source of construction funds at a time when Fred said he couldn't secure them elsewhere.[13]

Fred told Congress that he wouldn't have built Beach Haven if he had to invest all of his own money in it because the risk was too great. He also testified that he assessed Beach Haven's projected costs at inflated values and then held on to the extra money the government loaned him—about $4 million. Senators accused Fred of exploiting a loophole and pocketing taxpayer funds, an accusation he denied, claiming that the money was in a Beach Haven bank account and not in his wallet. The politicians also said Fred siphoned off about $1.4 million from Shore Haven accounts that he improperly classified as dividends. Fred, using a defense that other builders deployed, said he was entitled to extra funds left over on his projects as compensation for both the financial risk he bore as a developer and for cost savings he achieved through careful budgeting. But the Senate labeled the testimony of hundreds of builders who appeared before Congress—including Fred—as "outright misrepresentation."[14]

Fred was never charged with any wrongdoing in connection with the hearings, but the FHA subsequently banned him from participating in future projects. Fred avoided the media after the FHA hearings, rarely showing an interest in courting publicity. But several years later his political dealings in Brooklyn would land him in newspapers again.

A pivotal figure in Fred's real estate career was Abraham "Bunny" Lindenbaum, a Brooklyn attorney, fund-raiser, lobbyist, and political macher who enjoyed exceptionally close ties to City Hall. In the early 1960s Lindenbaum was a member of the City Planning Commission, the New York agency responsible for overseeing zoning and land use regulations in a city where fortunes were made and lost in real estate, and his client list was a roster of prominent New York developers—including William Zeckendorf, Peter Sharp, William Kaufman, and Fred. At a September 1961 fund-raising luncheon that Lindenbaum arranged for then Mayor Robert Wagner, most of Lindenbaum's clients, including Fred, pledged money to the Wagner campaign right on the spot. Fred offered to chip in $2,500. When the lunch drew press scrutiny, Wagner initially said he did not know everyone at the meal.

"How can the Mayor deny that he knew the identity of the builders and contractors doing business with the city when Fred Trump, one of the sponsors of the Coney Island housing project, appeared before the Board of Estimate in the Mayor's presence with Lindenbaum as his attorney?" one city official asked reporters the next day.[15]

The ensuing public outcry about the lunch and what was perceived as a seamy mix of politics, money, and access forced Lindenbaum to step down from the City Planning Commission and gave Fred his second lesson in the dangers of overexposure.[16]

Fred's last large development was Trump Village, an urban renewal project that broke ground in 1961 and would include its own shopping center and thirty-seven hundred apartment units when it was completed three years later. Fred, who prided himself on bringing projects in "on time and under budget" (a mantra Donald would later adopt), finished Trump Village eight months ahead of schedule and for $5 million less than its original projected cost of $55 million. But the scale of Trump Village—seven buildings, twenty-three stories each—was far greater than anything Fred had undertaken before. After just two of Trump Village's seven buildings were under way, Fred became overwhelmed by the project's logistics. He only managed to complete the project after securing help from one of New York's premier builders, the HRH Corporation. In the end Trump Village bore Fred's name and he reaped most of the profits from the site, but he didn't build it.

Trump Village was completed in the fall of 1964, at almost exactly the same time that Fred and Donald attended the opening of the Verrazano-Narrows Bridge. A little over a year later Fred found himself in front of another investigative committee, this time a New York State agency probing financial shenanigans at Trump Village. Like Beach Haven, Trump Village was publicly financed, and investigators trotted out familiar charges against Fred: owning a smorgasbord of companies that leased or sold equipment and services to Trump Village for usurious sums, banking excess funds from the mortgage that the state bestowed upon him, and channeling dubious project-related fees to Bunny Lindenbaum. Fred disputed these accusations and was never charged with any wrongdoing. But he left the hearings with his reputation tainted, and he never built another publicly financed property again.[17]

Over the following years, Fred purchased distressed properties, bought thousands of apartments outside New York, tended to his mushrooming fortune, and patrolled his Brooklyn and Queens developments on Saturday and Sunday afternoons in a navy-blue Cadillac with customized license plates bearing his initials, FCT. For his part, Donald, in the years just before the opening of Trump

Tower turned him into a business celebrity, would tool around Manhattan in a chauffeur-driven Cadillac that boasted customized DJT plates. Like father like son, though during Donald's early years the pair often clashed, and as he matured he and Fred became increasingly competitive. Through it all, however, they remained devoted to each other.

"We had a great relationship," Donald said of his father. "He was not an easy guy to have a great relationship. He was a tough guy. But we just had a great relationship."[18]

Donald was the fourth of five children and the second of three boys. Fred and Mary Trump raised their children to respect a dollar. Donald, a golf fanatic, grudgingly had to play at a public course when he was a teenager, and his father refused to buy Donald a pricey baseball mitt, telling his son he had to do chores and earn money to pay for the glove.[19] Still, the Trumps managed to cruise Queens in Rolls-Royces and Cadillacs, hardly standard-issue automobile fare for most New York families.

"Fred Trump used to drive around in this Cadillac stretch limo," recalled Robert Koppel, a neighbor and one of Donald's contemporaries in Queens. "He would always wear a dark suit, like he was a millionaire impersonating a chauffeur. And sometimes you would see Donald riding in the back of the car.

"This was at a time that you wouldn't see that many limos. It was an odd sight to see someone drive their own limo," added Koppel. "Fred Trump was well known in the neighborhood. He was an eccentric."[20]

The Trump clan also followed the power-of-positive-thinking teachings of the Reverend Norman Vincent Peale, who preached at Manhattan's Marble Collegiate Church. Among the Reverend Peale's teaching tools were a radio show, best-selling books, and a magazine featuring inspirational success stories that he targeted at businessmen and published with financial backing from Brooklyn Dodgers owner Branch Rickey and Gannett newspapers founder Frank Gannett. The Reverend Peale later presided over Donald's marriage to Ivana Zelnicek, and as an adult Donald would accentuate the positive, eliminate the negative, latch on to the affirmative, and never mess with Mr. In-Between. "The mind can overcome any obstacle," Donald said. "I never think of the negative."[21]

For his part the Reverend Peale, who died in 1993, had rather unusual insights into the budding entrepreneur's character. Donald, the minister once said, was "kindly and courteous in certain business negotiations and has a profound streak of honest humility."[22]

Donald told me that he grew up in a warm, close-knit household, but that it was also a highly charged, competitive home and his father was often away on construction sites; if the boys wanted time with their father, they joined him on the job (the girls stayed at home with Mom). Summer vacations found the Trump boys collecting rents for their father or lending a hand on one of his projects. Donald's older brother, Fred Jr., wilted under his father's expectations. He frequently quarreled with Fred Sr., decided to become a pilot rather than join the family business, and died of a heart attack and alcoholism at forty-two. "My brother didn't have a hunger for business, and he didn't do well at it," said Donald, who became a nonsmoking teetotaler. "I was devastated when he died."[23]

Donald's younger brother, Robert, followed him into the business and later oversaw his father's real estate portfolio at the end of Fred's life. One sister, Maryanne, became a federal judge. Another, Elizabeth, became an administrative assistant at a bank. In his early years Donald became a serial spitballer. He boasted in *The Art of the Deal* about giving his music teacher a black eye—as a second grader—and he kept his high jinks at a fever pitch right up to junior high school.

"He was a brat," said Donald's sister Maryanne Barry, to whom the developer remained close his entire life. "He admits it. He was on the tough side."[24]

Fred, who once described prepubescent Donald as "rough and wild," was not one to tolerate life's headaches for very long. He shipped Donald off to the New York Military Academy when he was thirteen.

"I was very bad. That's why my parents sent me to a military academy," said Donald. "I was rebellious. Not violent or anything, but I wasn't exactly well behaved. I talked back to my parents and to people in general. Perhaps it was more like bratty behavior, but I certainly wasn't the perfect child."[25]

Military school was a wake-up call for the problem child. "They used to beat the shit out of you; those guys were rough," Donald recalled. "If a guy did today what they did then they'd have them in jail for twenty-five years. They'd get into fights with you.

"They'd go pow! And smack you. And you know, all of the sudden a spoiled kid is saying, 'Yes, sir!' "[26]

Leyland Sturm, a 1957 NYMA graduate, said that no one, regardless of how wealthy his family might be, got an easy ride at the school during Donald's years there.

"Hazing was routine. When you're a plebe up there it's run almost like West Point," said Sturm. "You'd carry the cadets' laundry, shine their shoes, and get leftovers for dinner. There was a lot of hollering in your face and hitting you on your arms."[27]

Colonel Ted Dobias, who was Donald's baseball coach and residential adviser at NYMA, said he was "proud to be associated with" Donald and remembered him as an excellent, disciplined athlete who hit a clutch single to win a championship game one year. He also recalled that Donald had an awareness of appearances.

"He was very conscious of how his uniform looked—he always wanted his shoes to be shiny and he wanted to look sharp," said the colonel. "And boy, did he like to take charge."[28]

After military school, Donald said he became more focused academically and professionally. He spent two years at Fordham University, then transferred to the University of Pennsylvania's Wharton School of Finance, riding out the rock-and-roll era of the late 1960s studying business. Donald said that his time at Wharton transformed him.

"I was a little spoiled because I went to the Wharton School of Finance. And somehow, when you go to Wharton, you don't go back," Donald told me. "It's not a knock at Queens, because I love Queens and I love Brooklyn, I had a lot of good times there. You go to a school like that and you do well at the school and you know, somehow you want to break out of that mold. I think it brought me into a different world.

"I learned more from my father than anyone," Donald added. "He never wanted to come into Manhattan because it wasn't his thing. He was a wonderful negotiator and he couldn't understand how you could buy a foot of land in Brooklyn for 25 cents and yet you had to pay $1,000 for a foot of land in Manhattan. It wasn't his thing and it was the best thing that ever happened to me. If my father came into Manhattan, he would have been successful and you probably wouldn't be talking to me right now. You understand that? In a certain way, I would have been a son of a guy who made money. Making money in Brooklyn isn't the same; it's different."[29]

All of this eventually added up to Donald's break with Queens and Brooklyn, but it would be a long time before he did deals without his father's guidance and financial support. Donald depended on Fred's connections to launch his first deals, and despite any larger aspirations Wharton unleashed in him, he returned home after his graduation in 1968—and he worked there for about five years before he tried to strike out on his own into Manhattan. Fred's days of building big housing projects were well behind him by this point, and Donald's chores were not high end: Other than scrambling to structure a few real estate investments for his father, he said he went door-to-door in Brooklyn collecting rents, often accompanied by thugs who could protect him if tenants got nasty.

Pounding the pavement around projects isn't the stuff of budding billionairedom, and Donald's imagination constantly took him elsewhere.

"My father understood how to build, and I learned a lot from him. I learned about construction, about building. But if I had an edge over my father, it might have been in concepts—the concept of a building," Donald later told *Playboy* magazine. "It also might have been in scope. I would rather sell apartments to billionaires who want to live on Fifth Avenue and 57th Street than sell apartments to people in Brooklyn who are wonderful people but are going to chisel me down because every penny is important.

"You have to be comfortable with what you're doing or you won't be successful," he added. "I used to stand on the other side of the East River and look at Manhattan."[30]

Donald lived in Queens until 1971, when, at the age of twenty-five, he ventured across the East River and moved into Manhattan for the first time. He rented a one-room apartment on the sixteenth floor of 196 East 75th Street, near Third Avenue, and commuted to Brooklyn where he continued to help manage his father's stable of apartments.

"Moving into that apartment was probably more exciting for me than moving, 15 years later, into the top three floors of Trump Tower," Donald wrote in *The Art of the Deal*. "I was a kid from Queens who worked in Brooklyn, and suddenly I had an apartment on the Upper East Side."[31]

For most of America, looking in on New York from the outside through the glass lens of their television sets, Manhattan in the 1970s was *The Odd Couple*'s Manhattan, where Oscar and Felix avoided Central Park because that's where you got mugged; it was *All in the Family*'s Queens, where Archie Bunker dug in his heels; it was *Welcome Back Kotter*'s Brooklyn, where graffiti-laced subways delivered an ethnic hodgepodge of lovable misfits to a gritty high school. For Americans who went to the movies, New York was Gene Hackman busting a heroin ring in *The French Connection;* Robert De Niro stalking a politician in *Taxi Driver.* For Americans reading newspapers, New York was a city on the verge of financial collapse, unraveling amid blackouts and street crime. For Donald, a trust-funder with money to play the club scene, New York in the early to mid-1970s was a great place to get laid.

Donald frequented Studio 54 in the disco's heyday and he said he thought it was paradise. His prowling gear at the time included a burgundy suit with matching patent-leather shoes.

"What went on in Studio 54 will never, ever happen again. First of all, you didn't have AIDS. You didn't have the problems you do have now," he said to me. "I saw things happening there that to this day I have never seen again. I would watch supermodels getting screwed, well-known supermodels getting screwed on a bench in the middle of the room. There were seven of them and each one was getting screwed by a different guy. This was in the middle of the room. Stuff that couldn't happen today because of problems of death.

"You know, it's a whole different world today," he added. "I remember watching Truman Capote dancing with himself in the middle, spinning around. Elizabeth Taylor . . . Halston. Yves Saint Laurent. They had like forty superstars in the room."[32]

Being in the orbit of superstars was no small matter for Donald because his imagination was, and remains, decidedly cinematic. Before heading off to college he was fairly certain that he wanted a career in show business, not real estate. He said he planned to attend the University of Southern California to study filmmaking and had already produced a Broadway show called *Paris Is Out.*

Alas, Hollywood was not to have young Donald.

Just before he left for Fordham, Donald helped a Manhattan entertainment lawyer named Egon Dumler find an apartment and Donald said that the attorney, impressed with the depth of his real estate know-how, convinced him that his talents would be wasted on the West Coast. Donald said the lawyer told him that real estate, not movies, was his calling.

"I thought about it and then I said: 'You know what I'll do? I am going to go into real estate and I am going to put show business into real estate,'" Donald recalled. "'I'll have the best of all worlds.'"[33]

TrumpQuiz #3

To prepare yourself for billionairedom, in your younger years you should:

1) Perfect your hand–eye coordination by shooting spitballs.
2) Decide as a teenager that the world is out to get you.
3) Dodge bullets while collecting rent from pissed-off tenants.
4) Have a wealthy father.
5) Watch famous people and models have sex at legendary nightclubs.
6) Study mathematics and engineering.
7) Have a wealthy father who possesses an enviable list of political contacts.
8) Be kindly and courteous in business negotiations and have a profound streak of honest humility.
9) Have a wealthy father who possesses an enviable list of political contacts and knows how to wring every cent out of a construction project.
10) Get customized license plates.
11) Go to military school where, if you misbehave, the drill sergeant supervising you "smacks you and smacks you hard."
12) Think: *Ziegfeld*. Think: *Spielberg*. Think: *Trump*.
13) Have a wealthy father who possesses an enviable list of political contacts, knows how to wring every cent out of a construction project, and takes you under his wing.
14) Don't mess with Mr. In-Between.

TRUMPCITY

If you can think of any amenity, any extravagance or nicety of life, any
service we haven't mentioned, then it hasn't been invented yet.
—TRUMP TOWER BROCHURE, MID-1980s[1]

BECAUSE NEW YORK IS SUCH A SINGULAR TOWN—SEDUCTIVE, UNPRE-
dictable, challenging, maddening, inventive, abrasive, mon-
eyed, tolerant, explosive, diverse, insular, competitive,
inequitable, gritty, forgiving, intractable, cosmopolitan, and
rewarding—many of those who become famous or influential there
convince themselves that they embody some important part of the
city's character. There are also those—athletes, celebrities, local
politicians, artists, activists, financiers, the guy in Times Square
who plays guitar in his underwear—whom others see as embody-
ing important parts of the city's character.

And then there are those select few who convince themselves
that they embody New York, and whom others also see as personifications of the city. Connecting both sides of the equation for
more than just a camera flash is unusual. It requires a rare marriage
of massive egocentrism with an outré charisma that has staying

power in a city that spawned the notion that everyone on the
planet would be famous, but famous for just fifteen minutes. It also
requires that all that ego and all that audacity match up like clock-
work with broader social needs of the moment. In the 1980s Donald
Trump and Ed Koch were two such people. For that reason, among
many others, they loathed one another.

Both men adored basking in media coverage and both were catapulted into the public eye by forces larger than themselves, as
New York crawled out of the fiscal mess of the 1970s, grappled with
a complicated stew of social issues, and, as the city has always
done, reinvented parts of itself during the following decade.

Koch, who was New York's mayor from 1978 to 1989, identifies
with the city's attractions and foibles and admits to wishing he
were still in the middle of them. And he recalled his ascent to City
Hall, coming at a time when New York's future was up for grabs, in
almost messianic terms.

"I am a very retiring private person, which most people don't
accept when I say that," he said to me, grinning. "But I knew that
if I didn't become bigger than life, so to speak, and be seen as New
York City emerging, New York City returning, the cheerleader, that
we had no hope. And I did it."[2]

Koch, of course, didn't do it alone and had ample help resur-
recting the city's fortunes. In the years before he took office, New
York was sinking beneath a stalled economy, profligate municipal
spending, and $20 billion in public debt it could no longer man-
age. Simply rejiggering taxes or cutting services wasn't going to
make the debt go away, or make it possible to meet payments on it
of about $1 billion a month. Other solutions were needed.

"Do we want people 50 or 100 years from now to look back and
say that we here, today, sat back and allowed this city to die?" fin-
ancier Felix Rohatyn asked in the fall of 1975, as New York teetered
on the brink of insolvency and Gerald Ford's White House compared the city to a "wayward daughter hooked on heroin."[3]

The answer to Rohatyn's question, from New Yorkers at least, was no. Washington thought otherwise, memorialized in a famous *Daily News* headline: FORD TO CITY: DROP DEAD. So in 1975, New York Governor Hugh Carey and Rohatyn jointly orchestrated a bailout of the city's finances with Koch's predecessor as mayor, Abe Beame, who was overwhelmed by events but eager to stave off bankruptcy. In came fiscal discipline and an innovative way to raise fresh funds; out went financial independence for City Hall, leaving Beame and the office he occupied marginalized.

When Koch became mayor, fallout from the 1975 crisis still loomed (and the 1977 electrical blackout was a fresh memory), but he brought far more energy, imagination, and fiscal discipline to City Hall than Beame. Guided by Governor Carey and Rohatyn, and with Washington more willing to extend short-term financial aid to the city, Koch and others continued to clean up New York's finances. Their moves, combined with concessions and financial support from municipal unions and the tailwind provided by a resurgent economy, eventually put the debt crisis to rest—helping to uncork New York's effervescence in the 1980s.

Koch recalled several instances when he realized the city was turning a corner during his mayoralty, among the most memorable being one day in 1980 that he decided against making wage concessions to transit workers, triggering a strike. It was only the subway system's second general strike in its entire history, and because of the city's fiscal crisis transit workers had gone through a long dry spell without wage increases. Koch and the transit union had reached an impasse, which had climaxed in the April subway and bus shutdown. As Koch paced in an upper-floor office of police headquarters early on the morning of the strike, he worried about how badly New Yorkers would react to the city's entire public transportation grid being unavailable to commuters. But as he gazed out a window overlooking the Brooklyn Bridge, he saw tens of thousands of people crossing the bridge to work.

"It clicked in my head. This is our salvation. The people have to walk to work and they are willing to do it," Koch recalled. "I ran

over to the bridges. There was a huge amount of press waiting for
me there. And I rush onto the bridge. And it was like a force had
taken over my body. I am walking on the bridge, people are ap-
plauding: 'Walk over the bridge! Walk over the bridge! I am not going to let these bastards bring us to our knees!' People yelling,
screaming: 'Right on! Keep it up! Don't give in, Mayor!'

"Then, at that very moment, a guy walking a bicycle walks over
to me. 'You're a strikebreaker' [he shouted at me]. And I say to him:
'You're a Whacko!' That became a banner headline in every paper
the next day: KOCH CALLS UNION SUPPORTER A WHACKO."[4]

Koch's later years as mayor would come unwound by hubris,
tattered race relations, and a political scandal, but in the early
days when he lit up the bridges during the transit strike he gave
New York something it desperately needed: emotional liftoff. He
infused this charge with candid, confrontational voltage, and it
was candlepower that only a few other figures in New York at the
time could eclipse. One of them was a thirty-five-year-old developer who, in 1983, completed an East Side high-rise called Trump
Tower.

For Donald, cushioned by his father's wealth, the dog days of
the mid-1970s weighed lightly. The slump, he said, attracted him
because it meant Manhattan was a slumbering, depressed real estate market waiting to be reawakened.

"I worried about the future of New York too, but I can't say it
kept me up nights," he wrote in *The Art of the Deal*. "I'm basically
an optimist, and frankly, I saw the city's trouble as a great opportunity for me. Because I grew up in Queens, I believed, perhaps to
an irrational degree, that Manhattan was always going to be the
best place to live—the center of the world. Whatever troubles the
city might be having in the short term, there was no doubt in my
mind that things had to turn around ultimately. What other city
was going to take New York's place?"[5]

During his Studio 54 phase, Donald had begun to separate
himself from his father's orbit in the outerboroughs and started

looking at prospective deals in Manhattan, courting publicity along the way. On July 30, 1974, Donald landed on the front page of *The New York Times* in a story extolling him as a "major New York builder" (he was only twenty-six years old) who planned to buy a chunk of bankrupted properties for "more than $100 million" (he had no such financing lined up at the time). A year later *Business Week* picked up the ball, taking note of "a young and modish New York real estate operator" named "Don Trump" who, "despite the usual dreary news in Manhattan's depressed industry" had announced grand plans to buy Madison Square Garden and take over three properties made available by the Penn Central railroad bankruptcy: a swath of land along the Hudson River from 59th to 72nd Streets called the West Side Yards; a rail yard at 34th Street; and the old, run-down Commodore Hotel abutting Grand Central Station, a neighborhood so distressed that even the Chrysler Building was in foreclosure.[6]

Donald never got anywhere with the Garden, but he did secure options to develop the Penn Central properties—in part because he was able to trot out the mayor of New York, Abe Beame, for a meeting to impress one of the trustees managing Penn Central's assets. The mayor, a veteran of Brooklyn politics, had a longtime relationship with Fred Trump and had been the city official in charge of monitoring Trump Village's progress when it was originally built. The trustee later recalled Beame telling him at a meeting with the Trumps in the mayor's City Hall office, "Whatever Donald and Fred want, they have my complete backing."[7]

City Hall wasn't the only institution Fred and Donald toured together. Around the same time, Fred also walked his son downtown to Wall Street to meet with Conrad Stephenson, the head of real estate lending at one of New York's most venerable banks, Chase Manhattan.

"I knew that Fred was an important customer of the bank and he said he wanted to bring his son by to meet me," Stephenson told me. "Donald was an aggressive young man from the point of view of thinking he could get whatever he wanted because of the Trump name. He thought that he could just get the bank to give him money because of his father."[8]

Stephenson, who went on to develop a close relationship with Donald, said that Fred was well aware of his son's swagger. In fact, he thought that Fred—who was unfailingly polite and genteel—was secretly proud of Donald's oats. But Fred still sought to reassure Stephenson.

"I know he's moving fast, but I'll keep an eye on him and bring him along," Stephenson recalled Fred telling him as father and son left his office.

Although the *Business Week* story said the Trump family was worth $100 million, citing an "independent estimate" as the source, Penn Central officials valued the Trumps' holdings at $25 million in 1975 and believed that they were entirely under Fred's control. Even the options Donald secured on the Penn Central properties were held by one of Fred's companies.[9]

But the boy was audacious. The city planned to build a convention center on the 34th Street site and needed to buy the Trumps' option to do so. Donald sprang into action.

"Trump told us he was entitled to a $4.4 million commission on the sale according to his contract with Penn Central. But he told us he'd forgo his fee if we would name the convention center after his father—the Fred C. Trump Convention Center," said Peter Solomon, the city official who negotiated with Donald. "After about a month of knocking the idea around, someone finally read the terms of the original Penn Central contract with Trump. He wasn't entitled to anywhere near the money he was claiming. Based on the sales price we had negotiated, his fee was only about $500,000.

"But what really got me was his bravado. I think it was fantastic. It was unbelievable," he added, in a 1980 interview with *The New York Times*. "He almost got us to name the convention center after his father in return for something he never really had to give away. I guess he just thought we would never read the fine print or, by the time we did, the deal to name the building after his father would have been set."[10]

After the Trumps sold their 34th Street option to the city, Donald later let the option on the West Side Yards lapse. But he kept his option on the Commodore, an option he got without putting any money down. The Commodore, named after nineteenth-century railroad magnate Commodore Vanderbilt, was a sedate stone structure of a piece with other buildings in the landmark area around Grand Central. Donald, who equated shiny and spunky with classy, had no intention of being quiet when he overhauled the hotel. Fred loaned him money to hire an architect, and Donald's proposed redesign—all glassy, brassy exuberance—was the first hint that the power-of-positive-thinking had come to Midtown. To finance the hotel's $10 million purchase price, as well as more than $100 million in construction costs, he relied heavily on Fred's connections and deployed his considerable energies to forge new ones of his own.

Ben Lambert, a well-connected New York real estate investor, first met Donald in the 1970s at Le Club, an exclusive Manhattan nightspot that was a crossroads for investment bankers and deal-makers. Shortly after that meeting, Donald called him up and invited him to lunch at the 21 Club, one of Fred's favorite restaurants. Donald had unsuccessfully tried to woo Hyatt Hotels into a partnership with him on the Commodore and he knew that Lambert was close to the Pritzkers, the family who controlled Hyatt.

In a measure of Donald's talent for cultivating business partners when he chose to, he and Lambert would bid on the World Trade Center together a few years later, at a time when he had moved into a swank apartment in Olympic Tower and had begun dating a flashy Czech model named Ivana. But at this first lunch, Lambert initially didn't know what to make of the young wheeler-dealer.

"We got into his limousine, which was really his father's limousine, and he had these big renderings in the backseat of the Commodore," Lambert told me. "He was totally different. He had a flair. He had enormous creative spirit. He had a great deal of energy and incredible focus."[11]

Lambert was swayed. After the lunch he linked up Donald with the Pritzkers and the family, as well as Manufacturers Hanover Bank and Equitable Insurance, joined forces with Donald on the Commodore overhaul. (Fred and the Pritzkers had to guarantee a portion of Donald's loans because the younger Trump still hadn't earned complete credibility with the lending community.) But the most crucial key Donald turned to convince the banks and the hotel company to join him was to get Beame's administration to give his hotel project an outsize package of real estate tax breaks worth $111 million—the first ever given to a commercial property in New York and one that critics described as a sweetheart deal between political cronies.

Donald did little to dissuade people of this notion, including Michael Bailkin, an accomplished urban planner and one of the key officials involved in negotiating the terms of the abatement. "We were riding in his car, he always had a limousine, so we had to go to a meeting, and invariably when we were in the limousine he would get a call from the governor or some other high official," Bailkin recalled of a drive with Donald. "And I always believed that those were fake calls. I don't believe the governor would call him. He was like twenty-four, twenty-five at that time. He appeared to the world to be a rich man's son who was just playing around."[12]

City Hall was already friendly to Donald, and to win support in Albany he recruited Governor Carey's chief fund-raiser, Louise Sunshine, to help him lobby the state to get the tax break. Sunshine's proximity to the governor also extended to his payroll; the governor had given her a part-time job with a state transportation agency. She called Richard Ravitch, one of the state officials who would have to sign off on the abatement, to arrange a meeting with her and Donald. But Ravitch, a scion of the family whose construction company built Trump Village, opposed the abatement. During the meeting he ripped into Sunshine for representing

Donald and the governor at the same time, reducing her to tears. Ravitch offered Donald an alternative to the abatement, one that would still allow him to line up a $70 million mortgage on the Commodore, but the builder wouldn't consider it.

"It would not be fair to deprive the city of the real estate taxes if the hotel was successful," Ravitch told Donald. "But that at least would enable you to get the mortgage."[13]

"That's not good enough, I don't want to pay any taxes," Donald replied, according to Ravitch.

"I don't think that's good public policy," Ravitch responded.

Ravitch recalled that Donald blew up and threatened to have him fired. "I told him to get out of my office," Ravitch recalled. "And I haven't exchanged many words with him since then."

Donald—benefiting from family connections, his own determination, an economically struggling city anxious to get new construction under way, and banks ready to ramp up real estate lending again—ultimately got his tax break; Ravitch was convinced by other members of the Carey administration to sign off on it.

Donald "had the energy and vision and perhaps was hungry enough and maybe a little bit crazy enough to try to do things that were in the best interest of the city, whereas more traditional developers would never have taken on a task like this," said Bailkin, speaking about his decision to get Donald the abatement. "There were a lot of critics of the deal, both inside the administration and outside the administration . . . A lot of those people thought that Donald was all flash and that he would really get the mayor in trouble. And they probably had good reasons to believe that, but we just had a different judgment and I went with my judgment."[14]

When the new Commodore, rechristened the Grand Hyatt, opened up in 1980, it had cost about $120 million to renovate—about $50 million more than its original budget.[15] Fred had to come to Donald's rescue with a loan to help cover the overruns; he also convinced Chase's Stephenson to extend loans to his son to help cover the excesses.[16]

Had the Grand Hyatt failed, Donald would have been financially indebted to his father and others because of the cost overruns. Bankers also might have taken him less seriously on future projects. As it was, Fred got him over the hump, and the hotel was a sensation. Donald had chosen a great location, and the local hotel market was about to reignite on the back of a newly buoyant economy. Moreover, visiting conventioneers, sharing Donald's out-of-towner's love of glitz and sheen, adored the Grand Hyatt.

The lessons Donald learned packaging the Grand Hyatt deal teed him up for the Trump Tower launch, a project that remained his signature success until *The Apprentice* landed in his lap twenty years later.

The turf that Donald acquired for Trump Tower—56th Street and Fifth Avenue—was haute Manhattan, and it symbolized a part of New York as far from Trump Village as was imaginable. It was the ornamented stretch of Fifth Avenue that the old money of the industrial age once chose to call home, a boulevard that began in Edith Wharton's Gramercy Park, where the fault lines of nineteenth-century upper-class mores and exclusion were mapped and then continued past Central Park and some of the world's most important art museums before winding into East Harlem and neighborhoods underpinned by urban survivalism and blight. The 137-room Vanderbilt mansion used to be on Fifth between 57th and 58th Streets until the Bergdorf Goodman store replaced it in 1927. Theodore Roosevelt's teenage home was across the street, and the Rockefeller family once owned a series of homes on 54th Street between Fifth and Sixth.

Vanderbilt and Rockefeller wealth was "old" only in the American sense, where getting yours a generation before the nouveau riche got theirs qualified you as gentry. The roots of Vanderbilt and Rockefeller money—railroads and oil—were just as messy and plebeian as the roots of Fred Trump's much more limited fortune. But the turn-of-the-twentieth-century robber barons spent their funds—often ostentatiously; sometimes generously—to create an architectural vision of a New York where they wanted to live: restrained, European, classical, a place to stroll. It was a stuffy yet public aesthetic far removed from the glimmer, drawbridges, and moats dancing in Donald's imagination, but it was also an aesthetic that had come under assault long before Donald decided to erect Trump Tower.

Skyscrapers and mass-market retailers had been steadily encroaching on this part of Fifth Avenue from the 1920s on, pushing out smaller, more delicate limestone and masonry buildings that once lined the block. Even the Rockefellers themselves helped reorient the architectural standards of the neighborhood when Rockefeller Center opened in the 1930s, fronting Fifth Avenue. But Rockefeller Center and other skyscrapers of its era made use of setbacks to comply with Manhattan zoning laws that envisioned a pedestrian-friendly city rather than streets ribboned with canyons of concrete or glass that blocked out sunlight. Setbacks and caps on height allowed skyscrapers to be built near a street, but not to dominate it. That changed in 1961 when zoning law changes permitted towering skyscrapers; as long as builders provided atriums and other public spaces at ground level, they could add as many floors above as they desired. It changed even more in the 1970s, when the city introduced zoning changes meant to forestall the corporatization of Fifth Avenue. These zoning shifts allowed for bigger buildings in the neighborhood as long as they included residential and retail space along with offices.

But these laws did little to actually preserve the neighborhood's character. Raw height had an overwhelming power of its very own, regardless of how architects configured a skycraper's interior. The World Trade Center, a mixed-use monolith, illustrated this in the Wall Street area. Aristotle Onassis's Olympic Tower, the building Donald called home and a residential behemoth that inspired his own vision for Trump Tower, demonstrated the same point when it opened on 51st Street and Fifth Avenue in 1976.

"Zoning law paid no heed to the deadening effect on the streetscape that a huge, banal slab like Olympic Tower could have," observed architecture critic Paul Goldberger in *The New York Times*. "The building overwhelms Fifth Avenue like an aircraft carrier beside a row of sailboats."[17]

Before construction was completed in 1983, Trump Tower bore every hallmark of being just as smothering as Olympic Tower. It replaced the Bonwit Teller building, a small, handsome art deco structure that abutted and complemented Tiffany, the legendary jewelry store that was a Fifth Avenue landmark. When site preparation for Trump Tower began in 1979, Donald announced his arrival in the neighborhood by destroying two limestone sculptures and other ornamentation that graced Bonwit's facade and that he had promised to donate to the Metropolitan Museum of Art. In a vivid, out-with-the-old-in-with-the-new moment, a construction crew bashed the sculptures into dust in the dead of night. Donald had earlier argued that destroying the artwork was cheaper than preserving it (allowing him to save, at most, about $30,000 on a $201 million construction job). But he blamed the loss of the artwork on undocumented workers he had hired and whom he claimed acted on their own. Donald also said that he needed to raze Bonwits quickly in order to end-run architectural preservationists interested in, of all things, elegance and a legacy, if he had any hope of getting Trump Tower built.

"They were trying to landmark the building when I bought it, and they never saw a building get ripped apart so fast," he told me. "I will never say it was right or wrong, but I can guarantee you one thing: You wouldn't have a sixty-eight-story building there if I didn't [raze Bonwit]. They wanted to landmark the whole building. They wanted to stop me from building."[18]

(In fact, we don't have a sixty-eight-story building now. Trump Tower is only fifty-eight stories tall, but Donald added ten stories to his creation in conversation and on the tower's elevator panels.)

"In the end, my demolition contractor was terrible. He didn't know what he was doing. He was an animal," added Donald. "He could have taken [the artwork] down in a more genteel fashion.

But I was putting a lot of pressure on him to get this fucking building down."[19]

Another omen of the new mojo Donald brought to Fifth Avenue was the lawyer he had chosen to help him navigate Manhattan's back rooms: Roy Cohn. Tan as a catcher's mitt and as whippet-thin as Gollum, Cohn was a power broker who, until his death in 1986, prowled New York with a slippery, lethal pragmatism worthy of any Tolkien creation. Cohn sharpened his skills prosecuting Julius and Ethel Rosenberg for treason and helping Senator Joseph McCarthy round up alleged Communists in the 1950s before he turned his attention to counseling Mafia figures and fixing thorny legal woes that others shied away from handling. He had been sued and acquitted for fraud three times and was disbarred in New York shortly before his death for "particularly reprehensible" conduct.[20] Despite his sharp edges, Cohn engendered fierce loyalty from some, such as talk show host Barbara Walters and Yankees owner George Steinbrenner. Other New Yorkers, such as Ravitch, refused to meet with Cohn or simply left the room whenever he entered. Still others, like playwright Tony Kushner, were more direct in their appraisal; in his Tony Award–winning play, *Angels in America*, one of Kushner's characters fingered Cohn as "the most evil, twisted, vicious bastard ever to snort coke at Studio 54."

Donald, even after Cohn's death, remained a member of the loyalist camp. Cohn "did a very effective job," Donald told me in 1997, the first time we chatted about his lawyer. "I didn't know of his other relationships. You know how many lawyers in New York represent organized-crime figures? Does that mean we're not supposed to use them?"[21]

When Cohn was alive, Donald was known to whip out a picture of the lawyer and ask competitors with whom he was jousting: "Would you rather deal with him?"[22]

"Roy Cohn was a man that if he liked you, he was an unbelievable, loyal friend," Donald told me in 2005, when we spoke again about the role the lawyer played in the developer's career. "Roy was very, very connected . . . unbelievably. And Roy started introducing me to a lot of people. I got to know everybody.

"Roy was brutal, but he was a very loyal guy. He brutalized for you."[23]

Cohn did more for Donald than make introductions. The Justice Department sued Donald and his father in 1973, charging the builders with racial discrimination for refusing to rent to African Americans.[24] No shrinking violets they, Cohn and Donald countersued for $100 million, saying the government was trying to force the Trumps to rent to financially risky tenants. A judge quickly dismissed the countersuit, and two years later Donald signed a settlement in which the Trumps agreed to directly solicit African Americans tenants.[25]

Cohn also orchestrated Donald's political maneuvers and lawsuit against Ed Koch's City Hall that allowed the developer to secure a $26 million tax abatement on Trump Tower. But the lawsuit came later, after a hole had been dug, after tons of concrete had been poured, after a building had been built—after Donald deftly assembled all of the disparate pieces he needed to allow him to stamp his name in two-foot-high bronze letters on Fifth Avenue and begin his star trip into the national consciousness.

"From day one, we set out to sell Trump Tower not just as a beautiful building in a great location but as an event," Donald later recalled. "We positioned ourselves as the only place for a certain kind of very wealthy person to live—the hottest ticket in town. We were selling fantasy."[26]

Trump Tower was Donald's deal in almost every aspect, and he set it in motion independently from his father. When he read in a magazine that the company leasing the Bonwit building was in liquidation, he flew to Nashville to meet with the trustee and came home with an option to buy the lease for $25 million—without having to put a cent down. After newspapers reported the deal, other builders offered the trustee a better price for the lease. Donald threatened to take the trustee to court if he didn't honor his option. (Ever heard of Roy Cohn?) Donald got Bonwit. But Tiffany had air rights above its low-rise building that prevented anything loftier being built next door. Donald convinced Tiffany to sell him its air rights for $5 million. Equitable, the big insurer, owned the land under Bonwit. So Donald reeled in Equitable by giving the company a 50 percent stake in the project in exchange for an investment of about $100 million. Conrad Stephenson, witnessing what Donald had wrought, gave him a $100 million construction loan. Exhale.

There were two outstanding problems: public aversion to Trump Tower's size, which Donald couldn't yet control, and the workers who would pour Trump Tower's concrete, whom organized crime controlled.

Donald said he didn't believe that the city would approve the whole package because his tower would dominate its part of Fifth Avenue. Then on the day that Donald was to meet with city officials, Ada Louise Huxtable, architecture critic of *The New York Times*, called the building's proposed smoked-glass, zigzag design "a dramatically handsome structure." That observation, Donald said, tipped things in his favor.

"*The New York Times* is *The New York Times*, unbelievable power. These guys are sitting there, reading the review as I am going in for my zoning report," Donald told me. "I won three to two. Only three to two. I had no chance of winning, and every time I saw Ada Louise Huxtable, I made the sign of the cross. We totally would not have Trump Tower, or it would have been a thirty-story building or something. Because essentially, she represented establishment, she represented power."[27]

There were other powers Donald had to consider, however. In an unusual move, he built Trump Tower largely with concrete rather than the steel framing used in most modern skyscrapers. The concrete unions, and many of the concrete companies themselves, were mobbed up at the time and could shut a project down anytime they wanted. The city later started its own concrete plant on the West Side in the late 1980s to try to make a dent in the mob's monopoly, to no avail. Ultimately, prison terms did the trick. But when Donald was building Trump Tower, the mob still had full sway. Few people symbolized mob control better than John Cody, head of the union representing concrete truckers. Cody died in 2001 after serving prison terms for racketeering and other crimes, but Donald had to deal with him when he built his dream tower. And Donald said Cody maintained labor peace because he recognized that the builder was one tough customer.

"You know how I dealt with him? I told him to go fuck himself all the time," Donald told me, after asking me if Cody was definitely dead. "If you say it enough, if you say it enough, they go on and go after somebody else. This guy was one psychopathic crazy bastard . . . There was something wrong with him mentally. John Cody was real scum."[28]

Perhaps. But according to Barbara Res, the woman who oversaw the construction of Trump Tower, Donald and his wife Ivana were very friendly with a woman whom everyone associated with the project understood to be Cody's girlfriend. (For readers who need to instantly know more about Ivana, as well as Donald's other loves, please refer to chapter 7 of this guidebook: "TrumpStyle.") Donald sold three sprawling duplexes to Cody's girlfriend and allowed them to be customized, including the installation of an indoor swimming pool. Cody, who was also chummy with Roy Cohn, had his workers strike other construction projects around New York in 1982, a fate that Trump Tower avoided.

Concrete also gave Donald great flexibility in altering the design of Trump Tower even as it was under construction, allowing the builder to put up a new floor every two days—something he never could have done with steel.

"It kind of has to be a ballet and there are no concrete workers like New York concrete workers. Love 'em, hate 'em, they do incredible things," said Ms. Res, who also thought Donald was an unusual boss. "As much as he is with the Miss Universe thing, and with all the models, of all the men I have worked for he's the one who has taken the most interest in a woman's brain. He really cared about what I thought and what I had to say. People are surprised to hear that about him, but it's true."[29]

Indeed, two women, Ivana and Louise Sunshine, played key roles in helping Donald hone the Trump Tower aesthetic and then unleash a whirlwind of publicity around the building. Ivana selected acres of salmon-hued marble for the building's eighty-thousand-square-foot atrium, replete with an indoor, eighty-foot waterfall, and she outfitted Trump Tower's doormen in red military overcoats, gold braid, and black bearskin hats.

"I remember coming back to the city in 1983 and the Grand Hyatt had replaced the old Commodore Hotel and Trump Tower had just opened," recalled TV talk show maestro Regis Philbin. "And I went over to Trump Tower and there was this doorman with this huge fur hat on and I thought: *Who's putting out a doorman like this?* Well, lo and behold, it was the Trumpster! And he had a waterfall inside!

"I brought a camera crew down there right away and that's how we met. That's how I met the Trumpster," Philbin told me. "And let me tell you, he saved Fifth Avenue. It was not in good shape then."[30]

Donald and Sunshine pitched Trump Tower as the cushy choice for a cushy era (homeless people, then beginning to shuffle en masse around the city's streets, need not apply), and the media lionized the boy builder as the new face of Manhattan; the fiscal crisis of just seven years earlier seemed a distant memory. Steven Spielberg, Martina Navratilova, Johnny Carson, Dick Clark, and Sophia Loren lined up to buy some of Donald's 266 luxury condos, which were priced from $500,000 for a small one-bedroom to $5 million for a triplex when they went on sale in late 1982. Donald and Ivana kept a triplex for themselves; it had twenty-nine-foot living room ceilings, a gold-leaf couch and black-silk wallpaper, and a bathroom carved from blue onyx. *New York* magazine, citing a confidential source, wrote that Britain's royal family might bid on a $5 million, twenty-one-room spread in Trump Tower (they never did, but what seemed to be good enough for the royals swiftly became good enough for everyone else).[31]

"I think Donald got everybody's game up in terms of what was possible in building. He raised the bar in terms of quality and design," said Peter Kalikow, a New York developer whose father was also an outerborough builder and a friend of Fred. "He taught us that you needed to make a statement and think about everything from the basement to the roof.

"There was a time when we were all embarrassed to be in the real estate business. Donald really helped make real estate interesting again, and he made it cool to be in New York again—whether the real estate community wanted to recognize that or not. If you take away the hype and the veneer and the bravado, at his core he's a terrific builder."[32]

Trump Tower condo sales alone hauled in a pre-tax total of about $270 million for Donald and Equitable, and the partners told reporters that they each took in another $14 million a year leasing Trump Tower's retail space.[33] The building's forty-eight merchants, some of which paid annual rents as high as $1 million, included crème-de-la-crème outlets such as Charles Jourdan, Buccellati, Ludwig Beck, Harry Winston, and Asprey.

"We were selling bracelets in there for $100,000 and slacks for $1,000, it was just amazing," recalled Res. "It was so popular and was such a destination for high-end stuff. And we charged huge amounts of money for that space."[34]

Guests invited to Trump Tower's opening party received a small cardboard box in the mail. When they opened it, a black helium balloon with silver tinsel floated out, an invitation attached to the tinsel. The party itself featured orchestras playing on three floors of the building's atrium. And Fred was at the party, beaming at the fact that his son had realized his dream.

"Fred was absolutely ecstatic," recalled Jerome Belson, who attended the opening gala. "He said he couldn't have afforded the invitation."[35]

Trump Tower quickly became a major tourist attraction, but some people tried to dampen the party spirit. Sam Roberts, an urban affairs reporter for *The New York Times*, questioned how long retailers would pay sky-high rents at Trump Tower, and how long shoppers would be in a frenzy for a vertical mall (the answer in both cases turned out to be: not very long). Donald dismissed such questions, noting that tens of thousands of tourists passed through his atrium on Saturdays and that the space was always fully locked and loaded with vendors.

Ed Koch also got in the way, deciding two years after he had beaten back striking transit workers that he would stand up to Donald as well. He decided not to grant the developer a tax abatement on Trump Tower.

"The housing commissioner told me, he came in and told me 'We are not going to give him the tax abatement because the law, as written, doesn't require it,'" Koch told me. "I said: 'Good, it's a lot of money. [Trump] has the highest buildings and can make a fortune. It's just wrong to give him the money.' . . . Probably that's when he decided I was not his friend. And he was right."[36]

Donald launched Roy Cohn at Koch, winning the tax abatement after a series of court appeals. "Fuck Ed," said Donald. "Every building was given a tax abatement except me."[37]

Donald's battles with the mayor would escalate in later years and ultimately help undermine his chances of successfully completing a real estate project that perhaps more than any other—even Trump Tower—would have represented a leap beyond his father and Queens. Even so, Donald had already realized a lifelong ambition by traversing the East River and, at the age of thirty-seven, landing on Fifth Avenue like a supernova.

"Even to this day, if you asked me what's my favorite deal, it's always going to be Trump Tower," Donald told me. "Because it was sort of like: *What am I doing here? I have an office in Brooklyn. I am from Queens.*"[38]

Of course, there's a wide gulf between being a great marketer and being a great businessman, and sometimes a building is just a building, no matter how handsomely it's packaged or how often reporters write about it. In 1983, the same year that Donald completed Trump Tower, a real business revolution was afoot far away from Fifth Avenue—a little company called Microsoft announced a new product called Windows; another company called Cisco started a network routing business; Motorola began testing something called a cell phone; and Apple offered the first personal computer with a graphical user interface.

But in those first few years after Trump Tower opened, with casino deals beckoning and a tar pit of massive debt several years away, Donald was one of the most visible embodiments of the 1980s ethos. And he was at the top of his game.

"People might have laughed at the image that Trump gave, but the rest of the world fell for it," said Barbara Corcoran, one of Manhattan's leading real estate brokers. "It was the first recognized superluxury brand in America known outside the United States. He bullshitted about it, but by bullshitting about it, he made it sell. I don't know of anyone who is a better marketer."[39]

BEFORE FURTHER EXAMINING DONALD'S PLACE IN NEW YORK'S REAL ESTATE landscape, please work your way toward a billion-dollar fortune by taking the following quiz.

TrumpQuiz #4

To make the leap from small town to big city you should:

1) **Exchange your pit bull for an infamous lawyer.**
2) **Hold on to your dreams.**
3) **Use marble as if it were wallpaper.**

4) Get "psychopathic, crazy bastards" to work for you, not against you.
5) See an empty corner as a jigsaw puzzle waiting to be assembled.
6) Work harder than everybody else.
7) Abate, abate, abate.
8) Turn a skyscraper into a billboard for your name.
9) Use the word *brutal* as a verb. As in: "Roy brutalized for me."
10) Honor thy father.
11) Post men in furry hats in front of your building. Presto: Buckingham Palace.
12) Court the media and don't tie your tongue.
13) Go on a crusade against a mayor who has to approve development of almost every piece of land you buy.

CHAPTER FOUR

TRUMPLAND

This isn't just a building. It's the ultimate work of art.
I was in love with it . . . I tore myself up to get the Plaza.
—DONALD TRUMP, AFTER BUYING THE PLAZA HOTEL

Piggy, piggy, piggy.
—FORMER NEW YORK MAYOR ED KOCH

LATE IN THE SUMMER OF 1989, THE ROCKEFELLER FAMILY CIRCULATED two leather-bound portfolios to a select group of the world's wealthiest and most highly regarded real estate investors and developers. A Wall Street investment bank oversaw the offering, which quietly found its way to desks in New York, Tokyo, Frankfurt, and elsewhere and invited recipients to bid on Rockefeller Center, one of Manhattan's most legendary properties.

Completed at great financial risk over an eleven-year period starting in 1929, Rockefeller Center was the family's response to the Great Depression and a demonstration of their commitment to New York at a time when the city was swamped in economic despair. An art deco city-within-a-city, Rockefeller Center originally comprised six million square feet of space in fourteen buildings on twelve acres between 48th and 51st Streets and Fifth and Sixth Avenues, all of it completed at a cost of about $135 million in Depression-era dollars—or about $1.7 billion today.[1] The only other private properties in New York that boasted the same name recognition and legacy as Rockefeller Center were the Empire State Building and the Chrysler Building, and the men who dominated global real estate's leading ranks prized all three of them.

The Rockefellers originally leased the land under Rockefeller Center from the owner, Columbia University, but in 1984 they paid Columbia $400 million to buy the sprawling parcel outright, at that time the largest sum ever paid for a single piece of land in Manhattan. Four years later the Rockefellers decided to sell a controlling interest in the company that owned the center, seeking in part to appease an unwieldy collection of extended family members who wanted to cash in or diversify their holdings. So the word went out, bound in leather. But not to Donald.

"The Rockefellers were very careful about who they gave the material to," an individual involved in the sale told two *Manhattan Inc.* writers in 1990. "I don't think the Rockefellers were interested in having it called Trump Center."[2]

Donald, flush with flashy casino companies, a snazzy little airline service, Trump Tower, and a trophy property, the Plaza Hotel, was undoubtedly the most famous real estate developer in the country when the Rockefellers put their center on the auction block. Only six years had passed since Donald completed Trump Tower, but in the interim he had written a best seller, *The Art of the Deal*, engaged in deliciously public squabbles with business competitors and politicians, purchased his own 727 jet and a 282-foot yacht once featured in a James Bond movie, bought a 118-room Palm Beach mansion and an upstart football team, held Atlantic City's dominant gambling hand, was a fixture in gossip pages and on TV talk shows, and offered to broker a nuclear disarmament treaty with Russia. ("Gorby, Donald. Nukes are bad, man, bad.") In short, Donald did the one thing that the famously private and insular members of Manhattan's true real estate elite abhorred: He made a spectacle of himself.

Real estate in New York is a locus of commercial power, political influence, and social leverage (finance and media being the other two), and builders have shaped the city's character in much the same way that oil barons have shaped Houston and dreamweavers have shaped Hollywood. Unlike Texas oil wealth and California movie money, however, Manhattan's real estate establishment frowns on gaudy displays of affluence and public boasting. New York real estate money moves behind the scenes, endowing hospitals, universities, and art museums; handpicking senators, governors, and mayors; sponsoring charity balls and private auctions; scrambling for an edge on convoluted, complex deals; and whispering over the telephone about a hard-to-get-into hedge fund.

Although WASPs such as the Astors and the Rockefellers and Irish Catholic presidential patriarch Joseph P. Kennedy corralled enormous fortunes in New York real estate, Manhattan's modern land barons and construction magnates have largely been Jewish men with surnames such as *Uris, Rudin, Tishman, Durst, Speyer, Milstein, Fisher, Ravitch, Helmsley, Rose, Mendik,* and *Resnick.* None of them, save for one, has ever been a household name. Harry Helmsley, one of the most innovative minds in Manhattan real estate and a longtime manager of the Empire State Building, slipped into the popular consciousness at the very end of his life only because his second wife, Leona, had the brass, fangs, and tax-evading capacity of a small army.

Other members of Manhattan's real estate elite preferred anonymity and usually disdained slapping their names on their buildings. They didn't buy football teams or airlines or casinos or beauty pageants. They simply built, waited patiently to get rich, and donated huge sums to philanthropies. For the most part, no one in this crowd considered Donald a peer, either in terms of his tastes or his accomplishments. The Rockefellers, assessing Donald at his peak, dismissed him.

"I think the only arguably unique thing about Donald Trump is that he's a great showman, and he was able to persuade the media that he was somebody worth covering, because everybody paid a lot of attention to him," said Richard Ravitch, whose family once controlled one of New York's largest construction and real estate development firms. "He's a buccaneer in a society whose culture changed over the course of the past twenty-five years. He was not the cause of that change, he was a reflection of that change. It's a culture that put a primacy on public and social needs versus private consumer satisfaction, and Donald represented the latter.

"In that sense, he became a public person, but he became a public person because the media found him interesting."[3]

But more was at work in the disposition of Rockefeller Center than the anointment of a new owner or the Rockefellers' desire to diversify their investments. By 1989 New York's real estate market had been in full throttle for several years and much of the smart money—family money that for decades had watched markets ebb and flow, surge and collapse, enrich and impoverish—had begun pulling out a few years earlier. The values buyers placed on Manhattan's land, smart money had deemed, were overly frothy.

Jerry Speyer, steward of what is perhaps Manhattan's most formidable real estate operation, Tishman Speyer Properties, liquidated a substantial portion of his company's holdings in the mid-1980s. Harry Helmsley had also taken to the sidelines around that time, as had the Rudins, as had the Dursts. "Someone once said that the best way to double your money is to fold it over once and put it in your pocket," said Seymour Durst in 1985, a year in which a square foot of Manhattan land fetched $2,000, up from about $740 a decade earlier.[4]

About sixty new office towers were built in Manhattan between 1982 and 1986, Trump Tower among them, transforming the island into a small forest of skyscrapers. But New York's rampant real estate giddiness didn't deter some developers and buyers. With Rockefeller Center in play, the Japanese came calling.

After Mitsubishi bought a large stake in Rockefeller Center for $846 million, alarmists around the country sounded warnings that Japan was buying up much of the United States and therefore was buying its soul. But Mitsubishi's purchase was poorly timed. The subsequent implosion of the New York real estate market, a national recession, and Japan's own economic travails eventually forced it to walk away from Rockefeller Center and put the complex into bankruptcy. In 1996 Speyer and a large group of other savvy buyers with funds to spare snapped up Rockefeller Center for about $900 million. Four years later Speyer and a partner paid about $1.85 billion to take direct control of the center—an acknowledgment that the value of the property, post-bankruptcy, had doubled.[5]

Speyer's acquisition of Rockefeller Center was a classic, old-guard Manhattan real estate transaction: patient, methodical, built upon personal ties and the steady cultivation of trust, and, at the end of the day, lucrative. By 2004 Tishman Speyer controlled some thirty-three million square feet of property worldwide and had developed or acquired sixty-five million square feet of property worth about $16 billion during the previous twenty-six years—a portfolio that Donald's relatively modest Manhattan acreage did not come close to matching in size or value.[6]

To be sure, there was one Manhattan real estate legend to whom Donald bore a strong resemblance: William Zeckendorf Sr. From the late 1940s until the early 1960s Zeckendorf streaked across Manhattan and the front pages with flamboyant brio, selling the land under what became the United Nations to the Rockefellers, buying up suburban tracts and thousands of New York hotel rooms, and maneuvering to develop an expanse of West Side land that he planned to call Atomic City. Tubby as a jelly roll and with a long stogie always firmly in hand, Zeckendorf spouted grand plans like Vesuvius. On the eve of building the first new hotel in New York in decades (it would be called The Zeckendorf, of course), in 1965, he slammed into a wall of unmanageable debt and flamed out. Too impatient to wait until a deal was perfectly ripe, and both too premature and too old to find himself reborn on reality TV, Zeckendorf dissolved into a bewildered urban footnote: "How can they say I'm broke?" he wondered. "I owe a billion dollars."[7]

For Donald, the post–Trump Tower years were a heady rush into celebrity and entrepreneurial candyland as he snared one business bauble after another, sometimes in industries about which he knew next to nothing. While the vision he had shown in building Trump Tower remained, the discipline he had summoned to get the sky-scraper built evaporated. Emboldened by easy money and a lauda-tory press, Donald went on a massive and ill-considered shopping spree. Among the projects he juggled was a promising expanse on the West Side on the same turf where Zeckendorf wanted to erect Atomic City, and Donald gave the development-in-waiting an equally retro, Jetsons-like label: Television City.

As Donald wheelied along, fine-tuning his performance as the business world's answer to Evel Knievel, the media lavished whop-ping reams of attention on him. For the most part, reporters didn't cover Donald's ventures because what he did was smart. They cov-ered Donald's doings because what he did was fun to watch. Whether any of them recognized that what they were watching was a slow-motion car crash didn't matter. It was the '80s.

BLANCHE SPRAGUE, ONE OF DONALD'S LONGEST-SERVING DEPUTIES, CAN ISO-late the moment when she thinks the builder became a celebrity: April 8, 1984. On that Sunday, *The New York Times Magazine* ran a lengthy and richly detailed profile written by Bill Geist that cap-tured Donald in midflight and pinpointed what fame in America sounds like when it first arrives.

"Donald J. Trump is the man of the hour. Turn on the televi-sion or open a newspaper almost any day of the week and there he is," Geist's article noted. "Spending a day with Donald Trump is like driving a Ferrari without the windshield. It's exhilarating; he gets a few bugs in his teeth. . . . Just as the name Donald Trump is well-known to most New Yorkers, the name is now becoming rec-ognized throughout the country. He is fast becoming one of the nation's wealthiest entrepreneurs, able to buy practically anything he wants."[8]

Ms. Sprague, who worked as a project manager for Donald, said that she and her boss used to conduct business on the fly, conversing about plans and processes as they hustled along Manhattan's sidewalks. But things changed after the *Times Magazine* profile. Suddenly the pair couldn't walk down the street—they couldn't walk anywhere, in fact—without Donald being swarmed by autograph seekers or passersby waving at the developer and shouting his name.

"He was very good looking; blond, thin, athletic. He could talk to you, and I saw him do it, to famous and important people, he could talk to you, and these people felt like they were the only person in the world. It was like he hypnotized them," Ms. Sprague recalled. "I don't know how he did it, and I never saw anybody replicate it. He didn't make it up, he didn't hone it, he was always that way. He was born that way. He didn't become Donald Trump. He was always Donald Trump. He just had to let other people know that's who he was.

"He always knew what he wanted," she added. "He was always brash and aggressive about it. He never had to go to How-to-Be-Donald School. He just was."[9]

Behind the celebrity that was Donald was the business entity that was the Trump Organization, a teeny operation that catered to Donald's zealousness and preference for quick decisions. "People thought we were this humongous firm with billions of people," Sprague recalled. "In the New York office, there were only about eight or ten close 'executives'; the rest were secretaries and accountants and everybody did everything. Your job was to make sure that everything got done."

And Donald, during his salad days in the 1980s, was trying to do just about everything. With Trump Tower freshly minted, for example, Donald decided to take on the National Football League, one of America's most firmly entrenched entertainment monopolies. Given that the NFL was a lucrative juggernaut guided by a steely cast of owners and executives who rarely brooked outside intrusion, there was something delectable about watching Donald tilt at this particular windmill—and the press ate it up, regardless of the fact that it wasn't a completely logical business decision for New York's celebrated real estate maven. But businesspeople have always had a fetish for owning sports teams, a few of them actually made good money doing so, and Donald, an avid and lifelong football fan, wanted to be part of the club. After all, football ownership is a high-profile guy-thing (potato chips and Budweiser around a TV set on Sunday afternoon is a low-profile guy-thing), and men need to be boys. They can't help themselves. They like to run headfirst into one another. Donald and football almost had to happen.

The modern NFL took shape in the 1920s as player-managers like George Halas scraped money together to stage games at off-season baseball fields and recruited early stars such as Red Grange to drum up publicity and fans. Professional football teams meandered along until the 1950s, when the emergence of bona fide legends like running back Jim Brown and quarterback Johnny Unitas gave the sport greater traction. But it wasn't until 1960, when thirty-three-year-old Pete Rozelle—the Los Angeles Rams' former publicity chief and general manager—became NFL commissioner and brought his Hollywood touch to pro football, that the sport exploded into living rooms. Vince Lombardi and the Green Bay Packers arrived ready for prime time, and Rozelle went on to deftly wed the TV boom with athletic dramaturgy, corralling owners and warring leagues into a marketing goliath known as the Super Bowl. He also mixed marriage-destabilizing weekend sports extravaganzas and a novel diversion called Monday Night Football into a profitable brew of pigskin, showmanship, urban loyalty, hot cheerleaders, and gladiatorial excess. Rozelle constructed an athletic and financial powerhouse in the two decades before Donald and the United States Football League popped up, and it was Rozelle whom Donald, the football novice, targeted.

In September 1983 Donald agreed to buy the New Jersey Generals, one of the USFL's nascent franchises, from Oklahoma oilman

J. Walter Duncan. (Various reporters, quoting an unnamed source, say the price was anywhere from $6 million to $10 million, but Donald doesn't challenge a *New York Times* article stating that the actual price is about $1 million.[10]) Two months later Donald threw down the gauntlet. "It's definitely war between us and the NFL," he announced.[11] But Rozelle didn't seem troubled by Donald's battle cry.

"I've seen four of these 'wars' now," said Rozelle in a subsequent press conference. "You go back to the All-American Conference in the '40s, we had the American Football League for six years until we announced a merger, the World Football League and now this."[12]

The USFL's founders started their league in 1982 on the premise that shoestring salaries and budgets could muster enough athleticism and television ad revenue to offer football fans games during the spring and summer, when NFL teams weren't playing. Nurse the baby league's twelve teams along, the idea went, and eventually they would gather enough steam to either offer a permanent challenge to NFL primacy or merit absorption into the NFL itself.

The USFL got a TV contract with ABC, drafted but failed to sign college stars like University of Pittsburgh quarterback Dan Marino, drafted and successfully signed others like Heisman Trophy winner Herschel Walker and University of Miami quarterback Jim Kelly, and got former ESPN president Chet Simmons as its first commissioner. The challenge to the NFL looked credible. And into the league came Donald.

"I would prefer going up against a monopoly like the NFL—and I've been given very little chance of succeeding—than going out and just buying an NFL team," Donald told an Associated Press reporter in 1985. "I could have been one of them by spending a lot of money. But I'd rather spend a small amount of money and make this league work. I've always undertaken jobs that people said couldn't be done."[13]

Although the USFL comprised an unwieldy bunch of largely self-made men accustomed to financial arm wrestling and getting their own way, the league's original owners were completely unprepared for co-habitating with the whirlwind that was Donald, even when the publicity typhoon engulfing him had yet to reach full force.

"He was just a Donald, not The Donald," said Charlie Steiner, a radio sportscaster who announced Generals games, in an interview with an ESPN reporter. "He was a boy builder and then he bought the team. It was the best thing that ever happened to the USFL and the worst thing that ever happened to the USFL.

"He bought the back page of the *Daily News* and the *Post*. Suddenly, he was a man about town. He was building the greatest football team in history. Pretty soon, he was making Page Six [the *Post*'s gossip page]. It didn't matter to him if the league made it or not, he had already succeeded."[14]

From the moment he took over the Generals, Donald captured a majority of the USFL's media attention and engineered a plan of attack against the NFL that didn't mesh with the strategy other owners had already mapped. Sports leagues are fragile organisms that depend as much on publicity as they do on a unified front among owners who have to occasionally stuff their egos and their greed for long-term stability. Donald brought the USFL publicity, but he wasn't by any stretch someone who intended to check his ego.

"You buy a ball club and you're a local celebrity. You can get a seat at any restaurant. Bang. Just like that. It's almost like you're an athlete," observed veteran sportswriter Frank Deford. "With most business propositions, it's you on one side and another person on the other. But it's not like that when you own a sports team. You have to deal with a bunch of other owners and a commissioner. You can't wheel and deal the way you want to and the way Trump likes to."[15]

Years before Donald took on the NFL, New York Jets owner Sonny Werblin had shown that his upstart league, the American Football League, could contend with the NFL by signing and promoting high-profile players. Werblin struck gold when he hooked a young quarterback named Joe Namath, who proceeded to become the first pro to pass for four thousand yards in a single season. Donald went down the Werblin route after he bought the Generals. In February 1985 he signed Doug Flutie, a Heisman-winning Boston College quarterback who entered the national spotlight after hurling a Hail Mary pass for a winning touchdown in the final seconds of a game against the University of Miami a few months before. Donald paid Flutie $7.5 million for a multiyear contract, essentially blowing apart team salary caps that were key to the USFL's early financial viability. And Doug Flutie, while talented and tenacious, was no Joe Namath.

"Donald was always very supportive of my decisions. He said, 'If you believe in the players, sign them.' And we did, and he spent a lot of money on it," recalled the Generals' general manager, Jim Valek. "He was reasonable about it all. I know that when we were going after Flutie, Donald said something about how he'd probably have to pay what he was paying Herschel Walker. Once you make a statement like that, and the agent heard that, it made it tough to get a deal done. But we did.

"Donald wanted a team that was well representing of New York. He was a New Yorker, and he wanted to make sure the city could be proud of their team," added Valek. "Most of the ownership around the league looked to Donald as the leader. The others just got into line because they knew the power that Donald had."[16]

Donald, along with Chicago Blitz owner Eddie Einhorn, also pushed the league into head-to-head competition with the NFL by forcing other USFL owners to agree to play in the fall instead of the spring and summer. Although the AFL had played independently for six years in the 1960s before being absorbed into the NFL, Donald had no intention of allowing the USFL to wait that long to mature. He and Einhorn argued that the USFL would rake in more TV ad dollars by playing in the fall. A schedule change followed, but it was a disastrous decision for the USFL because the league was peppered with average teams populated for the most part by above average players. Side by side with NFL games, USFL matchups would be meager fare.[17]

"The league didn't want to do this, but basically Donald had them by a choke hold," said Steiner. "The feeling around the USFL was to wait another year. You know, wait until the NFL goes on strike because you'll have superstars falling out of the sky. Either the strike wouldn't have happened, or the USFL would have flourished. Donald just couldn't wait."[18]

Donald, as he did with most things he owned, enjoyed inflating the potential resale value of the Generals, on one occasion saying he could get $60 million for his team (at a time when established NFL franchises were fetching $70 million).[19] Donald generated scads of free press with his USFL foray, snaring headlines that New York Yankees owner George Steinbrenner had been used to having all to himself as the city's baseball majordomo. As owners and operators, however, there was a large gap between Donald and his crosstown media rival.

"Steinbrenner made one of the savviest moves in sports history. He bought the Yankees for $11 million or something like that. Anybody who looked at that knew it was a steal," said Deford. "CBS owned the team at the time, but Steinbrenner came in and was able to buy out the rest from his partners. He got the biggest and best brand in sports and got it cheap. Trump got a minor-league team in a deal that was no good. It's no comparison."[20]

As the USFL began to fray, wags dubbed it the Unusually Stupid Football League. Only weeks before Flutie was signed, the USFL's first commissioner resigned under pressure from Donald. And a few days after the Flutie signing, the league disbanded its scouting combine, essentially signaling that all teams were on their own in the hunt for football talent—whoever wrote the largest check could get the best players. That led to escalating salaries and a proliferation of agents in the USFL (and in the NFL as well). The Generals' payroll in 1984 was between $6 million and $7 million, smaller than the average NFL payroll of about $13 million, but still high enough to make it the second biggest in the USFL, where the average payroll was only about $2.5 million. Signing Flutie caused the Generals' payroll to bulge even farther.[21]

"Trump and those guys think they can buy success, but you can't. You have to work at it," complained the late Tampa Bay Bandits owner John Bassett in a *Toronto Star* interview. "We know how to run a profitable organization, we know how to market. We know it's better to go with local guys . . . who don't have gigantic salaries."

Bassett continued to other reporters, "These guys don't understand," after other USFL owners outvoted him in favor of moving the league's schedule to autumn. "They don't have any idea what they're doing. Maybe Donald Trump got to them. I couldn't care less. They'll go broke in the fall."[22]

Bassett was correct. TV networks didn't want to broadcast USFL games in the autumn, and as the league spiraled into extinction owner losses passed the $150 million mark. Donald later testified in court that he alone lost $22 million on his failed USFL gambit.[23] But making the USFL work had never been his real goal. From the beginning he wanted the NFL to absorb his team, and he was willing to subvert the USFL's larger goals to that end.

"I thought this would be a cheap way [to get into the NFL] because you couldn't get in; it was impossible to get in," Donald told me. "Spring football is third-rate, but I did believe the NFL had a monopoly. The USFL wasn't a big deal. It was a small deal. I didn't lose. It was a bid to get into the NFL on the cheap."[24]

In an effort to bring the NFL to the table, Donald launched a Hail Mary pass of his own: He sued Rozelle and the NFL in the fall of 1984. The anti-trust suit claimed that the NFL was a monopoly that neutered the USFL by locking it out of network TV coverage. The suit sought more than $1 billion in damages. Donald trotted out Roy Cohn for that one, and Cohn, who was dying of AIDS, dug back into his past for his opening salvo against the NFL. Invoking witch-hunting imagery from the McCarthy era, Cohn told reporters that a secret cabal within the NFL had plotted the USFL's demise (a claim he declined to substantiate but that was supported by records later introduced in court). But Rozelle unleashed a flotilla of very bright, white-shoe lawyers on Donald and Cohn, and their lawsuit was tied up for nearly two years before things came to a head in a trial during the summer of 1986.

Donald claimed in court that Rozelle had invited him to a private meeting in a Manhattan hotel and that the commissioner had offered him an NFL franchise if he dropped the anti-trust suit and didn't move the USFL schedule to the fall. Rozelle disputed all of this in his own testimony, saying that Donald had invited him to the meeting and that his goal was to find a back door into the NFL.

"He said, 'I want an NFL expansion team in New York,'" Rozelle recalled in court. "And he said, and I'm quoting him exactly, 'I would get some stiff to buy the Generals, my team in the USFL.'"[25]

Donald realized as the trial got under way that he had image issues. "I was part of the problem," he later recalled. "From day one, the NFL painted me as a vicious, greedy, Machiavellian billionaire, intent only on serving my selfish ends at everyone else's expense."[26]

In the end, a jury found that the NFL had acted as a monopoly but that the USFL's woes were the result of bad management, poor cost controls, and the shift to a fall schedule—not the overweening power of the NFL. The USFL was awarded just $3 in damages and several million dollars in court costs.[27]

The USFL suspended its operations in August 1986, only three years after Donald entered the league, and its teams never played another game. No real competitors to the NFL have emerged since. While Donald walked away from his USFL debacle a bit deeper in debt, the value of the publicity he received was incalculable. The attention he snared as the Generals' owner placed him more squarely in the public eye than any of the hoopla surrounding Trump Tower. Rather than being cast as a rash rich kid undone by impatience and scorched-earth tactics, Donald's run-in with the NFL solidified his image as an entrepreneurial underdog willing to take on all comers, no matter how much bigger they were than him. It was a theme Donald would mine again and again for the rest of his career.

ON MAY 27, 1987, DONALD AND ED KOCH ATTENDED A BLACK-TIE GALA together at the Waldorf-Astoria's Starlight Roof to celebrate their successful collaboration raising funds for a Vietnam War memorial in Manhattan. Donald had been a primary mover behind the campaign, generously donating his time and $1 million, and he and Koch put their mounting differences aside to offer cheery toasts at the Waldorf. But their charade masked the fact that both men were warily circling one another behind the scenes as they tussled over a familiar subject: land.

NBC had recently told City Hall it planned to leave its headquarters in Rockefeller Center unless New York offered it economic subsidies to stay in Manhattan. Donald wanted NBC to relocate to the West Side Yards, seventy-five acres between West 59th and West 72nd Streets that he'd paid $115 million to purchase in 1985 after letting his earlier Penn Central option lapse. Donald had borrowed $200 million to buy the Yards and had maneuvered stealthily to reclaim control of the property, one of the most desirable undeveloped parcels in the city. The entire stretch was a flash point between developers and residents with sharply different visions for the shape, texture, and quality of life in Manhattan. Builders wanted condos or office towers on the site; residents and good-government types wanted more parkland. Stuck in that vise, the Yards lay dormant for years, preventing Donald and predecessors like Zeckendorf from doing anything with the land. But Donald fully intended to build seventy-six hundred luxury condos and a sprawling TV studio on the site, and luring NBC to the property was a key to achieving that goal.

Donald applied to City Hall for a $700 million tax abatement to underwrite the construction of what he planned to call Television City, promising to share the tax benefits with NBC and profits from the site with the city. He also planned to build the world's tallest building on the Yards, a 150-story, rocket-ship-shaped skyscraper that would have cast shadows west to New Jersey and as far north as 96th Street.[28] But the Koch administration rebuffed his request the day before the Waldorf dinner. Incensed, Donald sent Koch a scathing letter that same day.

"Dear Ed, Your attitude on keeping NBC in New York City is unbelievable," the letter began, recasting the issue as one of how best to cater to NBC rather than ways of using the city's tax code to line Donald's wallet. "For you to be playing 'Russian Roulette' with perhaps the most important corporation in New York over the relatively small amounts of money involved because you and your staff are afraid that Donald Trump may actually make more than a dollar of profit, is both ludicrous and disgraceful. . . . I am tired of sitting back quietly and watching New Jersey and other states drain the lifeblood out of New York—and consistently get away with it for reasons that are all too obvious."[29]

Just before the Waldorf gala began, Koch fired off a response to Donald's missive, but he put his own, post-dated letter in the mail so it wouldn't arrive at the developer's office until after the celebratory meal was complete. And at the dinner, everything went swimmingly.

"Trump is the first one to be honored for his $1 million. And in response, he goes out of his way to give accolades to me: the best mayor, the most wonderful mayor," Koch recalled of the dinner. "I am sitting there [thinking]: *Wait until he gets that letter.*"[30]

The entire Trump clan was at the gala, and afterward Donald approached Koch with a request.

"Mayor, my father so much wants to have a picture with you," the mayor recalled Donald asking. "Could you take a picture?"

"Of course, Donald," Koch responded, before a dozen photos were snapped and the two men parted ways.

The next day Donald got the mayor's reply: "Dear Donald, I have received your letter of May 26. I was disappointed that you continue to believe that you can force the City's hand to your advantage through intimidation. It will not work. . . . I also refuse to

place hundreds of millions of dollars in future taxes at risk so that
you can more easily build a 15-million-square-foot luxury condominium and retail development. . . . If NBC chooses your site and
you make a profit, that's fine and the American way, but it will not
be on the backs of the New York City taxpayer. . . . I urge you to
refrain from further attempts to influence the process through intimidation. It should already be clear to you that this tactic is
counter-productive."[31]

Sometimes hand-to-hand combat in New York unfolds as
kabuki, with warring factions masking their mutual hatred through
the quiet pitter-patter of legal briefs. On other occasions brawls
never surface at all and are resolved after lawyers exchange confidential phone calls. But every so often the entire city gets lucky
enough to have front-row seats when two well-known people decide
to duke it out publicly and fill Manhattan with the clattering, un-
avoidable din of gargantuan babies' rattles. Confrontations between
Donald and Koch always fell squarely in the lattermost camp.

After haggling over the Trump Tower tax abatement, the two
men had traded barbs over the renovation of the Wollman Skating
Rink, a broad slab of Central Park ice that Donald successfully overhauled after the city's own efforts to do so were repeatedly delayed.
Donald courted the press like a magician during the Wollman renovation, an effort that culminated in a star-studded reopening that
Donald would recall throughout the rest of his career as one of the
highlights of his public life.

"The Olympics had just finished and Torvill and Dean were like
the biggest names. You know, the great Torvill and Dean. Peggy
Fleming, and this one and that one. We had every single gold-
medal winner in the last twenty years there on the ice for the opening," Donald told me. "In the history of ice skating, there has never
been an event put together like this. In fact, I joked, if you have a
silver medal, don't show up. That was my joke.

"There are moments in time that are so good, you can never du-
plicate them, okay? Number one, I was young," he added. "It was

like this incredible occasion. Best Weather. Best Skaters. Best Music. Best People. Everything was perfect."[32]

Donald used the Wollman reopening to pump up his image as a can-do entrepreneur while Koch went out of his way to point out the unusual hurdles and restrictions that the city faced in renovating the rink on its own. Donald took the mayor's comments as a rebuke.

"All I know is this, instead of getting up and thanking me for doing a great job, he got up and said he could have done a good job, too," Donald told me. "I said, you motherfucker, that's it."[33]

The Wollman Rink renovation was overdue and welcome, but by New York standards it was small time. In a city that regularly had to revamp or maintain underwater tunnels, a web of bridges, miles of roadways, parks, two major airports, sewage and electrical systems, courthouses, police stations, firehouses, jails, public housing, high schools, and hospitals, overhauling a skating rink didn't really measure up. Nor did it measure up to Donald's earlier accomplishment with Trump Tower or the vast undertaking that his $4.5 billion Television City proposal represented. Although Donald got extraordinary media mileage out of Wollman Rink, it was essentially a preamble to the final, mouthwatering face-off in the Trump vs. Koch saga—with Koch having learned a lesson about the advantages of making early publicity strikes.

The day after the Waldorf dinner celebrating the Vietnam War memorial, Koch leaped out in front of Donald in the spin cycle. The mayor held a press conference, announcing that he had decided against giving Donald his $700 million tax break for Television City. But, the mayor said, he would give NBC an $80 million tax subsidy if it stayed in New York. Then Koch released the nasty letters he had exchanged with Donald.

It got fun after that.

In his own press briefing, Donald gave the mayor some career advice: "He should resign from office. He can't hack it anymore."

Koch returned the shot: "If Donald Trump is squealing like a stuck pig, I must have done something right."

Donald fired back, calling the mayor a "moron" and advising New Yorkers that "this city is a cesspool of corruption and incompetence."

Koch parried, reducing Donald to three little words: "Piggy, piggy, piggy."

Well, said Donald, the mayor "has no talent and only moderate intelligence" and should be impeached. "Ed Koch would do everybody a huge favor if he would get out of office and they started all over again. It's bedlam in the city."

Bedlam! In New York!

"I have no intention of allowing this important matter to degenerate into a barnyard kind of contest," Koch said, about a week after he had already called Donald a barnyard animal.[34]

When Donald later took out full-page ads criticizing the White House's military spending overseas and advocating more financial aid for the homeless (yes, the homeless), Koch reminded New Yorkers of Donald's failed attempt to buy land in Moscow for a new hotel in the Russian capital.

"I mean, how bright do you have to be to know that in Moscow you can't own property?" asked Koch. "How bright? Is this the man we want dictating foreign policy?"

Donald slapped back with his own observations about Koch's pending visit to Central America.

"How can our idiot mayor go to Nicaragua when he can't even run New York City?" Donald asked. "The man is totally incompetent."[35]

Moments like these are why New Yorkers have trouble moving to Des Moines.

As ribald as things got with Koch, the stakes for Donald in the Television City smackdown were very real. The project was the biggest proposed in New York since Rockefeller Center, and whatever disdain the real estate elite felt for Donald, he would have vaulted to the top rung among Manhattan builders if he completed it. But he needed Koch's support in order to offer competitive rents on the site and to get it zoned for development, and he failed to do that. Moreover, New Yorkers who had rebounded from the fiscal crisis and then found themselves hemmed in by scores of new skyscrapers were more circumspect about King Tut–size developments like Television City that promised to add to the congestion. Residents, urban planners, and architecture critics assailed the project, and Koch said he would only support a development on the Yards that was about half the size of Television City. NBC ended up renewing its lease at Rockefeller Center after the city gave it tax breaks worth about $98 million.[36]

When Donald's blockbuster autobiography, *The Art of the Deal*, came out in late 1987, the forty-one-year-old builder devoted the book's penultimate chapter to Television City.

"There were some who told me that I was hurting my chances for zoning approval by taking on Koch in the media. They may well have been right," Donald wrote. "I've waited a long time to build on the West Side, and I can wait a little longer to get the zoning I feel is necessary. In the end, I will build Television City with or without NBC and with or without the current administration. . . . I'm lucky that I can afford to wait, because that way I'll be able to do it right."[37]

In reality, Donald couldn't afford to wait. Although he told the media that it only cost him about $3 million a year to carry Television City, his annual interest payments on the massive parcel actually climbed to $22 million—and the site wasn't producing any revenue.[38]

Other problems were also about to overwhelm Donald. Shortly before *The Art of the Deal* was published, the stock market suffered its worst single-day meltdown in history, with the Dow Jones Industrial Average losing about $500 billion of its value on "Black Monday," October 19, 1987. While the national economy later went into a recession, it was spared from any immediate devastation after Black Monday because regulators flooded the economy with money. But the crash laid particularly brutal siege to New

York's economy, where Wall Street was a driving force. Manhattan real estate prices would subsequently collapse. What all of this would mean for Donald, who had already begun gorging on bank loans to finance acquisitions and a lifestyle that his business holdings alone could never support, was lost amid the skyrockets of the burgeoning Trump phenomenon and the publication of *The Art of the Deal*.

While Donald hyped *The Art of the Deal*'s potential, boasting a first printing of 200,000 copies (only 150,000 were in the first run) and claiming that a *New York* magazine excerpt generated the best sales ever for the publication (it hadn't), the momentum around the book was still extraordinary.[39] Donald launched *The Art of the Deal* at a flashy Trump Tower party arranged by Studio 54 founders Ian Schrager and Steve Rubell and attended by Manhattan glitterati of almost every stripe. Comedian Jackie Mason emceed the event, which also featured a performance by fitness guru High Voltage (billed as "the world's first self-described Energy Conductor"), who danced in a purple spandex cape and bra.[40] Donald also landed guest appearances on the *Today* show, *The Phil Donahue Show*, *Late Night with David Letterman*, and *20/20* with Barbara Walters; conducted dozens of other live television interviews for local stations; and had reviews and excerpts in major newspapers and in *People* magazine. (*People* gushed, "This is the entrepreneurial mind at work if there ever was one." Huh? Compliment or insult?) Donald quickly found his book soaring to first place on *The New York Times* best-seller list, staying on the list for fifty-one weeks, reportedly selling about one million hardcover copies,[41] being translated into more than a dozen languages, and becoming one of the most popular bibles of American business know-how ever written.

Condé Nast owner Si Newhouse originally coaxed Donald into doing *The Art of the Deal* with a ghostwriter after the sales of one of Newhouse's magazines, *GQ*, soared when Donald appeared on the cover of an issue about "Success."[42] *The Art of the Deal* was a distillation of the Trumpster mojo, a nonfiction work of fiction that captured all of Donald's promotional chutzpah as he walked readers through a series of sometimes interesting and sometimes plebeian business deals he had orchestrated. The voice that sprang from the pages was entirely original, seemingly candid, relentlessly boastful, and refreshingly unafraid to take swipes, settle scores, and opine with an *I-am-what-I-am* gusto. *The Art of the Deal* was a tour of the business world according to Mister Id, and readers ate it up. The book also offered an eleven-step formula for business excellence that combined dictums inspired by the Reverend Peale's power-of-positive-thinking movement (Step 1, "Think Big": "One of the keys to thinking big is total focus. I think of it as controlled neurosis, which is a quality I've noticed in many highly successful entrepreneurs") with Donald's own homegrown, smoke-and-mirrors advice (Step 7, "Get the Word Out": "One thing I've learned about the press is that they're always hungry for a good story, and the more sensational the better. . . . The point is that if you are a little outrageous, or if you do things that are bold or controversial, the press is going to write about you. . . . That's why a little hyperbole never hurts. I play to people's fantasies. . . . People want to believe that something is the biggest and the greatest and the most spectacular. I call it truthful hyperbole. It's an innocent form of exaggeration—and a very effective form of promotion").

The Art of the Deal's eleven-step formula also included Step 10, "Contain the Costs": "I believe in spending what you have to. But I also believe in not spending more than you should. . . . I learned from my father that every penny counts, because before too long your pennies turn into dollars. . . . The point is that you can dream great dreams, but they'll never amount to much if you can't turn them into reality at a reasonable cost."

As hundreds of thousands of people around the country sopped up his business advice, Donald was spending more than he should, wasn't counting his pennies, and was pursuing great dreams regardless of their cost.

* * *

VISIBLE THROUGH A LARGE WINDOW DIRECTLY BEHIND DONALD'S DESK IN HIS corner office on the twenty-sixth floor of Trump Tower, and gleaming at him each evening like Jay Gatsby's green light from the corner of 59th and Fifth, was the Plaza Hotel. The Plaza was one of Manhattan's truly storied properties, steeped in wealth, glamour, power, and celebrity, and Donald snapped up the hotel up in 1988 for $407.5 million with $425 million in borrowed funds that he could ill afford.[43] This was Donald at high tide, however, when all he had to do to get a humongous bank loan was pick up the telephone. At meetings with bankers, Donald flashed a document the Trump Organization had prepared called a "statement of appraised value" that showed what his own auditors estimated his various properties to be worth. It was that easy. Donald never had a balance sheet also listing his outsize debts because, said a former member of Donald's company, the Trump Organization didn't have one.[44]

Wiser business minds took Donald to the cleaners on the Plaza deal, getting him to pay a price that the hotel's earnings couldn't support and successfully insisting that he commit to the purchase without performing any due diligence on the property.

To be sure, there was much to attract almost anyone to the Plaza. A stream of well-known guests had slept beneath the stately hotel's copper-green mansard roof over the decades, including Alfred Vanderbilt, Jay Gould, George M. Cohan, Frank Lloyd Wright, Cary Grant, Gary Cooper, Dorothy Parker, Marilyn Monroe, Truman Capote, the Beatles, John F. Kennedy, and a host of international dignitaries and heads of state. Films such as *Breakfast at Tiffany's, North by Northwest, Funny Girl*, and *Barefoot in the Park* had memorable scenes set in the Plaza. F. Scott Fitzgerald and his wife, Zelda, favored the hotel and were rumored to have danced in a drunken haze in its courtyard fountain, which featured a statue of Pomona, the Roman goddess of abundance. Ernest Hemingway, no stranger to drinking binges or the romance of hotel life, advised Fitzgerald to donate his liver to Princeton University but to will his heart to the Plaza.[45] Eloise, the young heroine of Kay Thompson's children's books, lived, of course, at the Plaza.

The original Plaza, built in 1890 for about $59 million in today's dollars on the site of a Central Park pond, was the first great New York hotel of the industrial age. Railroad tycoons and other grandees flocked to it, prompting the construction of the Waldorf-Astoria Hotel three years later. In 1907 the original hotel was torn down to make room for the imposing 805-room French Renaissance structure that cost about $234 million in current dollars to build and still graces the corner today.[46] Designed by Henry Hardenbergh, architect of the Dakota residences and other Manhattan gems, the Plaza was New York's only hotel designated a National Historic Landmark, and its motto was equally grand: "Nothing unimportant ever happens at the Plaza."

Donald bought the Plaza only four months after the stock market crashed, at a time when most other investors in Manhattan real estate were tightening their belts. His $407.5 million represented the most money ever paid for a hotel—amounting to about $500,000 per room—and the Plaza's operations would have to be juiced up to produce the cash Donald needed to pay interest on the hefty loans he incurred to buy it.

"This isn't just a building, it's the ultimate work of art," Donald said of his hotel. "I was in love with it . . . I tore myself up to get the Plaza." And, he said in the years that followed, any questions about price overlooked the Plaza's intangible cachet. "The spirit of the city is in this hotel," he said. "How can you possibly put a price on that?"[47]

In a 1988 piece in *The New York Times Magazine*, journalist William H. Meyers wrote a definitive story analyzing the Plaza acquisition. The story presciently identified all of the problems Donald would encounter running the hotel profitably. As the article suggested, and as subsequent events made clear, Donald had been bested in the deal by Robert Bass, the shrewd Texas investor who sold him the Plaza. Bass picked up a controlling stake in the Plaza as part of a larger hotel chain purchase in the fall of 1987, and though he was deeply enamored of the famous hotel he was concerned that it didn't generate enough cash to support his $300 million mortgage. So Bass, who had amassed a larger fortune and a much more solid track record as a dealmeister than Donald but had nary a scintilla of the fame that the best-selling author enjoyed, unloaded the hotel. Donald's purchase produced a tidy profit of at least $50 million for Bass's investor group just four months after it had bought the Plaza. And the deal left Donald holding a very expensive bag.

"The buying and selling of world class hotels is an emotional business," Donald later wrote in one of his books, *Surviving at the Top*. "When a place like the Plaza is on the block, the toughest negotiators become soft, and logic often gets tossed out the window."[48]

Donald had none of Bass's concerns about the Plaza's cash flow, even though the $425 million he borrowed from a syndicate of large Manhattan banks led by Citigroup was much higher than Bass's $300 million Plaza mortgage. The banks, digging deeper into a broader real estate lending crisis that would bring many of them to their knees, had the foresight to ask Donald to personally guarantee $125 million of his $425 million loan—something Fred Trump advised his son against ever doing and that Donald always said he never did in his deals.[49]

Being the 1980s, Donald was able to do unto others what had been done unto him. After he bought the Plaza, he sold Manhattan's St. Moritz Hotel for $180 million to Australia's "richest man," binge buyer Alan Bond (who ended up bankrupt shortly after the deal). Although Donald told the press that he had purchased the St. Moritz from Harry Helmsley for $30 million in 1985, he actually paid $74 million using an $80 million bank loan. Even so, the St. Moritz sale, net of its mortgage, grossed Donald a cool $100 million.[50] When Donald waited and found the right buyer, he could still hit home runs (though he had been stashing his mistress, swimsuit model Marla Maples, in a fourth-floor suite at the St. Moritz and was forced to find her a new place to stay, according to two members of the Trump Organization[51]). Donald said he poured most of what he made on the St. Moritz sale into the Plaza Hotel.[52]

Most investments and business deals are a mixture of aspiration and inspiration, and the best investors maintain their objectivity, balancing cool detachment and patience with any transaction's emotional and egotistical allure. Trump Tower was a model of an inspired, balanced business deal (sculpture smashing aside). Donald's execution of almost every other large-scale transaction he was involved in during the *Art of the Deal* years, including the Plaza Hotel, was not. For some of those working closely with Donald—whose much-publicized marriage to Ivana, newly installed as the Plaza's president, began unraveling amid his affair with Maples—his normally kinetic, impatient, restless need to deal gave way to something more intense and manic: He started to believe his own headlines.

"He was in an acquisition fever and he wasn't himself," recalled Barbara Res, who oversaw Donald and Ivana's renovation of the Plaza. "It was very hard to work with him at this time because he didn't focus and was always changing his mind. And he and Ivana were always at odds. He'd say up, she'd say down. It was an impossible situation dealing with Donald and Ivana and their problems."[53]

Some of this had become evident a year earlier. Weeks before the stock market crashed, Donald bought arms dealer Adnan Khashoggi's former yacht, the 282-foot *Nabila*, for $29 million from the sultan of Brunei.[54] Featured in Sean Connery's James Bond comeback attempt, *Never Say Never Again*, the *Nabila* had fifteen suites, a helipad, three elevators, a small swimming pool surrounded by bulletproof glass, a disco, and a mirrored grand piano that was a gift from Liberace. It was also one of the world's largest private vessels (though the ranks of bigger yachts included the 397-foot *Al Mansur*, owned by former Iraqi dictator Saddam Hussein who, like Donald, enjoyed putting his own name on lots of buildings).[55] Donald purchased the *Nabila*, which he renamed the *Trump Princess*, with borrowed funds and it was a pricey, headline-grabbing bauble, not an investment. The Plaza, Donald said, was "the ultimate trophy." On the other hand, the *Princess* was merely "the ultimate toy."[56] But wait! In *Surviving at the Top*, Donald revised his definition of the *Princess*, classifying it as "more a trophy than a personal toy." Wherever the yacht fit in Donald's dictionary, he moored the exotic craft in Atlantic City for part of the year, where he used it as a lure for high rollers (who, it turned out, wanted to stay ashore to gamble, not go on boat rides). Donald himself spent little time aboard the *Trump Princess*, other than to pose for photographs next to it with Ivana, the couple's first two fingers often raised in V-for-victory signs.

"Not many people live a life like Khashoggi, but I'm coming damn close," Donald said, referring to Khashoggi's lavish lifestyle and not the fact that the wealthy arms dealer lost his yacht when he went broke. The *Trump Princess*, like the Plaza Hotel, is "a masterpiece," Donald told the press. "It's beyond a ship or a boat or a yacht. That's what I love."[57]

Donald's buying spree continued unabated.

Only five months after buying the Plaza Hotel, Donald scooped up the Eastern Air Shuttle for $365 million in cash, personally guaranteeing $100 million of about $400 million he borrowed to buy it—even though he had no experience running an airline. The deal was arranged hastily, its details hammered out in Ivana's salmon-hued Plaza office and at Eastern's Rockefeller Center headquarters. The terms were nearly as restrictive as Donald's Plaza accord. Eastern precluded him from selling the Shuttle to an independent owner for five years; he was forbidden to sell to another airline for ten years. The price Donald paid for the Shuttle's aging fleet of twenty-one Boeing 727s also appeared to be steep. Eastern's own internal analysis a year earlier valued the Shuttle at $300 million; a later independent appraisal would place it at $150 million to $300 million, depending on market conditions.[58]

"I like buying Mona Lisas; the Shuttle is the single finest asset in the airline industry, the best," Donald said when that deal was done.

"I like collecting works of art. This is a work of art."[59] (Shades, again, of the Plaza: "For me this is like owning the Mona Lisa," Donald said of the hotel. "It's not just an investment, it's a work of art.")[60]

Donald renamed the Shuttle, which operated between Boston, New York, and Washington, Trump Air. He planned to put marble fittings in the Shuttle's bathrooms until his advisers told him that would make the planes too heavy to fly. But he managed to install gold-plated faucets in the lavatories.

As the 1980s closed out, Donald's image took a slight turn. While the lion's share of Donald's press remained laudatory, more pointed barbs began appearing. "Will Donald Trump Own the World?" *Fortune* asked in a 1988 profile. The magazine answered yes, he might, because the "no-fooling billionaire" was "an investor with a keen eye for cash flow and asset values, a smart marketer, and a cunning wheeler-dealer given to tough-guy tactics."[61] And *The Art of the Deal* made Donald universally identified with entrepreneurial genius. But then along came some zingers. Garry Trudeau routinely lampooned him in his *Doonesbury* comic strip; in one strip, Trudeau had Donald referring to the actress Meryl Streep as "that chick who does all the accents." *Spy* magazine, a short-lived and wickedly satirical monthly that was one of Donald's most unrelenting nemeses, invariably identified the builder as the "short-fingered vulgarian from Queens." On its "inherent loathsomeness scale," *Spy* gave Donald a ten.

Some developers—including Jerry Speyer—had built up a cash cushion that allowed them to ride out the real estate implosion that took shape in the late 1980s. Others had not, particularly those like Donald who did nothing incrementally and who owned properties that rose and fell in value while throwing off unpredictable, and sometimes paltry, amounts of cash. Donald's ability to keep playing depended on two things—borrowed money and casinos.

Donald enjoyed an almost mystical ability to keep convincing bankers to lend him funds. "The banks call me all the time—can we loan you money, can we this, can we that," Donald told New

Jersey casino regulators in 1988. "They want to throw money at you. I can give them security on their loan, 100 percent certainty. With me, they know they would get their interest."[62] And about a two-and-a-half-hour drive south of Manhattan, Donald owned casinos lined with slot machines and green-felt tables that in good times provided him with his own little seaside treasury.

Donald remained confident that the financial problems and bad business decisions surrounding him would never come home to roost.

"None of the debt is personally guaranteed," he told a reporter in 1988. "If the world goes to hell in a handbasket, I won't lose a dollar."[63]

TrumpQuiz #5

To add to your fortune once you've hit the big time as a billionaire, you should:

1) Convince opponents of your sprawling riverside development that two key benefits of your project are richer neighbors and better TV reception.
2) Convince your bankers that it's all about art, not money.
3) Convince journalists that it's all about art, not money.
4) Convince yourself that it's all about art, not money.
5) Convince the other boys in your football league that if they don't play by your rules, you're going home.
6) Convince an oil-rich Asian sultan to sell you a movie yacht that allows you to use a British accent and introduce yourself to friends as, "Trump, Donald Trump."
7) Convince your wife to run a big hotel that's just a few blocks away from where your mistress is hiding.
8) Convince business travelers on a one-hour flight from New York to Washington that it's worth paying more to have a golden toilet.

9) Convince low-income tenants forced from a building you're converting into a luxury condo that you truly stand behind your advertisements calling for increased federal aid to the homeless.

10) Convince readers that you stand behind one of your best seller's final thoughts: "The biggest challenge I see over the next twenty years is to figure out some creative ways to give back some of what I've gotten."

CHAPTER FIVE

TRUMPCHIPS

When you go to Atlantic City you're going to Trump City.
—RICHARD WILHELM, FORMER TRUMP CASINO EXECUTIVE[1]

I love to have enemies. I fight my enemies.
I like beating my enemies to the ground.
—DONALD TRUMP[2]

ONE PERSON WATCHING THE HELICOPTER PLUMMET FROM THE SKY ON an October afternoon in 1989 said the entire four-blade rotor atop the Agusta chopper stopped spinning, and then just snapped off from the rest of the craft. As the helicopter plunged thousands of feet toward a wooded median on New Jersey's Garden State Parkway, "it seemed like an eternity watching it" fall, the witness recounted.[3] All five people aboard the helicopter died in the crash; the impact left debris scattered across a quarter-mile stretch of highway.

Two of the people on board the helicopter were Stephen Hyde and Mark Etess, and they were the foundation of Donald's gambling operation in Atlantic City. The crash happened about thirty-five miles north of the small, faded resort town; the two executives were returning there from New York, where they had been promoting an upcoming boxing match at one of Donald's casinos. A subsequent investigation found that there were hard-to-detect fractures in one of the helicopter's forty-two-foot blades and that it splintered, causing the rest of the chopper to break up in midair.

Hyde, forty-three, was the father of seven, a well-regarded veteran of the gambling industry, and supervised all of Donald's Atlantic City casinos. Etess, thirty-eight, was a Columbia University graduate and a marketing whiz, the father of two, and had made Donald's casinos the leading Atlantic City boxing mecca. Etess also oversaw plans for the launch of the Trump Taj Mahal, a $1 billion mega-casino that Donald had gone deeply into hock to build, adding to the pile of loans he was already carrying for the Plaza Hotel, the Trump Shuttle, and other recent, conspicuous purchases.

The Taj was, as Donald likes to put it, very "Trumpy." When completed it would have a 135,000-square-foot casino floor, the largest in the world, above which would rise New Jersey's tallest building, a forty-two-story hotel. Atlantic City maharajahs could lay their eyes on a roof lined with seventy onion-shaped domes and mini minarets and on nine stone elephants weighing two tons each that guarded the driveway to the casino's entrance. The Taj's gourmet restaurant, one of twelve, was the Scheherazade, and high rollers could sleep off their losses in the Alexander the Great Suite for $10,000 a night. The interior was hung with $14 million worth of chandeliers and featured a fifty-two-hundred-seat arena for shows and boxing matches. Blinking and clinking away in the casino were more than three thousand slot machines surrounded by 160 table games, such as blackjack, baccarat, craps, and roulette. Some sixty-five hundred workers serviced the entire enterprise.[4]

Donald never liked to stay in Atlantic City for any length of time, and he loathed the daily grind of managing his casino operation. But he depended heavily on the cash that streamed out of his casinos, and he was on a financial tightwire with the Taj—the casino was set to debut only six months after the helicopter crash, and the cavernous gambling house needed to haul in $1.3 million a day in revenue just to break even, two to three times as much as any other casino in Atlantic City. There was a very real danger that the Taj would be a white elephant, far larger and more costly than any of the stone knockoffs lining its driveway. Meanwhile the entire Atlantic City market was in a slump; most of the casinos were hemorrhaging red ink. And now, with the snap of a helicopter's rotor blade, Donald had lost the two people he depended on to navigate a business he had little interest in managing, the two men with the firepower to make it all work.

On the day of Etess's funeral, Donald approached Steve Wynn, one of the savviest operators in the casino business, and asked him if he could join him the next day at Winged Foot, the exclusive Westchester club where Donald played golf. Wynn, who had led the resurgence of Las Vegas by unveiling a string of ever more exotically themed casinos, had been a competitor of Donald's in Atlantic City, and the two men were often at each other's throats. Hyde and Etess had once worked for Wynn before Donald lured them away. But Wynn thought Donald looked "forlorn" at the funeral, "as if the pegs had been cut out from beneath him,"[5] and he agreed to meet him the next day.

As the two men teed off on Saturday morning, Donald got right to the point.

"I don't know what to do. I'm lost. I don't even know the names of the people working for me in the casinos," he told Wynn.

"Go back to Atlantic City and bring in your department heads at each casino and tell them, 'Hey guys, I need your help, I need to learn,'" Wynn replied. "If you spend two full days at each hotel you'll learn everything you need to know."[6]

Wynn said Donald looked blankly back at him, without any enthusiasm.

"I could see in his own eyes that wasn't what he wanted to do. That wasn't his thing. His heart wasn't in it and he didn't go for it," Wynn told me. "He doesn't deny that's how he felt about it. So now you've got what you've got: A casino company that has his name on the door but doesn't have his heart inside. And that doesn't work.

"When Donald first entered Atlantic City it was about glamour and sizzle, but he's a New York real estate guy at heart," Wynn added. "Atlantic City is a gritty, operational place where you have to bear down every day, and that's not what Donald is about. Atlantic City has never been his love and a man can't be good at something that's not his passion."

If Donald wasn't passionate about Atlantic City, the town was certainly passionate about him. Over the years New Jersey regulators and law enforcement officials had gone out of their way to accommodate the developer, and he used that welcome mat to forge a hammerlock on Atlantic City gambling. Though Barron Hilton's association with Sidney Korshak, a heavyweight Hollywood lawyer with alleged mob ties, had cost the Hilton Hotel Corporation a casino license in Atlantic City, Donald's relationship with Roy Cohn never came up in his own licensing hearings. Though no one was supposed to own more than three of Atlantic City's twelve casinos, Donald at one point was briefly permitted to have four (and he purchased a fifth that had closed so he could have extra hotel rooms on the city's cramped boardwalk). Though regulators were supposed to strictly monitor the financial well-being of casinos and their owners, Donald was consistently given extra latitude to work through mounting money woes that left him teetering on the brink of personal bankruptcy.[7]

Atlantic City was passionate about Donald because the town had inhospitable weather for six months of the year, urban problems and racial inequities out of proportion to its size, a beach that even in the warmest months was a meager sight to behold, an economy that was wholly dependent on gambling, and acres of blue-haired old ladies sitting at slot machines who bore little resemblance to the mythic, black-tied high rollers of the Rat Pack era. Atlantic City needed that magic sparkle only Donald could bring: constant, glowing publicity, youthful energy, and a regular dose of spectacle. In return, Donald became so important to Atlantic City's fortunes that the resort was afraid to lose him.

Donald also became Atlantic City's most freewheeling and optimistic spokesman, extolling the town's hidden virtues and sometimes finding the slenderest of threads on which to hang his argument that Atlantic City was a gambling mecca unlike any other—even Vegas.

"It's got something Las Vegas and almost no other place has: the Atlantic Ocean," Donald told me when I interviewed him in 1996. "That's something you can't buy. In Las Vegas, if you turn on a sprinkler you have to pay a fine. I mean we have the entire Atlantic Ocean in Atlantic City."[8]

BEN LAMBERT, DONALD'S ERSTWHILE BUSINESS PARTNER IN NEW YORK REAL estate ventures, invited the developer to a dinner party in the garden of his town house on Manhattan's Upper East Side one spring evening in 1985 to meet one of Lambert's old friends, Barron Hilton. Donald and Hilton both shared a love of football. Donald had his USFL franchise, the New Jersey Generals, while Hilton was already in the big show as a co-owner of an NFL franchise, the San Diego Chargers. Both men also had stakes in Atlantic City. Donald had opened his first casino there a year earlier, calling it Trump Plaza. Hilton's company was building a new casino for about $308 million on an inland portion of town known as the marina district.

Lambert sat on Hilton Hotels' board of directors, and the dinner party was an effort to help Hilton find his way out of a bind. New Jersey's Casino Control Commission, the state agency responsible for reviewing prospective owners to determine if they passed the organized-crime-and-corporate-responsibility sniff test, had recently dealt a surprising blow to Hilton, telling him that Korshak's work for Hilton Hotels had scuttled his chances for a license. (*Playboy*'s Hugh Hefner had recently been bounced out of Atlantic City, also for associating with Korshak.) Even though Hilton Hotels had already spent hundreds of millions of dollars building its Atlantic City casino, Hilton suddenly needed a buyer. Lambert arranged the dinner party to introduce him to one: Donald.

But Hilton balked, unwilling to let go of the idea that he might still secure a license.

Shortly after the dinner party, Steve Wynn entered the picture, offering to acquire about 27 percent of Hilton Hotels' shares even though his own company, Golden Nugget, had profits that were about a sixth of what the hotel chain pulled down annually. Many analysts speculated that Wynn's real goal was Hilton's Atlantic City casino, not the entire company. And Wynn thought his bid had all the dynamics of a good game of poker.

"You know that point where you've drawn a good hand and it's late in the game. You've got a lot of money piled up in front of you and the guy across the table has a lot of money in front of him, maybe even more than you do," Wynn said to a reporter in 1985. "You think about it for a moment. Then you push the whole pile into the middle of the table, and you sit there with this sheepish grin on your face.

"Two things can happen: the other guy eyes the pile of money nervously and you know he is going to fold. Or else he says, 'Count it,' which means he is going to call you. That gives you a sinking feeling in the bottom of your stomach. That's where I am with Barron Hilton. Do I push in all my chips by making a public tender for the whole company, or don't I?"[9]

Hilton didn't wait to see if Wynn pushed his chips across the table. However serious Wynn's bid might have been, and whether or not he could have raised the funds to buy a chunk of a company as large as Hilton Hotels, the move lit a fire beneath Hilton. He recognized that he needed to shore up his company's cash position and focus on fending off Wynn's challenge, and he had no intention of allowing Wynn to snare the Atlantic City casino along the way. Almost overnight, he became much more amenable to soliciting an offer from Donald. So on an April weekend, Lambert and Donald hammered out a deal.

"We were a public company so we had to handle it very quietly, and Donald was one of the people I called," Lambert told me. "We met on a Sunday morning and I told him we wanted a full price for the hotel—$320 million. We negotiated night and day and by the end of the day he had agreed to buy it."[10]

With the stroke of a pen, Donald now owned two casinos in a town of about thirty-seven thousand people that billed itself as "America's Favorite Playground." And Donald, who began speculating in the stock market around the same time that he took the plunge in Atlantic City, felt right at home.

"The New York Stock Exchange happens to be the biggest casino in the world. The only thing that makes it different from the average casino is that the players dress in blue pinstripe suits and carry leather briefcases," he said. "If you allow people to gamble in the stock market, where more money is made and lost than in all of the casinos in the world put together, I see nothing terribly different about permitting people to bet on blackjack, craps or roulette."[11]

Atlantic City's streets inspired the names of properties for the board game Monopoly, and it had been home to gambling, legal or otherwise, for the better part of a century. Incorporated in 1854 by two entrepreneurs pitching it as a spa town for working-class Philadelphians, Atlantic City later turned its beach into a major tourist attraction by constructing a series of ever more elaborate boardwalks above the sand. The fifth and last boardwalk, built in 1896, was four miles long and forty feet wide and was lined with showy hotels, penny arcades, fortune-tellers' booths, beer gardens, and the world's first Ferris wheel.

As time went on, unusual displays and freak shows became Atlantic City draws. Among the attractions were midget boxing matches, giant typewriters, Siamese twins, horses leaping from diving boards sixty feet above the sea, eating contests, and electric billboards that made the night sky glow in the summer. Major vaudeville acts and the Ziegfeld Follies revue often opened in Atlantic City. Harry Houdini performed escape feats on the boardwalk; W. C. Fields juggled and cracked wise in a nearby theater. The

Miss America Pageant got its start in Atlantic City in 1921, with artist Norman Rockwell tapped as one of the early judges. To top things off, gambling, prostitution, and bootlegging thrived in the seaside town. Al Capone and Lucky Luciano prized the bays and inlets around town as transit points for illegal booze, and gangsters convened at least one sit-down of major mob families in Atlantic City in the 1920s.

Illegal gambling joints thrived in the back of cigar stores (with nickel betting limits) in the early twentieth century; later on more cushy joints appeared, such as Dutchy's and Levy's where $5 and $10 bets could be placed. By midcentury Charlie Schwartz's Bath and Turf Club and Skinny D'Amato's 500 Club (where Dean Martin and Jerry Lewis got their start) offered more elaborate venues for illegal gambling. But after Senator Estes Kefauver convened hearings in Atlantic City on organized crime in 1951, the swankier gambling joints disappeared. The advent of jet travel made it cheaper and easier for tourists to go elsewhere in the 1950s and '60s and Atlantic City withered, leaving a large population of unemployed African American hotel workers and steadily decaying neighborhoods.[12]

New Jersey legalized gambling in Atlantic City to try to reverse the decline. When the state gave gambling a green light in 1976, it did so on the premise that casinos were economic development tools and that a chunk of gambling profits had to be reinvested for senior citizens and the betterment of Atlantic City—in housing, schools, and other projects. Afraid that the mob influence that had hung over the town for decades might reassert itself, the state also established an elaborate review process to keep organized crime at bay—a process that for the most part proved successful after a number of minor Mafia blowups early on.

The trade-off, especially after gambling and lotteries became more common elsewhere around the country, was to take the wagering racket away from organized crime and turn it over to large corporations. Atlantic City was the first to experience this shift, but

it quickly spread elsewhere as corporate America poured more resources and sophisticated marketing techniques into the gambling
business than at any other time in the country's history. Legal in
only two states in the late 1980s, Nevada and New Jersey, casino
gambling would be welcome in more than thirty states by 2004.

Because mobsters spent most of their time skimming gambling
lucre out the back door of Vegas casinos rather than analyzing which
games sucked the most cash out of gamblers' wallets, they failed to
notice that the table games they prided themselves on in the 1940s,
'50s, and '60s—roulette, craps, and blackjack—were anemic money-
makers compared with slot machines. Corporate America didn't
miss a trick, however. Slots were fast, addictive, and had odds heavily stacked against the grandmas who used them, so corporations deployed the devices everywhere they could, relegating the old table
games to the sidelines and rapidly institutionalizing what had once
been an ancient and unruly pastime. In the decades after New Jersey
legalized gambling, wagering became the biggest entertainment industry in the United States in terms of dollars spent—more popular
than the movies, baseball, and Disneyland combined. Between 1993
and 2003, the amount American gamblers lost annually in casinos,
lotteries, and the like jumped from $35 billion to $73 billion.[13] And
Atlantic City was one of the first towns to find itself awash in the
slots tsunami.

"It was like the scene in *2001: A Space Odyssey* where the cave-
men are standing around looking at the monolith and not knowing
what to do with it," said former Atlantic City mayor Jim Whelan.
"That's what casinos were like in Atlantic City—nobody here was
prepared for the economic forces that were unleashed."[14]

Resorts International, the first company to score an Atlantic
City gambling license and a major financial backer of the legaliza-
tion push, had a legacy of mob ties that New Jersey regulators
somehow managed to overlook. While the state's Division of Gaming Enforcement later recommended that Resorts' temporary license be revoked, the Casino Control Commission, made up of

gubernatorial appointees, ignored that advice. What couldn't be ignored was the groundswell of enthusiasm gamblers had for Resorts. Some three hundred thousand people flooded Atlantic City on the day in 1978 when the new casino opened its doors. The crush to get inside Resorts to bet that day was so heavy, stories circulated about gamblers opting to wet their pants rather than give up their seats at the wagering tables. Resorts anticipated revenues of about $100 million in its first year; it made $225 million. Kaching! Over the next year, thirty-six corporations submitted new casino proposals to New Jersey regulators.

"I think we have committed ourselves to keeping this as a wholesome family resort," Atlantic City's mayor, Joseph Lazarow, deadpanned when Resorts opened. "From this day forward, I think we will see a city of growth and prosperity."[15]

By 1985, seven-years after Resorts debuted, twenty-seven million tourists a year flocked to Atlantic City, twice as many as Las Vegas. By the time Donald opened his first casino in Atlantic City, there were eleven gambling houses employing more than forty thousand people, taking in annual revenue of about $2 billion, and chipping in more than $300 million in state taxes. Crime rates and bankruptcies also escalated, compulsive gambling problems surged, African Americans were left out of the boom, and housing continued to wilt, making the city an eyesore. But the casinos, all of them largely indistinguishable barns lined up along the boardwalk like enormous cash registers with their backs to the city, were located in the country's most densely populated region, and they raked in money. Seniors busing their way into town ignored the sights and smells. They were there for the thrills.

"You're all alone, and the children are all grown and away. Or maybe you lost your husband. How much time can you spend cleaning your house?" an elderly New Jersey resident, Helen Piccola, told me. "When you go to Atlantic City it's like a magnet because it clears your mind of everything. It makes you feel like you're seventeen again and in a different world . . . Your blood boils when you get to Atlantic City. We just get out of the car and your blood boils. It's better than having a man."[16]

Donald first bought land in Atlantic City around the time that gambling was legalized, and the location he chose was impeccable. He assembled a site at the foot of the local expressway, at the point where drivers first entered the city. But Donald's partners in his first Atlantic City venture, Kenneth Shapiro and Daniel Sullivan, were more curious choices. Law enforcement officials and gambling regulators said both men were familiar with Atlantic City's underbelly—Shapiro as a street-level gangster with close ties to the Philadelphia mob and Sullivan as a Mafia associate, FBI informant, and labor negotiator.[17]

Donald told me that anyone buying land in Atlantic City during the early days of the gambling rush had to intersect with operators like Shapiro and Sullivan, that he dealt with both men through intermediaries, that he didn't care personally for either one of them, and that he wasn't worried about putting his reputation at risk by dealing with them. (In fact, Donald had previously used Sullivan to negotiate labor contracts when he was building the Grand Hyatt in Manhattan.[18])

But early on, when he was first testing Atlantic City's waters, Donald told casino regulators that he thought his real estate partners were model citizens.

"I don't think there's anything wrong with these people," Donald said of Shapiro and Sullivan in public testimony during his licensing hearings in 1982. "Many of them have been in Atlantic City for many, many years and I think they are well thought of."

Those thoughts contrasted with statements Donald made to FBI agents several months earlier, when he had concerns about the challenges of doing business in Atlantic City. According to a 1981 FBI memorandum (available for online viewing at www.thesmokinggun.com), Donald told the FBI that "he had read in the press media and heard from various acquaintances that Organized Crime elements were known to operate in Atlantic City" and that "he did not wish to tarnish his family's name." Donald and his brother volunteered to the FBI that Sullivan was a "labor consultant to their firm," that they were "aware that this is a very rough business" and that Sullivan "knows people, some of whom may be unsavory by the simple nature of the business."[19]

And when Donald reminisced with me more than two decades later about his first Atlantic City partners, his opinion of them had evolved even further.

"Some of those guys were tough guys. Shapiro. They were tough guys. In fact, they say that Dan Sullivan was the guy that killed Jimmy Hoffa," Donald told me. "They were tough guys and not good guys.

"I was able to handle them. I found Sullivan to be the tougher of the two. He would constantly bring up the name of friends of his who were in the FBI. He had many people in the FBI, who he would claim were his friends. And you'd say: You are talking to a saint almost. He would always talk about honesty. That everything in life was honesty. And yet he probably wasn't an honest guy.

"[Shapiro] was like a third-rate, local real estate mafia. Nothing spectacular. And you know, I get lucky. I heard a rumor that Sullivan—because Sullivan was a great con man—that Sullivan killed Jimmy Hoffa. Because I heard that rumor, I kept my guard up. I said, 'Hey, I don't want to be friends with this guy.' I'll bet you that if I didn't hear that rumor, maybe I wouldn't be here right now. If I didn't hear that rumor, I would have been much more prone to be taken into the whole crazy scheme of things."[20]

In addition to his real estate dealings with Donald, Shapiro also served as the conduit for bribe money paid to Michael Mathews, an Atlantic City mayor forced from office in a payola scandal.[21] According to investigative reporter Wayne Barrett, an early and dogged Trump biographer, Donald considered funneling campaign contributions to Mathews through Shapiro—which Donald disputed in an interview with me.[22] New Jersey law enforcement officials later investigated Barrett's assertions, including that Donald

failed to inform casino regulators about the federal racial discrimination probe of the Trump Organization in the 1970s—an omis-
sion that would have put his casino license in jeopardy. New Jersey
officials told me in subsequent interviews that their probes never
produced reasons to revoke Donald's license.[23] But after regulators
licensed Donald in 1982, they required him to buy out Shapiro and
Sullivan and end the partnership because of concerns about the
two men's backgrounds.

Donald initially lined up his casino license the old-fashioned
way. He was anxious to have a speedy, uncomplicated licensing review and hired a well-connected New Jersey lawyer, Nick Ribis, to
help him. Ribis, who later became the Trump Organization's president, convened a meeting in 1981 at his Short Hills, New Jersey,
law office with Donald, the state attorney general, and the head of
the Division of Gaming Enforcement. Trump Tower was making a
media splash at the time, and Donald's newfound celebrity status
made him a welcome presence in Atlantic City. According to people
with direct knowledge of the meeting, Donald pushed for an expe-
dited review, but state officials only promised that they would
move as quickly as possible without overlooking their duty to carefully vet the developer.[24] About a year after the meeting, Donald
had his license—not nearly as fast as he wanted, but with fewer nagging questions asked of him compared with other applicants.

Donald's Atlantic City land sat vacant until the early 1980s because he had difficulty finding money to build and banks were skit-
tish about the casino industry's historical ties to organized crime.
Donald had no track record as a casino operator, and he needed to
borrow money from his father to stay afloat in Atlantic City. But as
more straitlaced companies got into the business, and financiers
like Michael Milken opened the junk bond spigot to casinos, lining
up funds became simpler. Holiday Inns, a hotel company founded
by conservative Christians who originally didn't allow gambling,
liquor, or pornography on its properties, decided to broaden its
horizons by expanding into the gambling business; it purchased

Harrah's, a Nevada casino chain, and then opened an Atlantic City casino. When Holiday Inns decided it wanted a second Atlantic City casino, that gave Donald the opportunity to strike one of his best deals of the early 1980s.

Impressed by Donald's reputation as a building whiz, Holiday Inns and Donald began discussing a partnership only weeks before he might have had to abandon Atlantic City entirely. As Donald later recalled it, he was so short on money that when Holiday came calling, he ordered workers to move piles of dirt around on his site so it would look like he was actually building something. Holiday Inns bit. The company struck a deal with Donald that gave him 50 percent of the partnership's casino profits, a construction and management fee of about $24 million, and all of the financing needed to build the $220 million project. In addition, Holiday Inns planned to run the casino and protect Donald against losses for five years. All Donald had to do was relax and count his winnings. Without putting a dime into the deal, he got 50 percent of the earnings and an asset that threw off a steady stream of cash, something any debt-laden real estate investor would prize. But as often happened in the course of Donald's early business partnerships, he and Holiday Inns were at odds within months of Harrah's at Trump Plaza's 1984 opening.

Holiday Inns complained of construction flaws and cramped elevators at the property; Donald said the casino was poorly run. The casino lacked adequate parking because Donald delayed building a garage until casino operations changed and his name was used more prominently in marketing. Donald also had a different notion than Holiday Inns about which gamblers to court. Holiday was after the "Chevrolet crowd," said one analyst, while Donald, completely lacking in casino experience, pursued the "jet-set, champagne and caviar" class (who already roundly preferred Las Vegas).[25] Amid all of the confusion, Trump Plaza lost money in its first year. Then fate intervened. Barron Hilton ran into his licensing problems and just a year after opening his first Atlantic City casino, Donald had a second, which he christened Trump's Castle. But Trump's Castle was a neighbor of Holiday Inns' other Atlantic City casino. Uh-oh. Partners never like to be competitors, especially in the same small town, and Holiday Inns told Donald as much. Donald ignored his partner's complaints. Unable to resolve their differences amicably, Donald and Holiday Inns fought it out in court.

And in court, Donald took Holiday Inns to task for sullying something for which he had an unusual fetish: his own name.

"The Trump name has been so badly bloodied by your management of the facility that hopefully Trump's Castle Casino Hotel can do something to bring it back," Donald said in court papers filed as part of breach-of-contract charges Holiday Inns filed against him in 1985. Although Donald could only lay claim to two major buildings in Manhattan—the Grand Hyatt and Trump Tower, neither of which he owned completely—and was foundering as a football owner in the USFL, he leaped into the fray with panache.

He described himself in court papers as "an entrepreneur who has achieved national and international prominence, reputation, and recognition as the result of the outstanding success he has achieved in conceiving, developing, and promoting various enterprises . . . the Trump name has come to be identified in the public mind with quality, excellence, achievement, and success, and Trump has been the subject of innumerable articles in the press and of substantial media attention."[26]

Holiday Inns countered that Donald had "a more glorified view of the importance of his name in 1982 than we did at the time," but acknowledged that the opening of Trump Tower and the media typhoon that enveloped the builder afterward had made the Trump name a hot commodity. The conflict between the partners ended when Donald bought out Holiday Inns for $250 million in 1986—using $278 million in borrowed money. When Donald took control of the Hilton property for $320 million, he used $352 million—also in borrowed funds.[27]

In addition to larding a mounting pile of debt onto his business holdings, Donald's timing was bad. At the very moment that he began laying claim to Atlantic City, the entire town hit a wall. The absence of air service, traffic congestion, a shortage of hotel rooms, and the costs of exorbitant giveaways used to lure gamblers and bus in seniors who spent little and only stayed for weekends all combined to put a brake on the torrid momentum Atlantic City had built up during the previous decade. True, Atlantic City's ten casinos pulled in about $2 billion in revenue in 1984, more than the $1.7 billion Las Vegas's sixty casinos took from gamblers in the same year. But Las Vegas had room to grow; Atlantic City didn't. Las Vegas drew a diverse mix of gamblers; Atlantic City didn't. Las Vegas had fat profits; Atlantic City didn't. Most important, Las Vegas had imagination and Atlantic City didn't.

Between the mid-1980s and the mid-1990s, Las Vegas dropped garish, loopy, outré theme bombs up and down the Strip, peppering the city's main drag with expansive, inviting gambling palaces and nine of the world's ten largest hotels. Meanwhile Atlantic City did little to innovate along its boardwalk, choosing to just grind down gamblers in a desolate, gray locale. While Donald ramped up in Atlantic City, Steve Wynn, who ran the most profitable casino in town, the Golden Nugget, sold out in 1987. He then pocketed his Atlantic City profits and headed back to Las Vegas to build there. Wynn would try to return to Atlantic City in the late 1990s, and his comings and goings frequently prompted vitriolic exchanges with Donald that evoked the memorable, insult-fueled days of Trump vs. Koch.

Business spats often get papered over when warring factions decide there's good money to be made by putting old grudges aside. By 2005, some twenty years after Donald and Wynn first began feuding, the two men claimed that they had resolved their differences. They were building neighboring properties in Las Vegas and stood to benefit from cooperating with one another in Sin City. Wynn was even a guest at Donald's third wedding reception, and both men dismissed my and other journalists' coverage of their earlier mud fights as overdone.

"It was always professional, not personal. The press made more of it than it actually was—the size of the feud was exaggerated in the media," Wynn told me in 2005. "And once you guys in the press get ahold of something you never let go."[28]

"I agree with him," Donald told me. "I mean, we've had some bad moments because it was competitive . . . But we've had an amazing relationship."[29]

Hmmmm. So the media made too much of the casino titans' tiffs. Still, there once seemed to be something a tiny bit amiss between the two men.

When I mentioned to Wynn in the mid-1990s that Donald believed his Atlantic City holdings were far more valuable than the casinos and hotels that Wynn owned in Las Vegas, his reply sounded somewhat personal.

"It's very important for [Donald] to say these things, but you'd have to ask a doctor about why he does that," he told me.[30]

At various times in the 1980s and '90s Wynn labeled Donald a "lightweight, second-string adolescent," a "half-baked mentality," a "cartoon," and a "perverse exaggeration." During the same stretch of time, Donald called Wynn "disgraceful," a "blowhard," a "scumbag," and "nutty."

Nor, à la Trump vs. Koch, did the duo stop at single-sentence slights.

"Because he doesn't understand the gaming industry, he's capable of being confused. He's obsessed with being king of the hill, and he's probably threatened on more than one level," Wynn once said of Donald in *Fortune* magazine. "Basically, his fixation on me is so perverse that I'm inclined to excuse it all and forget about it."

Donald explained Wynn's animosity by extolling his own prowess at golf.

"A lot of it has to do with the fact that I have twice kicked his ass on the golf course," he said. "It seemed to be very important to him."[31]

Wynn has a degenerative eye disease, putting him at something of a disadvantage in a golf match, but over the years Donald also identified other forces undermining the casino owners' relationship.

"You know, I think Steve's got a lot of psychological problems," Donald told a *New York* magazine writer during a heated exchange with Wynn in 1998. "I think he's quite disturbed. That's just my feeling. I think he's a very disturbed person."

Wynn?

"No sane or rational guy would respond to Trump," Wynn responded. "His statements to people like you, whether they concern us and our projects, or our motivations, or his own reality, or his own future, or his own present, you have seen over the years have no relation to truth or fact. And if you need me to remind you of that, then we're both in trouble. He's a fool."

Donald? Ah, the golf game.

"We used to be friendly. Had a good relationship, would play golf. Which was always a problem. I kicked his ass in golf," Donald told *New York*. "He thinks he's a good golfer, but he's terrible. Not that I give a damn."

Wynn didn't sit that one out.

"What is the matter with him?" he asked. "How deeply is he disturbed? When he was a kid or growing up—who did this to him? I mean, a psychiatrist would know all this."[32]

To top things off, Donald strong-armed Wynn when he tried to reenter the Atlantic City market in the late 1990s, throwing legal and political roadblocks in the way of a tunnel Wynn wanted the state to build before his company, Mirage Resorts, would develop a new casino there. This brawl produced real brass knuckles, including allegations of corporate espionage, hidden cameras, hidden tape recorders, the theft of secret high-roller lists, and private detectives digging into each of the gambling moguls' colorful pasts. Wynn went so far as to accuse Donald of playing real-life monopoly in Atlantic City, filing an anti-trust suit in 1997 that claimed that Donald launched a "conspiracy to block Mirage's entry into the Atlantic City gambling and hotel market" and "illegally funded" a New Jersey politician opposed to Wynn's new casino. Donald denied the charges, arguing that state resources were being unfairly deployed to boost Mirage's prospects in Atlantic City.[33]

"Outperforming Donald Trump in Atlantic City is child's play," Wynn said shortly before he filed his anti-trust suit. "All his properties together have never made a dime."[34] But Wynn dropped the anti-trust suit in 2000, after his casino empire in Las Vegas came under siege in a takeover battle. Nonetheless, a side-by-side comparison of how he and Donald stacked up against each other as operators had actually already occurred nearly a decade earlier—when Wynn opened a casino in Las Vegas called the Mirage and Donald first offered the public the enchantments of his third Atlantic City venue, the Taj Mahal.

The Mirage's debut in 1989 was an event, not simply because it was the first new casino in Las Vegas in fifteen years and was a massive, $620 million gambling den that critics thought would be too big to survive. The Mirage was the first casino to offer undiscounted, premium hotel rooms and first-class entertainment that were moneymakers in their own right and not used solely as loss leaders designed to coax gamblers onto the casino floor. Wynn also wrapped the Mirage in a bright, pastel-hued package that Las Vegas hadn't seen before; added attractions included an exploding, forty-foot volcano near the street, white tigers in the lobby, a twenty-thousand-gallon aquarium with sharks at the registration desk, a dolphin tank near the pool, great service, five restaurants, a spa and beauty salon, and an upscale shopping mall.

None of this was an accident. Wynn, a student of meticulous hotel design, spent two years planning the Mirage. To hone its appeal, he oversaw a team of designers that examined the layout and operations of a number of Hawaiian hotels and the three biggest casinos in Las Vegas.

Wynn brought an unapologetic passion to what he was doing, and he brooked neither critics who questioned the scale of his aspirations nor activists and policy makers who questioned the social ills of casino gambling.

"Are we suggesting that our love affair with consumerism in America is all based upon real products filling a real need?" he once asked me in an interview. "Or is something else going on—people giving themselves something that they don't need, but they want? The idea that you can dictate how people should dispose of their income is ridiculous. And to suggest that betting on a football game or the outcome of a turn of a card is inherently immoral is preposterous."[35]

Gamblers apparently agreed with Wynn. The Mirage needed to generate about $1 million a day in revenue to break even. It did $1.12 million a day in its first year. In subsequent years the Mirage pulled down more than $2 million a day, while also setting cash-flow records and retiring a significant portion of about $900 million in potentially debilitating debt. By 1997 Wynn's company landed in second place on *Fortune*'s annual list of the most admired American corporations, bested only by the Coca-Cola Company.

Things were different on the East Coast.

A year after the Mirage opened, Donald offered the Taj Mahal to the world. The Taj was large. The Taj had big stone elephants. The Taj was an enveloping, vacuous warehouse, an aircraft hangar full of machines. For all of its attempts at grandeur, it was boring. In short, the Taj was completely overshadowed by the Mirage.

Named after an exotic, palatial tomb, the Taj was also very expensive, and its $1 billion price tag was more than Donald could afford. But Donald first set his sights on the Taj in the late 1980s, when he had leaped headlong into the debt-fueled buying spree that netted him the Plaza Hotel and the Trump Shuttle—a period in his life when Donald said he believed that he was infallible.

"I had a great string [of deals] and I think it was *Business Week,* and they had this great story: Everything he touches turns to gold. The fact is, you do feel invulnerable," he told me. "And then you have the tendency to take your eye off the ball a little bit and hunt around for women. And hunt around for models. And hunt around for shit instead of maybe doing what you're supposed to. Because you really feel it is easy. I mean, you feel it's easy.

"Let's put it this way: I'm much more cautious today than I was in the '80s. Much more cautious. Because I see what can happen. And I appreciate it much more today. In the '80s, I didn't even appreciate it. I figured, this is the easiest fuckin' thing."[36]

Resorts, the company that introduced gambling to Atlantic City, was the Taj's original proprietor, and the gargantuan casino represented Resorts' bid to reassert itself in America's Favorite Playground. But Resorts' founder died in 1986, leaving behind $700 million in debt and the Taj's skeletal beginnings. Aiming to sew up the Atlantic City gambling market for himself and lay claim to the Taj, Donald borrowed $80 million to buy a controlling interest in Resorts in 1987. Foreshadowing later shenanigans as the proprietor of a publicly traded company, Donald used his Resorts stake to extract cash from the company and to engage in scorched-earth tactics with the company's other investors.

When Donald bought his Resorts stake the stock was selling for about $62 a share; other investors complained that Donald's subsequent naysaying about construction problems at the Taj drove Resorts' stock price down to $12, allowing Donald to make a lowball, $15-a-share bid to secure control of the entire company. Although Donald attributed the stock's slide to the October 1987 market crash, he tried to mollify angry investors by sweetening his offer to $22 per share (while awarding himself a lush management contract from Resorts). In the midst of Donald's scuffle with Resorts investors, fate intervened in the unlikely form of talk show host and game show wizard Merv Griffin.

Griffin was, as they say in the gambling business, flush. In

1986 he sold his production company—which owned such TV hits as *Jeopardy!* and *Wheel of Fortune*—for $250 million. Two years later, at the urging of advisers whom casino regulators later said had ties to organized crime, he decided to go into the gambling business.[37]

For Griffin, life imitated art in Atlantic City.

"I love the gamesmanship," he confided to one interviewer. "This may sound strange, but it parallels the game shows I've been involved in."[38]

The entertainer did concede, however, that certain business matters eluded him.

"When I started hearing things like, 'Where's your subordinated debt?' I thought, 'God, I don't want them to think I'm stupid, but what the hell does that mean?'" Griffin admitted. "You really have to learn fast."[39]

Not fast enough, as things turned out.

Griffin sued Donald to scuttle the developer's attempt to buy Resorts for $22 a share, and on the eve of the first court hearing announced that he would pay a whopping $35 a share, or about $295 million, for the company. Regulators would later learn that one of the people advising Griffin's financial team had been buying Resorts shares in advance of the entertainer's outsize bid; the adviser was convicted of insider trading.[40]

"I knew that if I was going to make any impact on the shareholders, or the media that are going to monitor all this, I couldn't come in at $24 or $25 a share," Griffin told *The Los Angles Times*. "So I made a huge jump to $35 a share."[41]

Donald was more than happy to oblige the entertainer at that price.

"He said I had a fiduciary responsibility to sell the shares," Donald told me. "Fiduciary responsibility? . . . Are you fucking crazy? I had no intention of selling, but this offer was so fucking crazy . . . In fact, it was so crazy that I didn't think I should ask for more. You know, normally, I'd say, 'Merv, make it 40.' I was like,

'How can I ask for more? Maybe he won't.' So I sold the company to him."[42]

At the end of the day, both men said they had what they wanted. Griffin got Paradise Island, a Caribbean venue that Resorts owned, as well as all of the company's other properties except the Taj; Donald got the Taj for $230 million, broke even on his stock investment, and got a multimillion-dollar payment to end his management contract.

"So, I'll never forget, I do the deal, I shake hands with Merv," Donald told me. "Enjoy your Resorts, which is falling apart. Enjoy Paradise Island, which is the worst piece of shit you've ever seen. Have a lot of fun."[43]

While both Griffin and Donald crowed in the press that they had bested the other in the deal, the reality was that their ill-advised food fight and the money they borrowed to win sent each tycoon's business into titanic belly flops. Griffin used about $325 million of Michael Milken's junk bonds to buy Resorts, adding to the heap of debt already piled on top of the withering casino company. Less than a year later, Griffin was unable to make interest payments on about $1 billion in Resorts debt and the company was forced into bankruptcy. It emerged from bankruptcy, and lapsed back into bankruptcy again, before Griffin finally sold it.

The Taj opened in April 1990, a month and a half late and over-budget by $65 million.[44] Hyde and Etess had died in the helicopter crash about six months earlier, and Donald's casino team was woefully unprepared to manage the launch of an aircraft carrier like the Taj. Meanwhile, Donald had handpicked a person with no experience in the gambling business to run one of his other Atlantic City casinos—his wife Ivana. She had been an able adviser to Donald on Trump Tower and other projects, but her main value was that she was family; throughout his organization, Donald, paranoid about getting fleeced, often valued loyalty above capability, and he wanted someone he trusted monitoring the streams of cash sluicing through the Castle's coffers. Even so, Ivana, a former model, skier, and adviser to Donald, was hardly a casino veteran, and her presence in Atlantic City was an endless source of frustration for Hyde in the years before he died, according to John O'Donnell, an executive who worked closely with him.[45]

As Donald's semi-clandestine relationship with Marla Maples heated up in the late 1980s, he plucked Ivana from Atlantic City and put her in charge of the Plaza Hotel back in Manhattan. Then Donald ensconced Maples in a series of high-roller suites in Atlantic City, checking her in under the name of one of his bodyguards: Fitzsimmons. Donald allowed the Southern belle to indulge herself in spas, restaurants, and shopping, all paid for by the casinos.[46]

On the day that Ivana departed Atlantic City in 1988, she bid farewell to Castle employees at a send-off in one of the casino's ballrooms, breaking into a light sob as she offered them thanks from a stage. When Donald took the microphone from her, he gave attendees at the party a dose of management advice.

"Look at this," Donald said. "I had to buy a $350 million hotel just to get her out of here and look at how she's crying. Now, that's why I'm sending her back to New York. I don't need this, some woman crying. I need somebody strong in here to take care of this place."[47]

Ivana, interviewed years later about the incident, said she just shrugged off her husband's criticism.

"I did not really resent it. I know Donald better and he just cannot help himself, you know? He just couldn't help himself. But all my employees were devastated," Ivana told me, laughing good-naturedly about the episode. "I did not resent it because I know Donald and he does it to everybody."

Ivana added that Donald generally empowered the women who worked for him.

"Donald had respect for his mother and he respected me and he liked to have women work for him," she said. "Women, especially in management, I think they function better than men. Because, I don't want to infuriate men, but number one woman she always try harder, somehow she always try harder. Number two, she has more attention to the detail. Men sees the thing in the big scope and the banking and the financial sheets and all that stuff but if there's a little scratch on the table he will not probably see it for a year or two."[48]

But Donald did seem to have some limits when it came to which women he wanted in the workplace.

"I think that putting a wife to work is a very dangerous thing," Donald told a television interviewer. "There was a great softness to Ivana, and she still has that softness, but during this period of time, she became an executive, not a wife . . . you know, I don't want to sound too much like a chauvinist, but when I come home and dinner's not ready, I'll go through the roof, okay?"[49]

Donald had hired Al Glasgow, a gravel-voiced former cement contractor he credited in *The Art of the Deal* with alerting him to Barron Hilton's licensing problems, to advise Ivana at the Castle. Glasgow was wise to the ways of Atlantic City, had briefly been the target of a mob hit as a cement contractor in the early 1970s, and had an instinct for the way the casino industry operated.[50] But even after Ivana left the resort of last resorts, Glasgow thought holes remained in Donald's management techniques.

"I don't think Donald has the patience, or the interest, or the attention span to be a hands-on operator," Glasgow told me. "He's just a dealmaker. He blows in and then he moves on to the next deal."[51]

Donald also faced some unusual hurdles in Atlantic City—like managing heavyweights in the title fights his casinos sponsored. Shortly after Mike Tyson flattened Michael Spinks in ninety-one seconds in a 1988 Trump bout, the boxer, then married to actress Robin Givens, paid Donald a visit at Trump Tower. Tyson, a human pile driver who later bit off part of Evander Holyfield's ear during a fight, had a cordial, almost filial, relationship with Donald. When Donald heard Tyson was in his lobby he told his guards to send up his champion thumper.

Tyson sat down in Donald's corner office hundreds of feet above Fifth Avenue and the two men chatted for about fifteen minutes before the boxer got to the point. Donald recalled their conversation in detail.

"Mr. Trump, could I ask you a question?" Tyson asked.

"Whatever you want, Mike," Donald responded.

"Are you fucking my wife?"

"What?"

"Are you fucking my wife? Everyone's telling me that you're fucking my wife."

Tyson then pulled out a copy of *Vogue* magazine that featured a picture of Ms. Givens wearing a TRUMP PRINCESS hat from Donald's yacht.

"Everyone's telling me that you're fucking my wife and I think you're fucking my wife," Tyson said.

"Mike, let me tell you something: I never ever even thought about it. And I heard those rumors and they're disgusting. In fact, I called you a couple of times to tell you that I heard those rumors and it pisses me off. And I never, ever even thought about it. She's your wife, she's with you, she's loyal to you, and it's total bullshit."

(Donald told me years later that his life flashed in front of his eyes during the encounter. "That was a scary moment, you understand. He didn't say: *There's a rumor*. He said, 'Could I ask you: Are you fucking my wife?' Now if I froze, I'm dead . . . You would have zero chance . . . Here's the heavyweight champion of the world sitting there and he's a solid piece of fucking armor.")

"Mike it's absolutely bullshit, it's false," Donald reiterated. "I give you my word."

"Could I lie down on your couch?" asked Tyson.

"Why?"

"Because I'm so tired I just want to nap."

"Sure, go ahead."

Tyson then stretched out on a red couch to the right of Donald's desk. One of Donald's staffers later walked into his office and found Tyson asleep.

"Donald, Mike Tyson is drooling on your couch," the employee said.

"*You* wake him and tell him," Donald responded.[52]

Meanwhile, Donald's casinos were heading into serious financial problems. As long as Donald had able-minded people running things for him, some of the cracks in his casino empire might have been hidden. But the helicopter crash, and the deaths of Etess and Hyde, forced all of Donald's weaknesses to the surface.

Shortly before the Taj opened, alarms started to ring around the Trump empire. One of the first was sounded by a securities analyst named Marvin Roffman, who voiced doubts about whether the Taj could consistently generate the $1.3 million a day it needed to crawl out from beneath about $822 million of debt borrowed to build it.[53] Donald went on the attack after Roffman spoke up, and in a hallowed Wall Street tradition the securities firm Roffman worked for fired him for being honest.

"I've met with hundreds of the top corporate executives. The number one decision I make is on management, the people who run these companies," Roffman said in an interview fifteen years later. "If you get a bad guy in there, they can take down major companies, giants can come tumbling to their feet . . . Donald's troubles, aside from the financing, are from the management. I really don't think that Donald understands the day-to-day skills needed to run a casino. When it comes to the day-to-day operations, where Steve Wynn would understand the business, Donald doesn't have that."[54]

At about the same time that doubts were mounting about the Taj's viability, Ivana ran into Marla Maples in Aspen, Colorado. The two women exchanged words reported around the globe in wildly different variations.

"Stay away from my husband, Moola!" Ivana said to Marla, according to one news report.

"But I love your husband, and do you love your husband?" Marla asked.

"Stay away, we have a happy marriage!" Ivana responded.[55]

Marla later related how difficult, and inaccurately reported, the encounter was, particularly because Ivana apparently mistakenly believed that a friend of hers was the real Marla.

"She came up to [my friend] and said, 'Are you Moola? Are you?' And she said no," Marla recalled. "Then she came up to me and asked me if I was Moola. I said no, because well, that's not my name. I felt awful, just terrible."[56]

And Donald had his own revelations as a result of the episode.

"We were actually standing near the restaurant, getting ready to put skis on. And I was standing there like an idiot and Marla and Ivana were here," he told a reporter. "And there wasn't shouting, but you could obviously see there was some friction. And a man who was standing right next to me, who weighed about 350 pounds and wasn't a very attractive guy, said to me, 'It could be worse, Donald. I've been in Aspen for twenty years and I've never had a date.' And I'll never forget the statement and it sort of lightened it up a little bit for me. I'm saying, 'You know, I guess it could be worse.'"[57]

After her first encounter with Marla, Ivana hired a private detective. And shortly before the Taj Mahal opened, Ivana sued Donald in an effort to overturn the couple's prenuptial agreement.[58] Still, Donald lost none of his promotional chutzpah, telling reporters when the Taj opened that Wynn's Las Vegas casino couldn't measure up.

"This is really the biggest and the best. It's the most beautiful. People have come from the Mirage in Las Vegas, and they've said: This is far more beautiful," Donald offered. "And it is a far more beautiful casino, and, you know, that is very much of an honor."

Besides, said the same man who had a waterfall in Trump Tower's lobby and his name in gigantic letters everywhere else, the Taj was a model of restraint compared with the Mirage. "The Taj's special effect is the opulence," he said. "I didn't want to have a volcano on the boardwalk because it wouldn't be appropriate."[59]

On marched the Trumpster to the Taj's grand opening, where he rubbed an enormous genie's lamp in front of the casino, setting off a spectacular laser light show and igniting a starry fireworks display. Shortly after the Taj's doors opened, however, a cascade of problems began. Among other snafus, a section of the casino's slot machines went haywire and malfunctioned, forcing the floor managers to shut them down. And the Taj's staff and accountants lacked the proper systems that regulators demanded for tracking and counting cash on the casino floor.

When Donald later went on CNN to tell Larry King why the slots stopped, he offered the credulous host a novel explanation. Gamblers, enthralled with slots action at the Taj, had force-fed quarters to the little mechanical beasts so quickly that the machines exploded.

King: "So what, it blew out the slots, literally?"

Donald: "They blew apart. We had machines that—"

King: "It would be, like, too much use?"

Donald: "They were virtually on fire."[60]

No matter how much Donald scrambled, the Taj's heavily promoted kickoff failed to mask what had become increasingly obvious to everyone but Atlantic City's casino regulators: Donald was drowning in debt. Two months before the opening, when Donald's liaisons with Marla Maples spilled into the open, the tabloid fiesta that ensued produced an iconic front-page headline in the *The New York Post* beside a photo of a gloating Donald: BEST SEX I'VE EVER HAD. Yet just a brief spin of the news cycle later, Donald's debt woes had deepened and the *Post* had gone hostile. It dubbed the Taj the "eighth blunder of the world." The paper reduced

Donald's business prospects to a single, front-page catchphrase: UH-OWE!

In addition to Roffman, Neil Barsky, a *Wall Street Journal* reporter, was on to Donald's debt problems before the rest of the world. Donald threatened to sue the *Journal* if Barsky reported the severity of his cash squeeze, which the paper did anyway. The details Barsky unearthed in the spring and early summer of 1990 were revealing. Except for the retail space in Trump Tower and his half share in the Grand Hyatt Hotel, everything else Donald owned was losing money. The Trump Shuttle, Donald's airline, lost $85 million in the first year after he bought it. And Manhattan's West Side Yards, Donald's key to a future as an authentic real estate baron, was encumbered with $200 million in debt, generated no income, and had no interested buyers because the real estate market had deteriorated. And it looked as though he would need to sell much of what he owned to pay off his debts.[61]

Donald later revealed that Barsky, who won a prestigious journalism award for his coverage of the developer, had solicited boxing tickets from him, prompting the *Journal* to assign the reporter to a new beat. But sputtering like a downed power line, Donald argued that, despite the doubts of his bankers and the facts that Barsky was uncovering, he was as rich as ever.

"I've got a Shuttle that you can sell for a fortune, I've got the best real estate in the world, I've got everything else; do you . . . think I have a cash flow problem?" he asked a reporter. "Use your head. Who says that? Enemies say that? I have a problem with where to invest my cash."[62]

What cash?

All told, Donald was $3.2 billion in debt and had personally guaranteed about $900 million of that amount. And his businesses were all on the verge of seizures. An auditor retained by New Jersey regulators examined everything Donald had—his Manhattan real estate, the Shuttle, the casinos, everything —and

Donald and his parents, 1964.
(Courtesy of New York Military Academy)

Graduation from military school, June 1964.
(Courtesy of New York Military Academy)

Hot date, circa 1964.
(Courtesy of New York Military Academy)

Donald carries
the ball
at military school,
May 1963.
*(Courtesy of
New York
Military Academy)*

Donald and his father,
Fred Trump, atop Trump
Village in Brooklyn, 1973.
*(Barton Silverman, The New
York Times)*

Donald sits for a photo shoot, December 1975.
(Larry Morris, The New York Times)

Man About Town, November 1976.
(Chester Higgins Jr., The New York Times)

Donald with scale model
of Trump Tower, August 1980.
(Don Hogan Charles, The New York Times)

Fred Trump, Ivana, Ed Koch, Donald, and Mary Trump at City Hall, 1983.
(Holland Wemple)

Donald and the New Jersey Generals
introduce their quarterback, Doug Flutie,
February 1985.
(Fred R. Conrad, The New York Times*)*

Donald announces Television City
project on Manhattan's
West Side Yards, November 1985.
(Neal Boenzi, The New York Times*)*

Flyboy: Frank Lorenzo announces the sale of the Eastern Shuttle to Donald
for $365 million (in borrowed money), October 1988.
(Edward Hausner, The New York Times*)*

The Taj Mahal,
one of Donald's
three Atlantic City
casinos,
on the eve
of bankruptcy, 2004.
(AP/Wide World Photos)

Bill Rancic, Donald,
and Carolyn Kepcher
convene in
The Apprentice
boardroom.
*(Courtesy of Mark Burnett
Productions)*

You're Fired!
Donald in
The Apprentice
boardroom, 2004.
*(Courtesy of Mark Burnett
Productions)*

Tough Love: Donald and Melania at the Emmy Awards, 2004.
(AP/Wide World Photos)

Melania on the cover of *Vogue*, February 2005.
(Mario Testino, Vogue © The Condé Nast Publications Inc.)

The Mouth That Roared: Donald in character, 2004.
(Reuters)

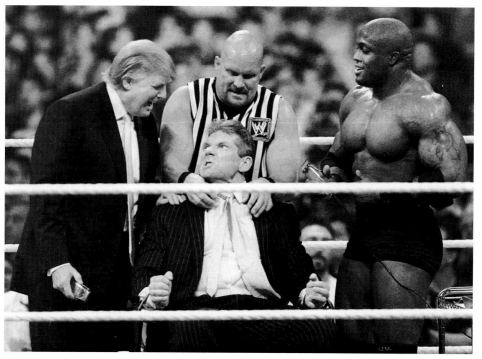

WrestleMania: Donald gives WWE chairman Vince McMahon a head shave.
(Bill Pugliano/Getty Images)

Newlyweds Donald and Melania celebrate their nuptials with the Clintons.
(Maring Photography, Getty Images)

It's About Me: Donald puts Jeb Bush on notice during a Republican presidential debate in 2016. *(Bloomberg)*

Performance Art: Donald decides that he's not taking Jeb Bush—or the Republican Party—seriously. *(Bloomberg)*

determined that the only property Donald owned that generated cash was the Trump Plaza casino; it was, the auditor noted, "the one asset within the entire Organization that historically has been capable of producing a healthy cash flow." But, the auditor warned, the cash squeeze draining Trump Plaza's coffers meant that it was likely that "this property may no longer be positioned as a crutch to prop up non-income producing or other cash-draining assets of the Organization."[63]

Shortly after the Taj opening, *Forbes* magazine published a cover story saying the developer was worth, at best, only $500 million, down from an earlier *Forbes* estimate of $1.7 billion. But Donald's situation was worse than even *Forbes* imagined. Given all of the debt Donald had piled on his holdings, it was unlikely he ever was a billionaire, much less worth $500 million. In fact, Donald only had about $17 million to $23 million in cash, and in the most optimistic scenario—one adopted by New Jersey regulators —his net worth was about $206 million.[64] But the debts on his properties were so massive that he owed far more than he had. In all likelihood, Donald was worth less than zero.[65]

Just two months after the Taj opened, a $41 million bond payment came due on one of his other casinos, the Castle—a payment Donald didn't have the money to make. So Donald's bankers, starting to recognize that they had tethered themselves to a borrower who could bring all of them down, gave him a $65 million emergency loan to prevent everything he had from sliding into bankruptcy. The magic of American capitalism impressed Donald. "I have gained a great and deep respect for the banking system and those who make it work," he said shortly after the banks gave him the handout.[66]

In return for the $65 million, and deferral of all payments on $2.7 billion in debt for three to five years, Donald gave the banks his ownership interest in his three casinos. The banks also put Donald on an allowance. He was forced to limit his personal and household spending to $450,000 a month (a tad more than the average American lived on, but Donald had been spending about $1 million a month, according to a person with direct knowledge of his finances). Donald's allowance was slated to drop to $375,000 a month in 1991 and $300,000 a month in 1992. His annual salary was not to exceed $200,000. He also had to submit a monthly business plan and budget to the banks.[67]

Even with the bank's first aid, the clock was ticking.

"Make no mistake about it. Trump is on his way down—and probably out," noted Allan Sloan, a financial writer who spent years cataloging Donald's more questionable financial maneuvers. "The question isn't whether his real estate–casino–airline empire will be drastically shrunk. The question is whether Trump will be left with anything at all."[68]

New Jersey regulators were like-minded.

The Trump "Organization as a whole is generating an insufficient level of cash flow to adequately support both daily operations and payment of debt service and the consequences of this shortfall will be compounded," the regulators' auditor warned. "Simply put, the Organization is in dire financial straits."[69]

Only eight years had passed since Trump Tower had opened; only three years had passed since *The Art of the Deal* became a best seller. In that brief span Donald had gone from being the country's most celebrated businessman to its most colorful flameout.

Still, Donald and his representatives said that his problems were overstated. And he found a new business tune to whistle: Yes, the real estate market was in a free fall, but that didn't matter because he didn't have that much at stake in Manhattan. His lawyer, Harvey Freeman, pointed out that Donald had sold all of the units in the apartment buildings he had built and most of the other real estate he owned. Other than the Plaza Hotel and the West Side Yards, there wasn't much left in Donald's portfolio.

"We just don't own that much Manhattan real estate," Freeman told *The New York Times.*

Donald agreed.

"Good or bad," he said, the New York real estate market "doesn't have any effect on me."[70]

All of this was, in fact, true. Donald owned very little real estate in New York and never would again. Creditors would take the Plaza Hotel away from him; control of the West Side Yards would also slip from his grasp.

But even without any exposure to New York real estate, Donald's situation remained perilous. The Taj didn't make enough money to pay down its debt, and in November Donald gave bondholders a 50 percent stake in the casino after he missed a debt payment. The Taj eventually filed for bankruptcy protection about a year after it opened. And Donald still had billions in debt, $900 million of which carried his personal signature.

As the casinos continued to wilt, the one person Donald could always depend on bailed him out—his wealthy father. As another big Castle payment approached in December 1990, promising to send Donald into personal and corporate bankruptcy, Fred Trump pulled off a neat trick. He bought $3.4 million worth of chips at the Castle and didn't cash them in, giving Donald the funds he needed to get past that hump. Fred's purchase flouted state casino regulations, but regulators gave Donald, the anchor of Atlantic City's gambling market, a pass.

Donald, struggling to avoid a financial meltdown, returned the favor by focusing his considerable energies on trying to rescue what he had left in Atlantic City. New York real estate, he said, was a second-tier endeavor.

"I think Atlantic City over the next two or three years will be far greater than anything I could ever do in Manhattan," he said in 1990. "I think it's far greater than anybody can do in Manhattan."[71]

TrumpQuiz #6

If you're a billionaire supplementing your fortune by entering the gambling market, you should:

1) Be sure that your first business partners have the right experiences on their résumés—like possibly murdering Jimmy Hoffa.
2) Challenge your chief casino competitor to golf games, even though he has trouble seeing. Make fun of his game.
3) Buy a casino you can barely afford, then appoint your wife to run it.
4) Take your wife and mistress to Atlantic City boxing matches—*at the same time and on the same helicopter.* Have an escort pose as your mistress's date. Assume your wife won't get suspicious.
5) Take your wife and mistress to Aspen *at the same time.* Assume they won't meet.
6) When your wife and your mistress intersect on Aspen's ski slopes and begin arguing, flee the scene. Forget that your wife skied competitively. Assume that she won't be able to catch up with you.
7) Play the *Wheel of Fortune* all-vowel game: IOU.
8) Install slot machines that blow up. The kids love 'em.
9) Charge your casino $5 million for the use of your personal yacht.[72]
10) Name your huge casino after a famous Indian tomb. Name the restaurant inside after a famous Arabian storyteller. Name the luxury suite upstairs after a famous Macedonian conqueror. Pretend the entire casino has a theme.
11) Enlist boxing promoter and fellow hair-raiser Don King to appraise your Atlantic City business skills: "Donald Trump don't mess around. He doesn't procrastinate or

vacillate but wants to titillate. He's built his own little empire here and it's growing all the time."

12) And the *Jeopardy!* answer is: This former talk show host wrote in his autobiography, "One morning in early 1989 I woke up and found myself responsible for $925 million worth of debt."

CHAPTER SIX

TRUMPBROKE

In a world of more than six billion people, there are only
587 billionaires. It's an exclusive club. Would you like to join us?
—DONALD TRUMP, *THINK LIKE A BILLIONAIRE*

B
Y 1993, WITH HIS CASINOS IN HOCK, MOST OF HIS REAL ESTATE HOLD-
ings either forfeit or stagnant, and his father slipping into
the fog of Alzheimer's disease, Donald, at the age of forty-
seven, had run out of money. There were no funds left to
keep him aloft, and as the bare-bones operation he maintained on
Fifth Avenue started to grind to a halt he ordered Nick Ribis, the
Trump Organization's president, to call his siblings and ask for a
handout from their trusts. Donald needed about $10 million to
fund his living and office expenses, but he had no collateral to provide his brother and sisters, all three of whom wanted a guarantee
that he would repay them.

The Trump children's share of their father's fortune amounted
to about $35 million each, and Donald's siblings demanded that
the developer sign a promissory note pledging future distributions
from his trust fund against the $10 million he wanted to borrow.

Donald got his loan, but about a year later he was almost broke again. When he went to the trough the second time, he asked his siblings for $20 million more. Robert Trump, who briefly oversaw Donald's casinos before fleeing the pressure of working for his brother to take over Fred's real estate operation, balked. Desperate to scrape some money together, Donald asked Alan Marcus, one of his advisers, to contact his brother-in-law, John Barry, and see if he could intervene with Robert and his other siblings.

"John and I spoke about it a few times," Marcus told me. "In fact, we spoke about it in the conference room in Trump Tower. John then went around and addressed it with the family."[1]

Barry successfully lobbied other members of the Trump clan and another handout was arranged, with Donald agreeing again that whatever he failed to pay back would be taken out of his share of Fred's estate.

"We would have literally closed down," said another former member of the Trump Organization familiar with Donald's efforts to keep the company afloat. "The key would have been in the door and there would have been no more Donald Trump. The family saved him."[2]

Donald disagreed with this version of events. "I had zero borrowings from the estate," he told me. "I give you my word."[3]

But Marcus and two other executives who worked closely with Donald all said that the family's financial lifeline gave the developer the support he needed to get through the rough waters separating his early years of overblown, overhyped acquisitions and the later years of small, sedate deals preceding his resurrection on *The Apprentice*. Both of Donald's parents died during that time, he parried with Ivana Trump in a bitter divorce battle that hinged on properly valuing his dwindling assets, he remarried and divorced again, and then he did what anyone else in his situation would do when confronted with limited options—he ran for president of the United States.

Before Donald could get to phase two of his career he had to muscle his way through the dismantling of his business empire and a thorny financial restructuring with his bankers and bond-holders that left him on the precipice of personal and corporate bankruptcy. As bankers who once fell over one another to throw money at him now lined up for their share of what was left over, Donald scrambled to hang on to whatever he could while maintaining his facade as America's most savvy entrepreneur. And in terms of maintaining his popular mojo, Donald proved to be remarkably resilient.

But the footrace that Donald's debt negotiations entailed in the early to mid-1990s landed him in the uncomfortable position of becoming something worse than a has-been; it brought him face-to-face with a specter who haunted all of Manhattan real estate's highfliers: William Zeckendorf Sr., the larger-than-life developer who fell to earth.

Zeckendorf "was a great, flamboyant guy who got crushed because of his appetite and his, you know, everything. But he was a great asset to the city. He was responsible for so many good jobs, but he ended up getting crushed," Donald told me. "You always have to watch that. I study him because you don't want the fate that happened to Bill Zeckendorf Sr. to happen to yourself. You don't want that . . . He could have done things that would have made him great. He was a great guy who ended badly, and that's not good.

"When I was in trouble in the early '90s, I went around and—you know, a lot of people couldn't believe I did this because they think I have an ego—I went around and openly told people I was worth minus $900 million. Because how are you going to make a deal with the banks when you are telling people you are worth millions of dollars, and, 'By the way, I want you to discount the shit out of the loan.' So I would openly tell people that I was worth minus $900 million. And then I was able to make a deal with the banks."[4]

Donald also gained two other insights into how financial dissolution could become a topsy-turvy process easily bent to his own devices. The first revelation was that when borrowers owed so much money that they resembled a foundering, third-world country that was simply too big to fail, banks wouldn't let them fail. The second revelation was that the bankruptcy process itself gave failed businesspeople ample buoyancy to levitate out of their own graves.

For Donald, all of this meant that the threat of walking away from what he owed, combined with as much artful dodging as possible, allowed him to attach himself to his casinos, the one part of his crumbling domain that promised financial salvation.

"You can delay these people for years from getting [what you own]," he said of his bankers and other creditors. "You understand: They can't get it. It takes years legally to get it."[5]

To survive a process as tortuous and unpredictable as a debt workout, however, requires a large dose of gumption. And Donald had gumption in spades.

"You're out there alone. I mean, it's not fun," he advised me. "It was like an exact opposite. I went from being a boy wonder, boy genius, to this fucking guy who has nothing but problems. And the sad part is, there were many other people in my same position but nobody gave a fuck about them . . . That's the negative to visibility."

IN SEPTEMBER 1982, WITH TRUMP TOWER A YEAR AWAY FROM COMPLETION, *Forbes* magazine published the Forbes 400, its annual list of America's wealthiest individuals and families, for the first time. (In 1918 *Forbes* had produced a list of America's thirty richest people, but that was a onetime event.) Chock-full of anecdotes about how the rich got rich and what they did with their richly deserved riches, the Forbes 400 was financial pornography of the most voyeuristic and delicious sort.

While there was a refreshing inclusiveness about the list (Mafia treasurer Meyer Lansky made the inaugural tally, for example), some on the roster held rank upon the loosest of foundations. For those whose wealth was based on a stake in a publicly traded company, calculating their Forbesworthiness was relatively straightforward—put a value on their stock. But for those with privately held money who weren't a Rockefeller, Mellon, du Pont, or Kennedy, the process of ascertaining their fortunes was trickier. *Forbes* relied on those people to willingly fork over an honest and somewhat exact self-appraisal of their wealth.

It also turned out that some big buckaroos, understandably averse to the avalanche of phone calls from charities or scamsters that would follow such publicity, loathed being on the list. Forrest Mars Sr., patriarch of one of the world's largest candy fortunes, actively kept his photo out of the press and, like others in his rarefied class, did not cooperate with *Forbes*'s researchers. Even Malcolm Forbes himself did not provide his list makers with an assessment of his wealth. Since he owned the magazine, no one bothered trying to guess. *Forbes* put Forbes in the four hundredth spot, without an estimate of his net worth.

Some people lobbied more actively against having their fortunes outed. After the first list was published, one millionaire, Kenneth Davis, sued *Forbes* to prevent his name from being on the Forbes 400. But a federal judge, David Belew, ruled against him in 1983. "A very significant proportion of our national wealth, land and industry is controlled by the Forbes 400," Judge Belew ruled. "Money is power and the wealthy wield great power and influence economically, socially and politically in this country and the American public has a right to know who they are."[6]

Others offered a more streetwise assessment of what the Forbes 400 was all about. The Hunt brothers of Texas, scions of an oil fortune who eventually lost billions after trying to illegally corner the silver market, made light of the list in 1983 after a congressional investigation revealed that they were very rich, but not as rich as *Forbes* had thought. Between year one and year two of the list, Lamar Hunt's wealth, according to *Forbes*, dropped from $1 billion to $500 million.

"Last year, I thought it was one of the greatest jokes I ever heard," Hunt said of the first *Forbes* list. "They create in the public mind some fairy tale type of situation."[7]

Nelson Bunker Hunt, sitting before a government panel grilling him about his silver purchases, told members of Congress that he really didn't know how much he was worth. Nor, he said, did he feel a pressing need to figure that out.

"A fellow asked me that once, and I said, 'I don't know,'" Hunt related. "But I do know people who know how much they are worth generally aren't worth much."[8]

Nonetheless, the Forbes 400 drew scads of attention from the very moment it was published. The list became capitalism's Rosetta stone, a decoding device for divining the American Way. Even prominent economists parsed it for social truths.

"At a trivial level, it is almost impossible not to be interested in *Forbes* magazine's annual list of the 400 wealthiest individuals, minimum net worth $150 million, and 82 wealthiest families, minimum net worth $200 million," observed Lester Thurow, an MIT economist, of the 1983 list. "Subconsciously, we read their biographies hoping to find the elixir that will add us to the list. While the elixir—a rich father—is to be found (all of the 82 families and 241 of the 400 wealthiest individuals inherited all or a major part of their fortunes), it doesn't help most of us to point this out to our fathers.

"Standard economics, after all, assumes that people accumulate wealth solely to provide future consumption privileges for themselves and their children. . . . But the standard assumption is incorrect," Professor Thurow continued. "Future consumption is not the motive that leads to large accumulations of wealth. If the 12 billionaires on the *Forbes* list were to treat their wealth as an annuity to be consumed before death, they would have to spend $630,000 a day for the rest of their lives. Clearly they do not have enough time left to spend their money, much less enjoy it.

"Great wealth is accumulated to acquire economic power. Wealth makes you an economic mover and shaker. Projects will happen, or not happen, depending upon your decisions. It allows you to influence the political process—elect yourself or others—and remold society in accordance with your views. It makes you an important person, courted by people inside and outside your family. Perhaps this explains why some people try to persuade *Forbes* that they are wealthy enough to merit inclusion."[9]

This, then, was the dividing line: Those who were secure enough not to reveal their wealth abhorred the Forbes 400, or at least tried to avoid it; those who were less secure, needed to keep score, and had their identities wrapped up in the concept of billionairedom, turned the list into a white-collar fetish. For the latter group, to be off the Forbes 400 represented emotional and social exile. Donald, paradoxically, was a loner who did not want to live in exile. He was obsessed with the *Forbes* list. And his propensity for inflation, matched with *Forbes*'s aversion to hiring the sizable staff it might need to accurately assess the wealth of each of its designated four hundred (as well as the advertising and publicity windfall the magazine enjoyed after inventing the list), got Donald on the magazine's inaugural list in 1982. *Forbes* gave Donald an undefined share of a family fortune the magazine estimated at $200 million—at a time when all Donald owned personally was a half interest in the Grand Hyatt and a share of the yet-to-be completed Trump Tower. That same year, New Jersey regulators gave a more realistic assessment of Donald's finances in his casino licensing report. The report said Donald earned a $100,000 salary working for his father in 1982, had $6,000 in savings, got a $1 million commission on the Grand Hyatt deal, and had a $35 million unsecured line of bank credit—in other words, short on cash and in debt up to his eyeballs.[10]

Donald and the Forbes 400 were mutually reinforcing. The more Donald's verbal fortune rose, the more often he received prominent mentions in *Forbes*. The more often *Forbes* mentioned him, the more credible Donald's claim to vast wealth became. The more credible his claim to vast wealth became, the easier it was for him to get on the Forbes 400—which became the standard that other media, and apparently some of the country's biggest banks, used when judging Donald's riches. In some years, Donald insisted on impossibly high figures for his net worth and then, in a faux fit of complaining, settled for an estimate that *Forbes* convinced itself was conservative—even though it was often wildly high anyway. The one gap in this mating dance was 1990 to 1995, when Donald didn't appear on the list at all. *Forbes* was apparently so chastened by the $2.6 billion difference in its estimate of Donald's wealth between 1989 and 1990 that the magazine needed a six-year hiatus before it had the confidence to begin helping him inflate his verbal fortune again.

Forbes's odes to Donald went like this over the years:

1982—Wealth: Share of Fred's estimated $200 million fortune. *Forbes* explains: "Consummate self-promoter. Building Trump Tower next to Tiffany's. Angling for Atlantic City casino." *Forbes* quotes Donald: "'Man is the most vicious of animals and life is a series of battles ending in victory or defeat.'" *Forbes* explains further: ". . . fortune estimated at over $200 million. Donald claims $500 million."

1983—Wealth: Share of Fred's estimated $400 million fortune. (Author's note: Observe that although 1982 to 1983 was a particularly brutal recession year, the Trump family's real estate fortune doubles!)

1984—Wealth: Fred has $200 million, Donald has $400 million.

1985—Rank: 51; Wealth: $600 million. (Donald becomes a solo Forbes 400 act; Fred disappears from list.)

1986—Rank: 50; Wealth: $700 million.

1987—Rank: 63; Wealth: $850 million.

1988—Rank: 44; Wealth: $1 billion.

1989—Rank: 26; Wealth: $1.7 billion. (Author's note: Observe that Donald's wealth has grown by $1.1 billion during a four-year period when he was borrowing huge sums to buy money-losing properties.)

1990—Dropped from the list! *Forbes* explains: "In 1990 the rich have been getting poorer. Trump is the most noteworthy loser. Once a billionaire, Trump's net worth may actually have dropped to zero." (That makes things clearer. Was he ever a billionaire? Maybe his net worth just stayed the same? Maybe it always had been zero? In later years, but not this year, *Forbes* acknowledges that Donald had a negative net worth of $900 million in 1990—that is, he was $900 million below zero.)

1991—AWOL.

1992—AWOL.

1993—AWOL. (These are the times that try men's souls. Hang in there, Donald.)

1994—AWOL.

1995—AWOL.

1996—He's back! Rank: 373; Wealth: $450 million. *Forbes* explains: "Trump, polite but unhappy, phoning from his plane: 'You're putting me on at $450 million? I've got that much in stock market assets alone. There's 100% of Trump Tower, 100% of the new Nike store—they're paying $10 million a year in rent!' Add it all up, said Trump, and his net worth is 'in the $2 billion range, probably over $2 billion.'" (Don't worry, Donald, one year from now *Forbes* will help you find another easy $1 billion.)

1997—Rank: 105; Wealth: $1.4 billion. *Forbes* explains: "The art of the comeback? With New York City real estate sizzling, the irrepressible Donald is back to billionairedom. . . . Net worth was negative $900 million 1990, but the Donald now claims to have $500 million in cash alone. Disputes our estimate. 'The real number,' he insists, 'is $3.7 billion.'"

1998—Rank: 121; Wealth: $1.5 billion. *Forbes* explains: "Unstoppable salesman, master of hyperbole. Net worth was negative $900 million 1990, now claims our estimate is low by a factor of 3: 'The number is closer to $5 billion.'"

1999—Rank: 145; Wealth: $1.6 billion. *Forbes* explains: "We love Donald. He returns our calls. He usually pays for lunch. He even estimates his own net worth ($4.5 billion). But no matter how hard we try, we just can't prove it."

2000—Rank: 167; Wealth: $1.7 billion. *Forbes* explains: "In The Donald's world, worth more than $5 billion. Back on Earth, worth considerably less."

2001—Rank: 110; Wealth: $1.8 billion.

2002—Rank: 92; Wealth: $1.9 billion.

2003—Rank: 71; Wealth: $2.5 billion.

2004—Rank: 189; Wealth: $2.6 billion. *Forbes* explains: "America's love affair with The Donald reaching impossibly new highs; his reality show, *The Apprentice*, was prime-time television's highest-rated series last year. . . . After nearly defaulting on its debt obligations, Trump's gaming properties to reorganize. . . . No matter. For Donald, real estate is where his real wealth lies. Over 18 million square feet of prime Manhattan space." (Author's note: We'll have fun with this *Forbes* audit later in our text.)

Forbes, if not entirely skeptical of Donald, had, of course, grown accustomed to his intense lobbying.

"There are a couple of guys who call and say you're low on other guys, but Trump is one of the most glaring examples of someone who constantly calls about himself and says we're not only low, but low by a multiple," said Peter Newcomb, a veteran editor of *Forbes*'s richlist.[11]

The Forbes 400, of course, has always loomed large in Donald's imagination.

"When you think of it, I've been on that list for a long time. I think they work very hard at the list," he told me in 2005. "It seems to be that they're the barometer of individual wealth. It doesn't really matter. It matters much less to me today than it mattered in the past. In the past, it probably mattered more."[12]

Donald's verbal billions were always a topic of conversation whenever we visited. In my first conversation with him, in 1996, he brought up his billions. In early 2004 one of his closest advisers called me to say that Donald was particularly rankled by a story my colleague Eric Dash and I had written in *The New York Times*. Although the story said that Donald had mismanaged his casino empire to the point of bankruptcy, the adviser conveyed that what really bothered Donald was that we were curious about the true size of his fortune and his self-proclaimed status as Manhattan's biggest real estate developer.

The *Times* story noted that another New York developer, Richard LeFrak, whose family controlled acres of apartments and projects around the city, extolled Donald's virtues as a builder and a real estate marketer, but that LeFrak was more circumspect about whether the Trumpster was New York's "biggest." I had called LeFrak at Donald's suggestion. "He's a dear friend of mine, but it wouldn't be accurate for him to say that," said LeFrak, noting that the LeFrak family owned the most residential units in New York. He added that if Manhattan was considered on its own, separate from the city's other boroughs, and size was measured in terms of the value of property sold, then Donald might be "up there" in the top tier of developers—though LeFrak was still hesitant to label Donald the biggest.[13]

When Donald and I spent time together one weekend in early 2005, the subject of his verbal billions inevitably came up. Donald had gamely and openly fielded a diverse range of questions all day, so I was curious to see where he would go when we got to money. When I popped the wealth question, he paused momentarily and scrunched his eyebrows. We had reached a crossroads. Out it came. He pursed his lips a little bit. Out it came. He blinked. Out it came, rising up from deep within him.

"I would say six [billion]. Five to six. Five to six."[14]

Hmmm. The previous August he told me that his net worth was $4 billion to $5 billion. Then, later that same day in August, he said his casino holdings represented 2 percent of his wealth, which at the time gave him a net worth of about $1.7 billion. In the same day, Donald's own estimates of his wealth differed by as much as

$3.3 billion. How could that happen? Was Donald living in his own private zone of wildly escalating daily inflation, a TrumpBolivia? And his $1.7 billion figure in August was well below the $2.6 billion *Forbes* would credit him when it published its richlist just a couple of months later.

Now Donald was saying he was worth $5 billion to $6 billion.

"Five to six. Five to six."

And on the nightstand in my bedroom at Donald's Palm Beach club was a glossy brochure that said he was worth $9.5 billion.

When I sat down in a Trump Tower conference room one afternoon with Allen Weisselberg, the Trump Organization's chief financial officer, he claimed Donald was worth about $6 billion. But the list of assets Weisselberg quoted, all of which were valued in very inflated and optimistic terms and some of which Donald didn't own, totaled only about $5 billion. Where might the rest have been? "I'm going to go to my office and find that other billion," Weisselberg assured me.[15] Did he ever return? No, he never returned.

A chart detailing Weisselberg's assessment of Donald's riches appears opposite, on page 155. This chart left me confused.

So I asked around for guidance. Three people with direct knowledge of Donald's finances, people who had worked closely with him for years, told me that they thought his net worth was somewhere between $150 million and $250 million. By anyone's standards this still qualified Donald as comfortably wealthy, but none of these people thought he was remotely close to being a billionaire.

Donald dismissed this as naysaying.

"You can go ahead and speak to guys who have four-hundred-pound wives at home who are jealous of me, but the guys who really know me know I'm a great builder," he told me.[16]

The real estate question also arose again in early 2005; Donald told me he was the biggest real estate developer in New York, bar none. The biggest. Donald suggested I call another New York real estate honcho, *Daily News* owner Mort Zuckerman, and talk to him about the Trumpster's edifice complex.

What Donald Owns in NYC	What Donald Says His Stake Is Worth
Trump World Tower 845 UN Plaza	$300 million
Trump Park Avenue 59th and Park	$160 million
40 Wall Street	$155 million
Trump Tower (commercial space/NIKEtown) 56th and Fifth	$565 million

Donald's Other Projects	What Donald Says They're Worth
The Apprentice	$100 million
Chicago skyscraper	$300–$350 million
Cash	$500 million
4 golf courses	$800 million
West Side Yards	$1.3 billion
"Other Land" (his term)	$200 million
Las Vegas condominiums	$250–$300 million
Miss Universe	$40–$50 million
"Condo inventory" (his term)	$400 million
Shopping centers	$40–$50 million
Palm Beach real estate	$100 million
"Profit sharing" (his term)	$100 million
Licensing/merchandising Trump name	$40 million

"I don't think Donald is the biggest guy in New York real estate, but he's a major player in residential real estate," Zuckerman told me. "He doesn't own anything like he did in the '80s. Everything now he does for a fee and a percentage of the profits and it means that someone else comes up with the money. That limits his upside, but it also limits his downside as well. And he's established a brand name out of his uninhibited genius for self-promotion . . . Donald is a character, a genuine New York character."[17]

However illusory, it was Donald's fixation on billionaire bragging rights and real estate prowess—in addition to the financial lifeline his siblings tossed to him—that kept his mojo rising during his brush with financial extinction in the early to mid-1990s. But the Donald who emerged on the other side of his business meltdown was a financial shadow of his earlier, acquisitive, debt-laden self, and would remain so right up to *The Apprentice*'s debut.

Donald entered the restructuring zone in the fall of 1990, and as the months wore on New Jersey casino auditors offered a gloomy assessment of his prospects.

"The overleveraging of this Organization, particularly in its recent acquisition of non-casino hotel assets, has created [a] crisis atmosphere," the auditors said of the Trump Organization. "It may very well be that the greatest hope for preserving remaining value lies in a quick and efficient reorganization and workout process—a privatized bankruptcy of sorts—outside the courtroom."[18]

Financial turmoil, of course, didn't stop Donald from spouting. The all-time howler award for a publication taking his verbal billions at face value belonged to *Playboy*. In early 1990, just a month before the Taj Mahal opened in Atlantic City and began a slide that would take Donald's empire down with it, the magazine profiled the developer and said that he had amassed "a fortune his father never dreamed possible," including "a cash hoard of $900,000,000," and a "geyser of $50,000,000 a week from his hotel-casinos."[19]

In the real world, New Jersey casino auditors estimated that as of September 1990, Donald was worth about $206 million—almost all of which was tied up in hotels, an airline, casinos, and other properties that were devaluing rapidly or about to be taken away from him. Donald's cash on hand was only $17 million, and that was dissolving quickly as well.[20]

Regulators projected Donald's 1991 income from trusts and rentals at $1.7 million, offset by $9.7 million in debt payments, $6 million in personal business expenses, and $4.5 million to maintain his Trump Tower triplex and estates in Greenwich, Connecticut, and Palm Beach for the year—meaning he would be about $18.5 million in the hole at the end of 1991. Regulators projected Donald's income for 1992 to sink to $748,000 and his 1993 income to drop even farther to $296,000—with all of his debt payments and personal expenses continuing to pile up. At the end of 1993 his personal cash shortfall would amount to about $39 million, and there would still be $900 million in personally guaranteed loans hanging over his head.[21]

In the midst of all of this, Donald reached a property settlement with Ivana following their divorce. The March 1991 agreement called for the former Mrs. Trump to get a $10 million payment, the Greenwich estate, $350,000 in annual alimony, $300,000 in annual child support, a $4 million housing allowance, use of some Trump properties, and a $350,000 salary for running the Plaza Hotel. The settlement nearly bankrupted Donald because he didn't have the $10 million to pay his ex-wife; he ended up using part of the $65 million banks had loaned his business the prior year to pay her.[22] Even so, regulators noted that the payment to Ivana "depleted most of Trump's personal cash."[23]

Throughout early 1991 and into the summer, Donald helped his banks begin to dismantle his holdings so he could pay off $3.4 billion in business debt and release himself from the $900 million in personal arrears attached to that pile. Absent an overhaul, Donald would be wiped out.

The little ray of sunshine in all of this for Donald was that the seismic real estate collapse sweeping the country in the early 1990s left banks with wads of bad loans in their coffers. They could choose to put their borrowers out of business, and be left owning companies they didn't want to run, or force debtors into messy bankruptcy proceedings that would involve paying whopping legal fees and suffering through years of delays. Neither alternative appealed to banks, and Donald got the first glimmer of this one afternoon in early 1991 when Boston Safe Deposit and Trust, the bank holding the $29 million loan he used to buy his über-yacht, the *Trump Princess,* called to ask the fallen developer to cough up some cash for an insurance payment.

Donald didn't have the money for the payment. Nor, having paid Ivana's divorce settlement, was there a line of credit into which he could tap. If the Boston bank called the loan, the first domino in Donald's financial universe would fall, triggering the collapse of everything else. So Donald and Stephen Bollenbach, a well-regarded financial adviser he retained to appease the banks and salvage his holdings, gambled. They told the Boston bank that they didn't plan to make the insurance payment.

"We told them, you got the mortgage payment on it and there's an insurance payment due so you should make it," Bollenbach told me. "And they did. I think that's when we knew that we had some room to maneuver and negotiate.

"It was so complicated that I think Donald had an advantage in terms of knowing where all the pieces fit, whereas many of the creditors had a much more limited view. It became more important to creditors to get a fair share of whatever pie was left, rather than the size of the pie itself."[24]

The yacht standoff opened Donald's eyes as well.

"We said, 'You pay the fuckin' insurance. We're not paying it.' Half a million dollars worth of insurance annually," Donald recalled. "They said, 'We're not going to pay it, you have an obligation. We're going to foreclose it and blah, blah, blah. I said, 'I don't give a fuck: You pay it.' And we waited, and the deadline came. And they paid it.

"That was sort of the bottom of the heap. Deep trouble. They could have really done a big number. There was a personal guarantee on the loan," Donald told me. "My father was a pro, my father knew, like I knew, you don't personally guarantee. So I wrote a book called *The Art of the Deal,* which as you know is the biggest of all time. In the book, I say, 'Never personally guarantee.' . . . And I've told people I didn't follow my own advice."[25]

Not that the grind of eking out bankruptcy agreements and scrounging around for money fazed Donald. Staring insolvency in the face, he called on that Norman Vincent Peale huzzah inside of himself and accentuated the positive, eliminated the negative, latched on to the affirmative, and didn't mess with Mr. In-Between.

"He has this very optimistic approach to the world. I would have been looking for the nearest building to jump off of and he just remained upbeat all of the time," said Bollenbach. "I never suspected that he lost a moment's sleep."[26]

Donald's lenders became increasingly pliant as the debt talks continued. And Bollenbach decided that in exchange for giving up all of his major real estate holdings, as well as the Trump Shuttle, the yacht, and other assorted moneylosers Donald had overpaid for in the 1980s, he could strip away most of the debt Donald owed and give him a shot at holding on to the casinos—a business that barely passed the sniff test with most of the banks and one that they certainly didn't want to own and operate.

Of course, Donald's struggles did leave some people gloating, particularly real estate competitors who had grown weary of his shtick—most particularly competitors with acid in their veins. Leona Helmsley, whose husband, Harry, had been a role model for Donald when he entered the Manhattan real estate market, unleashed a torrent of abuse on Donald in the early 1990s (thus assuring herself a spot alongside Ed Koch and Steve Wynn in the If-Donald-Smacks-You-Smack-Him-Right-Back Hall of Fame).

In the course of a 1990 interview with *Playboy,* Ms. Helmsley referred to Donald's then girlfriend Marla Maples as "Marpa Meeple,"

"Marble Maple," "Marlo Mipple," "whatever her name is," "Maple Marble," "Maypo Marla," and "Marla Mipple," before savaging Donald's budgeting abilities.

"Donald Trump is no Harry Helmsley. Can you imagine Harry assuming $2 billion in debt and guaranteeing $500 million of it personally?" Ms. Helmsley asked. "Egomaniac. Just plain stupid. All so he could have his little airplane, his little hotel and his little boat. He's great at playing O.P.M.—Other People's Money. Why not? It's not his. Then the egomaniac has the nerve to think that putting his name on everything makes it better. You watch: He's going to be left flat on his can and it couldn't happen to a nicer person."[27]

Ms. Helmsley's fusillade was inspired by Donald's own broadside against her several months earlier, also in *Playboy*.

"Leona Helmsley. She is a vicious, horrible woman who systematically destroyed the Helmsley name," Donald opined. "Also, Leona was not a great businesswoman but a very bad one.

"She set the women's movement back fifty years. She is a living nightmare, and to be married to her must be like living in hell," Donald added for good measure. "She's out of her mind. Leona Helmsley is a truly evil human being. She treated employees worse than any human being I've ever witnessed and I've dealt with some of the toughest human beings alive."[28]

Donald said you ruined your husband's good name, Ms. Helmsley. What of it?

"I'm sure that his father, a respectable man in real estate, is enthralled with what his son has done to his name," she retorted. "He's smeared it. I wouldn't believe Donald Trump if his tongue was notarized."

Ms. Helmsley even offered Ivana a dollop of advice on how she had mishandled Marla.

"I wouldn't have done what Ivana's done," she said. "I wouldn't leave a young, good-looking, very rich husband alone to work in Atlantic City four days a week. Gorgeous girls go after a cripple if they hear he's got billions."[29]

Several years later Donald got the last word in.

"Leona is without question one of the truly mean people around," he observed. "She is, in fact, the Queen of Mean. A mean sucker and dangerous, no question."[30]

Donald's gift for penning best sellers also waned during his flirtation with bankruptcy. His sequel to *The Art of the Deal,* a book called *Trump: Surviving at the Top,* was on *The New York Times* bestseller list for seven weeks after it debuted in 1990, but bookstores returned about half of its initial five-hundred-thousand-copy printing to Random House, its publisher. Another of Donald's nonfiction works of fiction, *Surviving* had these untruths to say about his airline, the Trump Shuttle: "The Shuttle is now profitable. Frankly, I'm glad I saved it. I'm proud of the way it's been improved. It is now the best."[31] *Surviving* also offered a perplexing take on Donald's view of the Forbes 400.

"It always amazed me that people pay so much attention to *Forbes* magazine," wrote Donald, who always paid a lot of attention to *Forbes* magazine. "Every year the Forbes 400 comes out, and people talk about it as if it were a rigorously researched compilation of America's wealthiest people, instead of what it really is: a sloppy, highly arbitrary estimate of certain people's net worth."[32]

Which "certain people"? Was this Donald's attempt to follow one of the key rules his book expounded for surviving at the top: "Be Honest"? Hard to tell. (Other *Surviving* rules included "Be Disciplined," "Don't Think You're So Smart You Can Go it Alone," and "Stay Close to Home.") *The New York Times* reported at the time that publishers concerned about the slumping marketability of celebrity tell-alls like *Surviving* began saying "that they don't want a 'Trump' on their hands."[33]

Donald managed to weather the slings and arrows of Ms. Helmsley and other doubters during these lean years and hunkered down with his bankers and with his debts.

One of the first restructuring meetings in early 1991 took place one evening in a Citibank office near Fifth Avenue, where more than three dozen bankers were waiting for Donald to arrive. Donald was throwing a party on his yacht—which he couldn't afford to maintain—to celebrate his ownership of the Trump Shuttle—which he shouldn't have bought to begin with, which had lost money, and which the banks were going to force him to sell.

"The call was made to Mr. Trump for him to attend the meeting. And he said, 'I cannot attend the meeting because tonight we're having a party,'" recalled Harvey Miller, a lawyer representing Citibank. "And he was told in a very gentle fashion that it was very important that he go to this meeting. And he said, 'Really?' 'Yeah [the bankers responded], really.'

"About a half hour later, Donald arrived with his whole team. Including his brother, his lawyers, the accountants, some other advisers, and I think they had come straight from the yacht. Donald then went around, like a true politician, to shake hands with everybody there. And by the time he got finished, people had already settled in around the table in their chairs. And when he got finished, he looked around, and there was no empty chair, and he suddenly looked up, and he said, 'Is this what it is like being poor?' I think that was sort of a revelation to him that there was something serious going on here.

"Donald listened and said that he would cooperate fully. I'm not sure if it was that meeting or thereafter where he started talking about his future with casinos. That's really where he wanted to devote his time and attention. And then that was followed by trying to figure out all of Donald's projects, financial positions, et cetera," Miller recalled. "And that's when it was discovered that he had all of these different projects with different banks, and that each bank syndicate had different collateral. And basically, that's what saved Donald. It was spread out."[34]

As the negotiations progressed, Donald's bankers looked for every alternative they could find to bankruptcy, because none of the banks wanted to contend with the mess that would ensue if the talks collapsed. And the Trumpster kept singing a happy tune. "He was always upbeat," Miller said. "One thing I'll say about Donald, he was never depressed."

Nor did he let the Trump Organization staffers get depressed. To give them a boost, he claims he became a sloganeer, a preacher, and very Pealesque.

"The bad time was from 1992 to 1995 and I had an expression: 'Survive till '95,'" Donald recalled. "I'd tell my staff: You motherfuckers, survive till '95. I used to go around preaching it."[35]

In a June 1992 conference call, Donald's bondholders debated whether they should seize the Trump Castle casino in Atlantic City because Donald was about to miss a debt payment. *The Washington Post* obtained a tape recording of the discussions and discovered that Donald's bondholders also wanted to avoid bankruptcy. One participant in the call warned that a bankruptcy was "a huge wild card" that would be a "really drawn out, very, very nasty process." Most of the bondholders "expressed contempt for the way Trump had managed the casino. But their cynicism about the bankruptcy system outweighed their cynicism about Trump," the *Post* reported.

The *Post* story noted that Warren Foss, who was advising the bondholders, thought it wise to pay Donald a $1.4 million annual management fee at the Castle, if only to buy off his support so they could all avoid bankruptcy court.

"What is he providing for the million and a half?" one bondholder asked, as participants on the conference call broke into laughter.

"We hope as little as possible," Foss replied, prompting even louder guffaws. "We hope it becomes characterized as a non-management fee."[36]

Unbeknownst to his creditors, Donald was just as worried about a bankruptcy as they were. He later told me that he wanted to avoid bankruptcy at all costs because he felt it would permanently taint him as a failure or a quitter.

"I did a lot of workouts in those days on behalf of Chase, with a lot of real estate developers who had similar problems, and big ones," said Sanford Morhouse, an attorney representing Chase Manhattan bank in the Trump negotiations. "Almost all of them, at one point or another in that era, filed for bankruptcy protection. And Donald, to his credit, did not."[37]

Donald also looked to Fred for support, which his father, steadfast and true, provided him despite the onset of Alzheimer's.

"People would say: 'Oh, Donald's in trouble.' And they used to love it, you know, because, you know, they're jealous assholes," he told me. "They would go to my father and say, 'Oh your son bit off more than he could chew. He's in trouble. He's in trouble.' And my father would say, 'Don't worry about Donald. Bet the ranch, he'll never be in trouble. Donald will be fine.' "[38]

By 1992, dozens of banks had written off several hundred million dollars in loans to Donald, his Atlantic City bondholders had agreed to forgo debt payments for five years, and Donald had whittled down his mammoth personal debts to $155 million by forfeiting his yacht, his jet, his 50 percent stake in the Grand Hyatt, and the Trump Shuttle. The Trump Organization now owed $2.2 billion instead of $3.4 billion. A year later Donald's personal debts fell to $115 million, but he had barely enough cash to remain in business, spurring his call to his siblings to rescue him with a financial handout guaranteed by his share of Fred's estate.[39] Two years later, in 1995, Donald narrowly averted personal bankruptcy yet again when the deadline arrived for paying back all of the $115 million; he got out of that corner when his banks gave him another three years to pay back the debt.[40]

"Sure, it crushed my ego, my pride," Donald wrote of this period in his third nonfiction work of fiction, *The Art of the Comeback*. "I hated having to go to the bankers with my hat in my hand. And yes, my lifestyle was a little cramped for a while. I guess that's all important. But getting a deal on the table—without filing for bankruptcy—was the most important thing of all."[41]

Huge chunks of what Donald had in Manhattan fell into other

hands. Chase Manhattan, which loaned Donald $200 million to help pay the $115 million purchase price of the West Side Yards and then watched the property bleed about $23.5 million a year in carrying costs, forced a sale of the prized tract to a Hong Kong development group in 1994 for about $85 million.[42]

Letting go of the site where he had planned the world's tallest building, and even eventually forged a partnership with community groups to get it zoned, tore at Donald. Just four years earlier he had spoken glowingly of the site's prospects in a television interview with Larry King.

"It's an opportunity to build a city within the greatest city, and I don't think anybody's ever had that opportunity," he said.[43]

Though Donald would claim after the Yards were sold that he remained a principal owner of the site where he once planned to erect Television City, property records and condominium offering plans for the parcel did not list him as such.[44]

According to former members of the Trump Organization, Donald didn't retain any ownership of the site—the Hong Kong group merely promised to give him a 20 to 30 percent cut of the profits once the site was completely developed. Until that time, the Asian investors kept Donald on to do what he did best: build. They gave him a modest construction fee and a management fee to oversee the development. They also allowed him to slap his name on the buildings that eventually rose on the Yards because his well-known moniker allowed them to charge a premium for their condos. Retained for his building expertise and his marquee value, Donald was a glorified landlord on the site; he no longer controlled it.[45]

Of course, giving up the West Side Yards to his bankers and to other developers wasn't Donald's only option. In 1989 William Zeckendorf Jr., son of the once high-flying developer, offered him $550 million for the site. Although closing documents were prepared and ready to be signed, at the last minute Donald decided not to sell. The real estate slump set in shortly after that, and potential buyers disappeared.[46] As much as he liked to buy, Donald found it almost impossible to sell, even when extraordinary deals came his way.

As bankers continued to dismantle Donald's empire, he hoped to retain control of the Plaza Hotel, the jewel at 59th and Fifth that he bought in 1988, and Mar-a-Lago, his Palm Beach manse. But Citibank, which loaned Donald the $425 million he used to buy the Plaza for $407.5 million, took control of the hotel and sold it for $325 million in 1995.[47] Donald had better luck in Palm Beach. After a game of chicken with his Mar-a-Lago lender—and with the help of a new mortgage loan from a politically connected New York construction union—Donald held on to the estate.

Meanwhile, Bollenbach departed the Trump Organization and Nick Ribis, the company's president, took over the job of keeping Donald focused on his Atlantic City casinos. Miracle of miracles, the angel of Donald's deliverance from the purgatory of bankruptcy and unrequited debts turned out to be . . . the stock market!

Even as the national real estate bubble was bursting, fresh funds began rushing onto Wall Street, fueling a historical run-up in both the stock market and initial public offerings of often barely viable companies. Between 1980 and 1995 the total annual value of IPOs leaped from $1.4 billion to $30.2 billion (in 1993 alone, IPOs worth $58 billion took flight).[48]

Although some high-quality companies like Microsoft went public in that crop of IPOs, a large portion were little stinkers. Of all new companies that went public between 1985 and 1995, only half were still trading in 1995. Even promising companies went on wild IPO rides: Netscape, the pioneering but unprofitable Web browsing concern, went public in 1995 at $28 a share, was trading at $171 three months later, and then fell to $57 by the end of 1996.[49]

If you had a good story and a prominent name, it suddenly became quite easy to sell stock. And it turned out, against all odds, that investors were willing to gamble on Donald's name— even though they were getting a chief executive whose sense of his responsibilities as the steward of a publicly traded firm and the guardian of other people's money were somewhat ill defined.

"Something gnawed at me, and I knew what it was—the whole head-of-a-public-company routine," Donald wrote in *Surviving at the Top*, relating his previous experience as a manager of Resorts. "Although I certainly agreed with the theory of stockholder-owned corporations and was absolutely committed to fulfilling my fiduciary duties, I personally didn't like answering to a board of directors."[50]

In a masterstroke of financial maneuvering, and in a tribute to the sucker-born-every-minute theorem, Donald and Ribis managed to take two of the Trump casinos—the Plaza and the Taj Mahal—public in 1995 and 1996, at a time when Donald was unable to make his bank payments and was heading toward personal bankruptcy. The stock sales allowed Donald to buy the casinos back from the banks and unload huge amounts of debt. The offering yanked Donald out of the financial graveyard and left him with a 25 percent stake in a company he once owned entirely. Trump Hotels & Casino Resorts traded at $14 a share and, along with a fresh bond offering, the new company raised about $295 million. When Donald later folded the Taj into Trump Hotels, he was able to foist $795 million of that casino's debt onto the backs of his new shareholders.

Voilà, in one fell swoop someone else became responsible for the debts that almost sank Donald and the Trumpster went from gaming the bankruptcy system to gaming the world of publicly traded companies.

Exactly what investors thought they might get for their Trump Hotels investment wasn't entirely clear. Donald had already demonstrated that casinos weren't his forte, and investors were buying stock in a company that was immediately larded with debts that made it difficult, if not impossible, to upgrade the operations.

Even so, Trump Hotels' shares rose to about $36 in 1996, giving Donald, who owned 25 percent of the shares, a stake worth about $290 million. With little real estate left to speak of in Manhattan,

Donald's wealth was centered on his casinos.[51] Bollenbach, now running Hilton Hotels, was amazed.

"I didn't think anyone could do it," he said in 1996, before slightly inflating Donald's newfound wealth. "I know of no other case of someone going from almost a billion down to over half a billion in net worth."[52]

Indeed, Bollenbach was so impressed that, according to three people familiar with the offer, he tried to buy Trump Hotels in 1996. He offered Donald about $39.50 a share for Trump Hotels in a take-it-or-leave-it offer. Donald wanted $45 a share.

Donald wouldn't budge, and Bollenbach went on to purchase another company that became one of Donald's most troublesome competitors in Atlantic City.

"He's the worst seller ever," the person familiar with the talks said of Donald. "That's why he'll constantly get hurt, because he just won't let go. There's something emotional that won't allow him to do it . . . He always believed there's another penny behind every offer he gets, so he won't let go."[53]

In the years after Donald failed to sell Trump Hotels, its stock price tanked. Had he tried to pare down some $1.8 billion in debt smothering the casino company, and spruced up the operation, he might have ridden a reignited gambling boom and grown his newly seeded fortune. Instead, Trump Hotels, which never earned a profit in any year between 1995 and 2005, became Donald's private stockpile of ready cash.

Allan Sloan, the financial writer who had opined with great accuracy on many things Trump, offered a fair warning to Trump Hotels' investors: "Shareholders and bondholders have to be total fools ever to think that Donald Trump will put their interests ahead of his own."[54]

Lo and behold, Donald spent several years proving Sloan correct.

Just a few months after Trump Hotels absorbed the Taj, Donald sold his last Atlantic City casino, the Castle, to the public company. That is, Donald sold his own casino, with all of its heavy debts, to a public company he controlled. The $490 million price tag for the Castle was about $100 million more than analysts thought it was worth. A later valuation by Trump Hotels itself pegged the Castle's true price at $314 million. Nonetheless, Trump Hotels paid $490 million, sending the company's stock into a nosedive from which it never recovered. In 1996 alone, the shares fell to $12 from $35.50.[55] About a decade later, the New York Stock Exchange delisted the shares entirely and any kid with a quarter could buy the stock.

When I interviewed Donald in 1996, he was effusive about his casinos and somehow seemed to forget that he owned very little property in Manhattan anymore.

"The thing people don't know about me is . . . Donald Trump is in two businesses," he told me. "I'm not in one. You take a Wynn, a Circus Circus, they're in one business. I'm in two businesses. I'm probably the biggest in real estate in New York and it's a big business. . . . I own most of my stuff. I own one hundred percent of Trump Tower. My buildings I own, for the most part. . . . I have this huge company that's real estate. I also have this huge company that's gambling. So I have two huge companies."[56]

Although Trump Hotels' shares were sinking and there were no earnings to be seen, Donald paid himself $7 million for his handiwork at the company in 1996. The hefty payout wasn't a surprise to one compensation analyst interviewed about the package.

"It's bad, but you wouldn't expect any less from Don Trump, would you?" offered Graef "Bud" Crystal, an expert on corporate pay, at the time. "Don Trump's a pig is not a breaking news story. Don Trump's a pig has been the story from day one. That's been, I think, why many of his enterprises have collapsed."[57]

While investors didn't seem to mind Donald's shenanigans at Trump Hotels, some journalists cataloged the fun and games. Jerry Useem at *Fortune* took note in 2000 of Donald's "disquieting" tendency to "use the casino company as his own personal piggy bank." In addition to the multimillion-dollar bonuses Donald was lifting out of Trump Hotels, Useem pointed out that "the pilots of his personal 727 are on the casino company's payroll" and that in 1998 Donald "had the already cash-strapped company lend him $26 million to pay off a personal loan."[58] In a separate development, regulators later questioned how the company was managing its accounts. In 2002 the Securities and Exchange Commission imposed a cease-and-desist order on Trump Hotels for producing "misleading" financial statements in an earlier quarter.[59]

Though Donald seemed preoccupied with finding different ways to loot Trump Hotels, he made time in 1999 to mount a run for the presidency. America needed him!

Donald said he was inspired to make a stab at public service by former wrestling star and bodybuilder Jesse Ventura's successful run for governor of Minnesota. Ventura's "breakthrough in Minnesota caused me to start thinking about the role people outside government must play to help our country," Donald intoned.[60] Guided by Roy Cohn's former acolyte, political strategist Roger Stone, Donald's political platform was no-nonsense: good schools, safe streets, national security, economic growth, and an improved Social Security system. Stone commissioned a poll to test Donald's viability as a candidate, and Donald wrote about the results in his 2000 campaign treatise, *The America We Deserve.*

"It was no surprise to me that 97 percent of the American people knew who I was," he wrote. "It was also no surprise that I was particularly popular with some segments of the American population. Working people, African Americans, Latinos, and people making under $25,000 a year all had a favorable opinion. Rich people did not like me. Rich people who don't know me *never* like me. Rich people who know me like me."[61]

Donald jumped into the race as a candidate in Ross Perot's Reform Party, but shortly after Ventura left the party, Trump left the race. Still, Donald's words echoed through the voting booths.

"I'm not worried about whether or not the intellectual/journalistic/political establishment thinks I've got the stuff to talk about saving the American Dream," Donald offered. "I believe in the American Dream. My business experience shows me that it works, and I want to do everything possible to see that regular Americans can enjoy the same opportunity for success and security that I have had.

"Maybe our next great leader—one with the cunning of Franklin Roosevelt, the guts of Harry Truman, the resilience of Richard Nixon, and the optimism of Ronald Reagan—is walking down Fifth Avenue right now, straight through the heart of this land of dreamers and shakers—this land that I love."[62]

Gosh.

Meanwhile, back on Fifth Avenue, Donald had already spent time carving out a new niche for himself in New York real estate. One of his acquaintances from his restructuring talks launched his new career. Sanford Morhouse, the attorney representing Chase in the negotiations, had taken a liking to Donald during the talks and decided to introduce him to his acquaintances at General Electric. In 1994 GE was looking for someone to refurbish the old Gulf & Western building on Columbus Circle in Manhattan. Morhouse thought that Donald fit the bill and pushed for him at GE.

"At the end of the day, he's a tremendously talented and smart and experienced builder," said Morhouse. "The common description of Donald is that he is a great salesman. He is a great salesman, but he also happens to be a very, very good builder. He's smart and he works hard."

GE brought Donald aboard and, according to one person with direct knowledge of the deal, paid him a management fee of about $25 million to oversee the rehabilitation of the property. Like the Asian investors who bought the West Side Yards, GE found value in letting Donald put his name on the building and gave him a cut of the condo sales. Presto, the renovated skyscraper was christened Trump International Hotel and Tower. Even though Donald didn't own the building, it later flashed across the opening credits of *The Apprentice* as if he did.

Donald does own 40 Wall Street, which he spent about $35

million to buy and refurbish in 1996. The building has about $145 million in debt attached to it, and New York City assessors value the property at about $90 million. Donald values it at $400 million.[63] He also owns Trump World Tower, which a South Korean conglomerate financed before Donald bought out its interest for about $25 million, according to records of the deal (Donald's financial adviser, Weisselberg, originally told me that the South Koreans gave their interest away to Donald *for free*—which, had it been true, would have been an unusual example of charitable giving by a major corporation). And he owns Trump Park Avenue, which GE financed initially. Donald then borrowed $140 million to buy out GE; the building has yet to sell out, but Donald projects total sales of about $300 million.

Donald's recent golf course ventures have produced some sterling new courses, but the value the Trump Organization assigns those deals appears to be hyperinflated. Donald's Palm Beach course, for example, has about 285 members who paid $250,000 for memberships, for a total of $71.25 million. Donald borrowed about $47 million to build the course and a new clubhouse. So he banked about $24 million on the deal, before other costs. He leases the land beneath the course from Palm Beach County—he doesn't own it. But Donald carries the course on his books as an asset worth $200 million.[64]

Donald doesn't control other Manhattan properties that bear his name or are closely associated with him today, including Trump Tower (where he still owns his own triplex and some commercial space below). As Zuckerman noted, Donald gets the financial backing of other people who give him a cut of the action to make sure projects arrive properly at the finish line.

Forbes, in bestowing a $2.6 billion fortune on Donald in its 2004 richlist, credited Donald with owning eighteen million square feet of Manhattan property, which certainly is an impossibility. On one occasion Donald told me that the West Side Yards, which he doesn't own, will have ten million square feet of salable space when the site, now known as Riverside South, is completed (Weisselberg told me the site actually would have about five million square feet of salable space[65]). However measured, the Yards was by far the biggest property in Donald's former Manhattan real estate portfolio. *Forbes* described the Yards in its 2004 assessment of Donald's holdings as "an 80-acre parcel bought for $80 million in 1985," when it is, in fact, a 77-acre parcel bought for $115 million in 1985 and sold to others for $82 million and the assumption of about $250 million in debt in 1994. Donald gets a management fee of about $2 million a year to oversee the property, and a cut of the profits after all sixteen of the project's buildings are completed and the group he sold it to gets all of its expenses repaid.[66]

In June 2005, the Asian investors who controlled the West Side Yards sold the entire site for $1.8 billion—about half the amount that Donald had told me it was worth. Although Donald told me that the site was debt free when the Asians sold it, others involved in the transaction said the Yards carried a substantial amount of debt and expenses that had to be deducted from the sale price. Although Donald declined to detail how much money he realized personally on the sale, it was certainly a fraction of the $1.3 billion he had told me that the Yards would add to his bank account after a sale. The sale further undermined Donald's already flimsy claim to being Manhattan's biggest real estate developer.

Between 2000 and 2004 *Forbes* allowed Donald's verbal billions to grow by $1 billion, a period when the stock market bubble burst, his stake in his casinos—his most valuable asset until *The Apprentice* came along—had fallen in value to $7 million (around $300 million less than Bollenbach would have paid him for it), and, despite Manhattan's red-hot real estate market, Donald owned much less real estate there than he let on.

Donald said that his casinos' myriad problems—no profits, suffocating debt, disappearing cash—did not mean that he had failed in Atlantic City. Instead, he described his management of the casinos as an "entrepreneurial" success, defining *entrepreneurial* as his ability to take cash out of the casino company and use it for other things.

"Entrepreneurially, not as a person who drives up stock but as a private person, it's been a very good deal," he told me. "In many years, it's been good.

"I've loved Atlantic City. It's been very good to me and I've been very good to it. But it's been disappointing in the sense that things could have been done, which would have made it unbeliev-able," Donald added. "Various politicians and others decided to go a different route and that's too bad because it was a great opportunity. If I would have worked Atlantic City the way I worked real estate, I would probably be the biggest casino company in the world rather than just a nice company, et cetera, et cetera."[67]

There was, of course, a method to Donald's madness. His ability to float above the wreckage of his financial miscues and magically add zeroes to his bank account ensured that he remained an object of fascination. Besides, as an Idahoan named Bill Cope pointed out in *The Boise Weekly* in 2005, Donald did have an authentic bond with some members of the Forbes 400.

"Lucky billionaires. They don't have to worry about reality as you and I know it," he wrote. "So they have all this extra time to dream up new ways to make reality more to their liking.

"We hundredaires and thousandaires are so fascinated with billionaires: that power they have over their own reality. It's not because they're so good looking, and it's certainly not because they have such pleasing personalities. Just try to imagine Donald Trump without all his money, and basically we'd be talking about a guy who couldn't pick up a drunk hooker at a Holiday Inn happy hour," Cope added. "If I'm jealous, it's because billionaires are like, well . . . they're like hippies in a way, aren't they? Hippies with Lear jets. People that rich sort of float above the normal flow of human events, hovering over a sea of trials and tribulations and bad credit ratings without ever getting wet. That's it, they're like hovercraft. Hippy hovercraft."[68]

<u>TrumpQuiz #7</u>

If you're a billionaire encountering unexpected and sudden poverty, you should:

1) Beg.
2) Borrow.
3) Steal.
4) Accentuate the positive.
5) Eliminate the negative.
6) Latch on to the affirmative.
7) Don't mess with Mr. In-Between.
8) Repeal *The Art of the Deal* for a presidential seal.
9) Play the *Wheel of Fortune* acronym game: IPO.
10) Keep your head when all about you are losing theirs and blaming it on you.
11) Trust yourself when all men doubt you, but make allowance for their doubting, too.
12) Meet with Triumph and Disaster, and treat those two impostors just the same.
13) Make one heap of all your winnings, and risk it all on one turn of pitch-and-toss, and lose, and start again at your beginnings, and never breathe a word about your loss.
14) Force your heart and nerve and sinew to serve your turn long after they are gone, and so hold on when there is nothing in you, except the Will which says to them: "Hold on!"

CHAPTER SEVEN

TRUMPSTYLE

I've always thought that Louis B. Mayer led the ultimate life,
that Flo Ziegfeld led the ultimate life, that men like Darryl Zanuck and
Harry Cohn did some creative and beautiful things. The ultimate job for me
would have been running MGM in the Thirties and Forties—pre-television.
—DONALD TRUMP[1]

In my opinion, the social scene—in New York, Palm Beach, or anywhere
else for that matter—is full of phonies and unattractive people who often
have done nothing smarter than inherit somebody else's wealth—
the Lucky Sperm Club. . . . I prefer, on most nights, to sit in bed
with the TV tuned to some movie or sports event.
—DONALD TRUMP[2]

DONALD IS STANDING NEXT TO A RED FERRARI IN THE COBBLED DRIVEway of Mar-a-Lago, a Palm Beach estate he bought with an unrecorded $8.5 million loan in 1985. It's Saturday morning and he's dressed for an early round of golf. He holds up the keys.

"Wanna drive?" he asks me, smiling.

(I consider this. I tend to drive too fast. I like to drive very fast, except when my kids are in the car. I wonder about the look on Donald's face if he was strapped in next to me and we zipped off too quickly for him to unroll himself from the Ferrari's passenger seat, if we began weaving through traffic on Ocean Boulevard, clipped a lamppost cornering onto Worth Avenue and dented his $160,000 chariot, peeled out onto I-95 and shot down to Miami, to South Beach, to Joe's Stone Crab in time for lunch. I love Joe's. We could get there quickly. Would Donald be terrified, eyes bulging?

Would he yank out his cell phone on I-95 and call the cops, tell them his Ferrari's been hijacked? Would he call Melania? One of his bodyguards? Maybe he'd just go along for the ride, consider it a little adventure. I know he'd like Joe's. Everybody likes Joe's. Or we could get really ambitious. Haul straight up the East Coast and get to Manhattan in time for a very late dinner at the Russian Samovar. No, Manhattan is too far away. Donald would jump out at the first gas station or at my sister's house when we visit her in Virginia.)

"That's okay, you drive," I respond, smiling back at him.

Donald, away from his office, ready for a golf game and at home with a woman he loves, is a happy, engaging man, and he opines randomly on almost everything he sees. He steers the Ferrari toward a lovely new golf course he's built in West Palm Beach and tells me about the history of Mar-a-Lago, about its original owner, Marjorie Merriweather Post, and about her architect, Joseph Urban.

"He was a great architect. He also did all of the sets for Flo Ziegfeld," Donald says. "Marjorie Merriweather Post was said to be the richest woman in the world. She inherited Post cereals. She then married E. F. Hutton. He quadrupled her money through great investments and everything. Unfortunately, he liked screwing maids. And after the fifth time, she just said, 'I can't do this anymore.' You know, they were married for like ten years. But they would have these gorgeous maids working at Mar-a-Lago. Dina Merrill grew up in Mar-a-Lago in a room designed by Walt Disney, a young Walt Disney, before Walt Disney was big."[3]

Dina Merrill, a leggy, refined actress, was Marjorie Post's daughter, but Disney was working in Los Angeles when Mar-a-Lago was built. He never had a thing to do with the mansion. Donald's Mar-a-Lago staff adore him, as do most of the small coterie of people who have worked closely with him, but they wince whenever he tells the Walt Disney story. Urban, however, did design sets for Ziegfeld during vaudeville's heyday, and his connection to Mar-a-Lago has an understandable appeal to the Hollywood showman and set designer lurking inside of Donald.

"There is no place like Palm Beach in terms of wealth," he tells me. "This is the wealthiest community in the world. You know they say the difference between Palm Beach and Beverly Hills is that there are no mortgages on the houses. In Beverly Hills, you have four, five, and six mortgages."[4]

Donald was thirty-nine when he first became a Palm Beach homeowner. His arrival in a balmy, pristine locale that observed baroque social rules freighted with barely disguised anti-Semitism and lily-white racial aspirations was, to put it mildly, seismic. On one occasion Donald's houseguest, African American clothing and hip-hop impresario Sean "Puffy/P.Diddy/Puff Daddy" Combs, decided to tryst alfresco on Mar-a-Lago's sands. Fellow beachcombers asked a guard to intervene. Combs went ballistic, complaining that the guard was "ruining his concentration."[5] Donald's neighbors, members of the über-WASPy Bath & Tennis Club, shared the same beach, and Combs's exertions didn't amuse them.

Palm Beach also frowned on projects that threatened the town's architectural balance or its delicate fortification as a quiet haven for the wealthy. Since Donald lacked enough money to maintain Mar-a-Lago over a long period of time, he decided shortly after buying it to convert the entire spread into a pay-for-play club and hotel. Palm Beach, and Ms. Merrill, would have none of it.

"Dina Merrill, who was also a great beauty like her mother, was born with her mother's beauty but not her mother's brain. And they went fuckin' nuts about me. Because she's one of the sacred few," Donald recalled. "They went nuts. The bottom line is that after litigation and all sorts of shit, I ended up winning and I got the right to turn it into a club. Very traumatic, very long arduous task . . . They hated me."[6]

As we near Trump International Golf Club, which Donald built in 2001 in a working-class, racially mixed West Palm Beach neighborhood featuring a strip joint and a run-down shopping center, he slows the Ferrari. He points out the club's landscaping, its palm trees, its $350,000 membership fee (his financial manager later tells me the fee is $250,000), and its handsome new clubhouse. Trump International is also next to a noisy airport and a twelve-story jail (inmates on upper floors are known to whistle catcalls at female golfers on the third hole), but we don't dwell on those points. Donald takes special note of the attendant at the club's entry gate.

"Look at the guard. Is that Central Casting? Look at him," he says. "We have the richest people in the world at this course."

There are more than 140 golf courses in Palm Beach County, but nearly all of them are uniformly flat. Donald, who reinvented himself as a golf course developer in the years between his financial demise and The Apprentice's debut, leased the land beneath Trump International from the county and created an immaculate, lovely golf course that swells with berms, rolling fairways, undulating greens, and elevated tees. Donald ambles off to play and returns to Mar-a-Lago later that day to pick me up again.

As we coast through Palm Beach in the Ferrari, on the way to a house Donald recently bought near The Breakers hotel, he points out the homes of various grandees. At a stoplight an older couple wearing tennis togs and driving a light blue Mercedes convertible stare over at Donald. They have broad smiles on their faces. They chatter excitedly with each other and look back at Donald again. Donald is staring straight out the windshield, telling me about local gossip from a few years back that still irks him. Membership in the Bath & Tennis Club is a badge of exclusivity in Palm Beach society, and Donald said that newspapers inaccurately described him as making a fruitless effort to join the club.

"I don't want to get in. I have a better club than them. It costs $30,000 to join Bath & Tennis. It costs $150,000 to join Mar-a-Lago. Mar-a-Lago is a much bigger property, a much better property.

"I can get in if I wanted to. If I wanted to, I can get anything," he adds. "I'm the king of Palm Beach. They all come over, they all eat, they all love me, they all kiss my ass. And then they all leave and say: 'Isn't he horrible.' But I'm the king.

"I hate to tell you this because I'm embarrassed by it but I think I've become very much part of the establishment. I have the place that everyone comes to."[7]

Later in the day Melania, Donald, and I have dinner in a new, Versailles-like ballroom he's built on Mar-a-Lago's grounds and where the couple had a lavishly publicized wedding reception two months earlier. Donald is clearly enthralled with Melania as he chats away with another couple at the table, Regis Philbin and his wife, Joy. Tony Bennett is performing on a stage at one end of the ballroom; Mar-a-Lago's members have paid $250 for dinner and the show (as a nonmember, my ticket sets me back $350; my room, at $2,000 a night, sets me back even further). The ticket is worth it. Bennett, ever the gentleman as he nears eighty, sings for almost an hour and goes out of his way to compliment each member of his band. Toward the end of his show he belts out "Fly Me to the Moon" without a microphone; every lyric is in tune and crystal clear.

After dinner, there is dancing by the pool. Mar-a-Lago is bathed in floodlights, and its peach walls glow against a purple sky. Donald has set up an array of large speakers, many of them the size of my body, on the patio and inside a smaller ballroom nearby. Most of the music is stellar, vintage rock amid a smattering of cringe-inducing 1970s and '80s flotsam. I retreat for a drink as soon as the DJ spins Barry Manilow's "Copacabana." When I return, Wild Cherry's "Play That Funky Music White Boy" is cranking into the night. Donald, wearing a navy Brioni suit and a baby-blue tie, is biting his lower lip, forearms raised rib-high, doing his own halting version of a suburban disco dance. He's happy. He turns to me and leans in toward my ear.

"I bet they can hear this fucking music up and down Palm Beach," he shouts. "And I bet it's driving them nuts, the stuffy cocksuckers. And you know what? I don't care."

In the back of a limo on the way to the airport the next day, as

Bennett is in the middle of telling me his favorite Frank Sinatra story, Donald tells me Mar-a-Lago paid the singer $300,000 to perform the night before. I'm not sure if Bennett wants me to know this, but he smiles and nods. Melania, gentle as a swan, compliments Bennett on his performance. Shortly after Donald's jet takes off, he rolls *Sunset Boulevard* on the plane's movie screen. Joy Philbin makes popcorn for Regis. Bennett says hello to my sister into my tape recorder, tells me that Billy Wilder is one of his favorite directors, and then finishes telling me his Sinatra story.

Sunset Boulevard reaches a classic moment. Gloria Swanson and William Holden are seated together on a couch, smoking, watching a Norma Desmond silent film.

"Still wonderful, isn't it? And no dialogue," Swanson says to Holden. "We didn't need dialogue. We had faces. There just aren't any faces like that anymore. Maybe one. Garbo." Swanson ponders the arrival of talkies and the demise of Norma Desmond's career. She springs to her feet, outraged. "Oh, those idiot producers. Those imbeciles! Haven't they got any eyes? Have they forgotten what a star looks like? I'll show them. I'll be up there again! So help me!"

As Swanson pivots into a tunnel of light generated by the projector's lamp, her profile is limned in smoke and noir shadow. Donald leans over my shoulder.

"Is this an incredible scene, or what?" he whispers. "Just incredible."

IN 1959 EARL BLACKWELL AND CLEVELAND AMORY COMPILED THE FIRST *Celebrity Register,* a thick tome containing mini biographies of more than two thousand people, mostly men, whom the authors deemed "celebrities."

"We think we have a better yardstick than the *Social Register* or *Who's Who,* or any such book," the authors wrote. "Our point is that it is impossible to be accurate in listing a man's social standing—even if anyone cared; and it's impossible to list accurately the success or value of men; but you *can* judge a man as a celebrity—all you have to do is weigh his press clippings."[8]

Celebrity is a global commodity today, but its roots lie in a singularly American co-mingling of mythmaking and commercial logic. When the *Celebrity Register* was first published, the celebrity-making machine was entering its third and most nuclear stage.

Stage one in celebrityland was the advent of the modern commercial press at the end of the nineteenth century. Publishers quickly realized that stories chronicling the exploits of larger-than-life characters sold newspapers. Charles Lindbergh, before winging to France solo aboard the *Spirit of St. Louis* in a legitimately enthralling feat of derring-do, cut a deal with *The New York Times*. When Lindbergh landed on the other side of the ocean in 1927, the only reporter he would speak to was a *Times* reporter because he had sold the paper exclusive rights to his story. In exchange, the aviator got several pages of the paper all to himself the next day. He returned home a phenomenon, his every movement grist for the newly forming celebrity mill.

Lindbergh represented . . . what exactly? American know-how? Bravery? Technological prowess? The binding together of the world? All of these things? As an explorer and as a risk taker, was he greater than Captain Cook? No. Was he more famous than Captain Cook? Yes, definitely. Lindy, memorialized in song and script, was a celebrity.

Hollywood, laying down the foundations of its studio system at the same time that Lindbergh returned home to ticker-tape parades, provided stage two in the creation of the modern celebrity. Shrewdly packaging actors not simply as thespians, but as members of the cosmos, points of light in the firmament, white-hot symbols of eternity—as "stars"—Hollywood raked in money and tapped into the dream life of everyone willing to surrender themselves to the dark intimacy of a movie theater. Film lifted celebrity off the dusty pages of newspapers and wound it at light speed right into our consciousness. You could almost touch a star on the screen in front of you. Stars on the screen were, quite literally, larger than life.

Stars, as the gossip mags and celebrity shows endlessly informed us, also lived lives imbued with passionate romance, baronial homes, scandalous excess, unbridled freedom, clawing addictions, and trendsetting fashion. But the quality of Hollywood celebrity varied. For every Spencer Tracy or Katharine Hepburn there was a Robert Taylor or a Lana Turner; for every Johnny Depp or Cate Blanchett there was a Ben Affleck or a Drew Barrymore. Still, the Hollywood glamour apparatus spread celebrity worldwide. It gave us Marilyn.

Television, the nuclear fuel of stage three, brought celebrity out of the theater and into the home, and into the home on a daily basis. Like newspapers, television offered celebrity in the living room. Like film, television offered celebrity in motion. TV made celebrity present at the flip of a switch, and the quality of tele-celebrity was even more divergent than in Hollywood. For every Rod Serling or Jean Stapleton there were many, many more Bob Denvers or Eva Gabors; for every James Gandolfini or Edie Falco, there were many, many more Ryan Seacrests or Hilary Duffs. Celebrity also became more fleeting because novelty faded faster in the television era. But the unavoidably potent calculus of televised celebrity worked: The more a star's face was in front of our face, the more significant he or she appeared to be by virtue of sheer ubiquity.

Just two years after the *Celebrity Register* was published, historian Daniel Boorstin took note. Celebrities, as Boorstin indelibly put it in *The Image*, are those singular beings who have made a profession out of being "known for their well-knownness."

"While heroes are assimilated to one another by the great simple virtues of their character, celebrities are differentiated mainly by trivia of personality," wrote Boorstin. "To be known for your personality actually proves you a celebrity. Thus a synonym for 'a celebrity' is 'a personality.' Entertainers, then, are best qualified to become celebrities because they are skilled in the marginal differentiation of their personalities. They succeed by skillfully differentiating themselves from others essentially like them.

"With the mushroom-fertility of all pseudo events, celebrities tend to breed more celebrities. They help make and celebrate and publicize one another. Being known primarily for their well-knownness, celebrities intensify their celebrity images simply by becoming widely known for relations among themselves. By a kind of symbiosis, celebrities live off one another."[9]

Once celebrity's Ferris wheel began spinning, even artistes wanted to hop on for the ride. Novelist Norman Mailer adopted a royal distance from himself after landing a $4 million book contract in the early 1980s, when he advised readers of serious literature that "of necessity, part of Mailer's remaining funds of sensitivity went right into the war of supporting his image and working for it."[10]

But celebrity came relatively late to the business world. While scores of businesspeople were renowned in their day—beginning with self-made, Gilded Age titans like Andrew Carnegie and John D. Rockefeller Sr. and continuing through Henry Ford and all of his corporate and entrepreneurial successors—none of them was embraced (or even bothered to promote himself) as a celebrity. It wouldn't be until the 1980s, amid Ronald Reagan's pageantry of economic renewal, that the idea of businessperson-as-celebrity even became viable. And it fell to the charismatic son of Italian immigrants with a very good story to tell to break that particular ice.

In 1984 Lee Iacocca, a former Ford executive who'd taken over Chrysler five years earlier, published his blockbuster autobiography, *Iacocca*. Once upon a time, Iacocca's book related, there was a nearly bankrupt, moribund automobile manufacturer that a visionary, plain-speaking CEO revived into a profitable, dynamic enterprise. This CEO paid himself only $1 during his first year at Chrysler's helm and, mirabile dictu, wrought wonders.

"There are times in everyone's life when something constructive is born out of adversity. There are times when things seem so bad that you've got to grab your fate by the shoulders and shake it," Iacocca wrote. "Fortunately, Chrysler recovered from its brush with death. Today I'm a hero."[11]

Iacocca sold six million copies and was a best seller for a year. President Reagan asked Iacocca to oversee the restoration of the Statue of Liberty, and the Chrysler CEO was considered surefire presidential timber. Gallup polls in 1984 and 1985 placed Iacocca on the top ten list of the country's most admired men, making him the first businessman to earn such a ranking since Bernard Baruch landed there in 1958.[12] Iacocca also went on a whirlwind romance, bought an opulent Italian villa, starred in dozens of TV ads, marketed his own wine, and made a guest appearance on the TV cop show *Miami Vice*.[13] Other CEOs, displaying the kind of needy, narcissistic brio once largely limited to Hollywood and Vine, also got starry-eyed.

"I envy Iacocca," said Jerry Sanders, head of semi-conductor maker Advanced Micro Devices. "If they asked me, I'd do a *Miami Vice* episode. I'd even do *Hill Street Blues*."[14]

Iacocca's managerial contributions notwithstanding, Chrysler survived because the federal government provided the company with mega-doses of assistance: an injection of more than a billion taxpayer dollars to bail out the sinking giant and a comfy trade restriction on Japanese auto imports. Moreover, the American auto industry as a whole never made the fundamental changes needed to compete effectively with Japan.

Even though Chrysler's profits seesawed, Iacocca's $1 paycheck leaped to the princely height of $20.5 million two years after *Iacocca* was published, and his annual compensation stayed in the multimillions. By the mid-1990s, *The Wall Street Journal* noted, the CEOs of about thirty major corporations hauled in annual pay packages 212 times greater than what the average American worker received.[15]

"That's the American way," *Iacocca*'s author told reporters who questioned his whopper-size paychecks. "If little kids don't aspire to make money like I did, what the hell good is this country? You gotta give them a role model, right?"[16]

And role models we got. Iacocca ushered in the era of the glamorized, phantasmic, imperial CEO, a run that lasted until the implosion of two companies called WorldCom and Enron temporarily popped the businessperson-as-celebrity balloon in the early years of the twenty-first century. Before that bubble burst, post-Iacocca CEOs snared the same kind of celebrity stroking on the covers of glossy business magazines that Hollywood luminaries enjoyed on the covers of *Vanity Fair* and *People*.

But celebrity CEOs were just as human and fallible as the Hollywood stars swimming in the entertainment industry's talent pool. For every Jack Welch or Bill Gates who oversaw authentic transformation in corporate America, there were many Jerry Levins or Carly Fiorinas who wore empty suits. In a class by themselves were the Emperor-Has-No-Clothes CEOs like Ken Lay and Bernie Ebbers, whose enterprises floated on fraud.

Celebrity CEOs "are corporate fictions. If they didn't exist, we would have to make them up," observed Eric Guthey, an associate professor at the Copenhagen Business School in Denmark. "They get these high salaries that connect market myths with American myths. It's physically impossible to see a corporation, but they have to be visible, so it comes through their leaders. People don't really connect to these people in personal terms. They are personifications of capitalism. They are cultural icons in the purest sense of the word."[17]

Did someone say cultural icon? Enter the Trumpster.

Iacocca may have launched the celebrity sweepstakes that took hold in America's business community in the 1980s, but Donald was the tycoon who played the celebrity game most deftly—and with unfettered glee. Donald published *The Art of the Deal*, the Rosetta stone of entrepreneurial pizzazz, three years after *Iacocca*.

And Donald's best-selling, nonfiction work of fiction gave his stature the same effervescent bounce already uncorked by Iaccoca's literary endeavors. But Donald's book and his celebrity had much longer legs. Donald's celebrity, rooted in his image as the republic's reigning can-do guy, forged such a high-voltage, intercontinental bond with every mogul-in-training that he spent two decades striding the business landscape like Thor in Valhalla, like Donaldus Rex, dealmeister of all he surveyed.

In the year 2000, when what Donald owned was a husk of what he owned before and after he had barely dodged financial obliteration, a Gallup poll still ranked him the most famous businessperson in America. Some 98 percent of the poll's respondents recognized his name. As *Fortune* noted, Bill Gates and Ross Perot were the only other businesspeople to score in the poll's 90th percentile. Warren Buffett, the legendary investor-manager with decades of tangible, demonstrable achievements to his name and a cult following of his own to boot, ranked even farther behind.[18]

Many celebrities who have stayed in the spotlight as long as Donald have been cultural chameleons, changing hues willy-nilly or simply shedding personas like layers of skin as fans' passions shifted. Andy Warhol and Madonna, two maestros of celebrity, owed their durability to the Zen-like precision with which they changed clothing, crowds, and "artistic" pitches, rearranging their graphics, song, and masks at will. Other celebrities who endured, like Oprah, used the familiarity of TV to create an intimate, neighborly bond with their audience, something film stars rarely could do because movies were a more distant, Olympian medium than the tube.

Unlike most businesspeople, Donald was telegenic and quite willing to jump into the fray without a script. And he was just as willing as Oprah to let his fans inside his life and his most intimate thoughts. He let them—he *wanted* them—to partake of the Trump mojo. But Donald defied Madonna's chameleon act, simply remaining very Trumpy, very himself, from the 1970s into the new millennium. He kept the suit, kept the tie, kept the hair in unusual configurations, and week after week, year after year, kept his tongue wagging in exactly the same way.

Donald came across, blazingly, as the unreal real thing.

TrumpQuiz #8

This is the first of two essay exams in this chapter. They're both designed to help speed you along to billionairedom. Think about the questions, write down your own answers, and then see how closely your response corresponds with answers from a famous New York real estate developer.[19] The Trump Organization will examine vocabulary and penmanship when judging submissions:

1) *Are big houses important?* "I have fun with big houses. And are they important? No, not at all."
2) *Do cars matter?* "Only for fun. They don't matter."
3) *Do clothes make the man?* "No, but they can break the man . . . if a guy walks into my office and walks in with an undershirt, he truly doesn't have a chance."
4) *What do you love most about your hair?* "I've combed it the same way for years. For years. And I don't love anything about my hair. To me, it just is. One of the things I like about Melania. They say: 'Why don't you change his hairstyle?' [She says:] 'Well, I don't like to change his hairstyle. I like it.' How nice is that, right? You know, Marla would say I want to change your hairstyle."
5) *Your favorite memory?* "Always my parents."
6) *Worst memory?* "The death of my brother, Fred. He was a good guy. He died of alcoholism and he was a great guy. You know, alcohol got him. That was the saddest part in what I've been through."

7) *Best person you've ever met?* "I've always said that the best person is my father, but it's my mother and father. But my father was more directly related to me because we were very business-oriented."

8) *Worst person?* "The list is too long to name. I've met more shit. I've met more scum. There are too many to name. I'd insult too many people by leaving somebody out. I can only say I know so many bad people, it's amazing."

9) *How would you define success?* "I think real success is if you find contentment and happiness at the same time, because they are not necessarily the same words . . . Ultimately, if you can be happy and enjoy your life, that's the ultimate success."

10) *Why does money matter?* "It's only a scorecard. It matters to live. Beyond a certain period and beyond a certain amount of money, it doesn't really matter. Maybe it matters psychologically."

11) *Why does being a billionaire matter to you?* "It doesn't matter . . . No, no. Fact is important to me."

12) *What's your favorite book?* "*The Art of the Deal*, because I made a fortune from it."

13) *Which businessperson do you admire the most?* "I love that question and it's not something that I think about a lot because I don't like to admire anybody. Obviously, a simple answer is Jack Welch."

14) *Which businessperson do you least admire?* "I guess I'd rather not give names because I don't want to embarrass anybody. Interesting questions, by the way."

15) *What's your favorite movie?* "*Citizen Kane* . . . I loved Orson Welles. He was totally fucked up. He was a total mess. But think of his wives. Think of his hits . . . He was like this great genius that after twenty-six, never ever did it. He became totally impossible. He thought everybody was a moron, everybody was this, everybody was that; if he

had a budget, he'd exceed it by twenty times and destroy everything. He became impossible. I loved that."

16) *Favorite music?* "Some of the Beatles' music was so great . . . I think Eminem is great . . . He's the king of that world. He's like the biggest. His [last] name is Mather, M-A-T-H-E-R, like Dan Rather, but he's much smarter. I love Neil Young."

17) *What's your favorite food?* "Meat loaf . . . Oreos . . . Pastas . . . The Atkins Diet is a total fraud, but because of it I eat a lot of steak and I feel better about it. And hamburger and all of that. You know, Atkins, he did hit his head but he was dead before he got to the ground. He exploded. You know that, right?"

18) *When you're sleeping, what's your most frequent dream?* "Always sexual. It's always fucking."

19) *Any recurring nightmares?* "Every once in a while, you have something. But basically, I don't have those sicko deals."

20) *Would you ever do therapy?* "I have found I am not a disbeliever in it. But I look at reports that psychiatrists have by far the highest rate of suicide than anybody—that means they're pretty fucked up, and I don't have the time for it."

21) *Why do you think people are curious about you?* "I have absolutely no idea . . . I don't see in me what other people do. I don't think about it, and I think I don't want to think about it. It's sort of like an athlete or a golf swing, when you start analyzing it too much, you lose it."

A SMALL, SOMEWHAT SECRETIVE, AND VERY INFLUENTIAL LONG ISLAND company called Marketing Evaluations measures and tallies an elusive celebrity barometer known as a Q Score—with Q (meaning "quotient") being a yardstick of an entertainer's appeal and familiarity. Founded in 1964, during roughly the same window of time that birthed the *Celebrity Register* and Boorstin's seminal analysis of the fame game, Marketing Evaluations is a vital cog in the entertainment industry because it quantifies likability. Q Scores often determine which actors get certain movie and TV roles and which do not. Film stars Julia Roberts and Tom Hanks have lofty Q Scores; hence, the thinking goes, their box-office magic.

Out of the 1,750 celebrities Marketing Evaluations studies, the majority are from the television and cable industries, followed by film stars, comedians, and sportscasters. The smallest group the company examines is businesspeople. The average celebrity, on a scale of 0 to 100, has a familiarity rating of 33, a positive Q Score of 16, and a negative Q of 25. Marketing Evaluations said Hanks has had the company's highest ratings for years—a familiarity score of 93, a Q of 55, and a minuscule negative Q of four.[20]

In a study from the winter of 2005, Donald's familiarity score was 80, his Q was 11 and his negative Q a lofty 48. In the same survey, Apple Computer founder Steve Jobs had a familiarity rating of 30, a Q of 12, and a negative Q of 27; Disney CEO Michael Eisner had a familiarity of 55, a Q of 9, and a negative Q of 40. In a Marketing Evaluations survey from the summer of 2003, conducted just before *The Apprentice* debuted, Donald had a familiarity score of 69, a Q of 8, and a negative Q of 49.

"The conclusion from the set of data is that Donald is well known, and mostly not liked," said Steve Levitt, Marketing Evaluations president. "He is despised by some, threatened by some, envied by some, and four times as many don't like him as do like him.

"He could hardly be characterized as a host, but I don't know a better word. A host can have low ratings and the show have a high rating," Levitt added. "I'm old enough to remember Ed Sullivan. He had horrible numbers, but it was always the highest-rated show. It was a talent show that happened to be hosted by somebody that the public didn't like. People liked the program, the concept of the program. It's the totality of the package that the public is interested in."[21]

Many in the entertainment industry bemoan Q Scores, saying they can fail to capture the real appeal of celebrities and instead force producers and programmers to follow homogeneous agendas when handpicking stars. Whether Donald's Q really reflects the totality of his appeal, all of the mojo behind his celebrity, is debatable. He is a magnet for talk show audiences, for a broad swath of aspirational Americans, for white rappers like Eminem, and for African American singers such as Usher.

No less an authority on celebrity than Barbara Walters, talk show doyenne and a seasoned interpreter of the ephemeral, made Donald a perennial regular on her TV shows, as did CNN's gabfester Larry King. Walters attributes Donald's staying power to a number of things, perceived and real.

"First of all he's extremely successful—even when he's down he's up. He's got great charm and charisma and he's very good to friends," she said. "This is a man who tells you what he thinks and I think people respond very strongly to that. He's one of the more original people of our time, and we don't have very many of them. He's got the women and the money and, by the way, he also has great children. He very often says what he thinks even when what he says isn't politically correct and will get him in trouble."

In sum, said Walters: "He takes chances where other people wouldn't and I think people are fascinated by that."[22]

Agreed, said Steve Wynn.

"He's so atypical. He does things that are countercultural. Most of us middle-class Americans are taught not to brag about money and to keep our chins down. Donald walks around with his chin up and he brags about money all the time. What makes it acceptable is that he does it with a wink. You always think he's giggling about it and that he's in on the joke. That's why he's gotten away with it for so long."[23]

Melania?

"He's a great man. He should live forever."[24]

Enduro-celebrities like Donald also snag semi-permanent slots in our imaginations because they are adept at spinning and doling out their own fables. Serializations fascinate an audience much more than one-act shows, and if the story is very good fans will keep coming back for the next chapter. An expertly crafted celebrity myth is outré and engaging, a little spark in an otherwise mundane world. It allows us to play, too. It's fun. And Donald has had more chapters (and threats of Chapter 11s) in his story than all of those hardworking, predictable, plain-vanilla businesspeople. He has had his romances, his expensive toys, his meteoric rise, his meteoric downfall, his buoyant self-promotion, and his determination to be a cultural Phoenix, constantly reborn in different media, industries, and generations.

Fascinated by celebrities, particularly Hollywood stars, Donald claims that he rarely focuses on his own star power. Magazine covers and photographs of Donald plaster the Trump Organization's walls and he maintains an electronic clipping service that alerts him to how often his name appears in the media each day, meeting the 1959 Blackwell-Amory rule that to "judge a man as a celebrity—all you have to do is weigh his press clippings." Donald weighs his own, daily. He also loves to wade in among people who line up in restaurants, on street corners, and at parties, craning their necks for a glimpse of him. He adores grand entrances.

"To be a celebrity is very unique," Donald confided to *Women's Wear Daily*, telling the magazine that maintaining his celebrity status was hard work. "I know a lot of people with money but they could never transform themselves into celebrities. . . . It takes a look . . . a certain personality—not always necessarily even a good personality, but a unique personality."[25]

But really, he tells me, he hasn't a clue.

"I'm not aware of even being a celebrity," he told me. "Melania will say, 'You are the biggest celebrity.' I say: 'Excuse me?' [She says:] 'You are the biggest. There's nobody bigger than you.'"[26]

Mr. Big does admit to a bit of playacting, however. In public, on *The Apprentice,* he yanks the wings off errant worker bees and exiles them from the boardroom. In private, while still capable of tyrannical fits and outbursts, he prides himself on being caring and loyal to his closest employees and business partners. He has plucked a number of them out of relative obscurity, sometimes on only a hunch, and given them serious responsibilities and rewarding jobs.

"He took a risk on me," said Greg Cuneo, a contractor who got his start with Donald's help. "I had nothing. My mother was a schoolteacher and my father was a social worker . . . His show, where he says 'You're fired!' all the time and he comes off heartless—he's not."[27]

True, said Donald.

"People don't realize that about me. They think I'm a fuckin' flamethrower," he said. "Historically, I've had people that stay with me for a long time. I think that's probably counter to the image. The image would be, you know, you're fired. You're fired. You're fired."[28]

And Donald knows that his celebrity endures because, as needed, he wears different masks. "A great actor is an actor who's an actor on the stage and when he leaves the stage he is gonna be a different person than he is on the stage, in his show," he told me.[29]

Donald has been on stage from the moment his first big Manhattan real estate project, the Grand Hyatt, started getting local attention in the late 1970s. In most of the intervening years prior to his *Apprentice* renown, he strutted on stage, sometimes playing Howard Hughes and at other times playing James Bond. Most of the time he played the role he was made for, Donald Trump, and he played it so effectively that his name became synonymous with glitz and money. Thereafter, sentences could be uttered, such as "That's so Trump!"—with a meaning that was perfectly clear.

In front of an audience, any audience, Donald riffed openly about the price of glossy baubles, about business transactions that others kept hush-hush, about politics, sex, family, money, children, foreign policy, money, marriage, sex, sports, money, movies, human frailty, sex, race relations, money, real estate, gossip, music, sex, greed, revenge, money, victory, sex, and . . . his toys. Donald not only let people look at the toys his bank loans bought, he took America on guided tours of his trophy case —the sleek plane, the fabulous homes, the football team, the yacht, the cars, the Manhattan skyscrapers, the helicopters, the hotels, the casinos, the babes.

Often the premier showcase for Donald's wares, and a keystone of his early celebrity, was *Lifestyles of the Rich and Famous*, the champagne-wishes-and-caviar-dreams TV smoochathon that aired from 1984 to 1995. Donald was a *Lifestyles* fixture, and the show, which used wide-angle lenses, gauzy filters, and reverential narration to make celebrityhood even more splendiferous than it already was, wrapped the Trumpster in the robes of a giant.

"Rome wasn't built in a day, but it might have been—and at a handsome profit—if this man lived there: Donald S. Trump," a *Lifestyles* announcer cooed in a 1984 episode, botching the young developer's name. "Even his peers, few that there are, hold him in awe. He puts deals together like other people play Monopoly."

Donald was thirty-eight, slender and boyish, and *Lifestyles* filmed him for that episode at his Trump Tower desk, busily working his telephone.

"I believe in spending extra money," Donald told the camera. "I believe in spending maybe more money than other people would think almost rational." (Author's note: See chapters 5 and 6 for examples of what Donald meant by this.)

Robin Leach, *Lifestyles'* host, producer, and inimitable Cockney carnival barker, helped make his show the first acid trip taken legally and en masse by the American public. And like Mark Burnett twenty years later, Leach had immigrant's antennae that zeroed in on Donald's bionic intersection with the American Dream.

"The Reagans came to the White House and were living what *Dynasty* was projecting on the television screen," said Leach. "Then *Lifestyles* came along and said the reality was even bigger and more fantastic than what you saw on TV or in the White House. And Donald was the biggest symbol of what all that meant. He made it okay to be rich again, to not be ashamed for being rich and brazen.

"In England we don't have the opportunity for achievement that you have in the United States. As an outsider you really appreciate that extraordinary spirit," Leach added. "Donald's arrival was so spot-on that the marketing of him and what he represented came together in a perfect storm."[30]

As Donald aged and mellowed, he still surfed TV's celebrity waves like the Big Kahuna, popping up here, there and everywhere, and sharing his myth and his toys with an ever broadening circle of stargazers.

In 2002 award-winning documentarian Errol Morris put Donald in front of the camera to expound about the movie *Citizen Kane,* part of an aborted project in which Morris asked famous people to analyze films in which they might have starred ("Isn't it possible that in an alternative universe Donald Trump actually starred in *Citizen Kane?*" Morris wondered on his Web site, http://errolmorris.com, where footage of Donald's exposition can be viewed).[31]

"The wealth, the sorrow, the unhappiness, the happiness, just struck lots of different notes," Donald told the camera. "*Citizen Kane* was really about accumulation and at the end of the accumulation you see what happens and it's not necessarily all positive. Not positive."[32]

Donald narrated a pivotal scene from *Citizen Kane*, showing Orson Welles and Ruth Warrick dining together at a table that grows longer as the couple becomes progressively alienated from one another.

"I think you learn in *Kane* that maybe wealth isn't everything, because he had the wealth but he didn't have the happiness," Donald told Morris. "The table getting larger, and larger, and larger, with he and his wife getting further and further apart as he got wealthier and wealthier—perhaps I can understand that. The relationship that he had was not a good one for him. In real life I believe that wealth does in fact isolate you from other people. It's a protective mechanism. You have your guard up much more so than you would if you didn't have wealth."[33]

Most of the time, however, Donald brought much less gravitas to the money game. Usually, like a kid in a candy store, he just wanted to have fun.

Hip-hop mogul Russell Simmons, founder of Rush Communications, recalls vacationing in Mar-a-Lago with his younger brother, the rapper Reverend Run, a member of the Run-DMC trio. While Simmons and the Rev were chillin' in the club's steam room, Donald appeared in the mist, still tightly bound inside his suit and tie, asking if he could get either of them some orange juice.

"The most important thing is that he's a real-life Richie Rich—he shares his toys," Simmons told me. "A lot of rich white guys want to thumb their noses at you and have their cake. They're fucking cake-aholics. That's not Donald.

"The hip-hop community is a branding community and they decide where value is. They love Donald for having the knack for branding himself and everything around him. Mainstream America loves Donald because he's successful and because he enjoys it. He enjoys his money. Most white businessmen who've had the success he's had are more about getting the toys than enjoying the toys. Donald enjoys his toys and he plays with his toys. He's the official bling-bling white man."[34]

And Palm Beach, brought to life by a Gilded Age oil tycoon named Henry Flagler, is the spot where Donald's bling, and the bling-draped women in his life, have often intersected the most memorably.

Flagler was born in 1830, the son of a Presbyterian minister who led Ohio's temperance movement. He had the good fortune to cross paths in Cleveland with John D. Rockefeller, and the two tyros eventually built Standard Oil into the world's first industrial monopoly. In the late 1870s Flagler began wintering in Florida to help his sickly wife convalesce, and after becoming disenchanted with the local offerings he decided to pour part of his oil fortune into Florida hotels and railroads.

Flagler built casinos in all of his hotels and, perhaps to hedge his bets, built chapels on all of his properties as well. St. Augustine's Ponce de Leon Hotel, for example, offered guests both the Bacchus Club and the Memorial Presbyterian Church.[35] In 1888, when Flagler opened a massive new hotel in Palm Beach, the Royal Poinciana, the town became a favorite winter watering hole for East Coast gentry. Large swaths of Florida were inhospitable swampland, traversed by railroads Flagler built to outposts such as Miami and Key West. But Palm Beach was his jewel and in 1902 he built Whitehall, an emblematic industrial age manse that became the center of the town's charity balls and holiday parties.

"I think Palm Beach has always been a place where somebody who had done well in business could settle in and find a place," said John Blades, executive director of the Flagler Museum in Palm Beach. "Newport was tougher and there was a much less flexible society there. Flagler was a self-made man, and he made the character of Palm Beach early on."

If Donald, the beneficiary of Fred's deep pockets, was not exactly self-made, he was certainly sui generis. And his arrival in Palm Beach after he bought Mar-a-Lago might have marked the entry of just another well-heeled, déclassé mogul into the town's cushy embrace. But Palm Beach, like anyplace where slightly older money sniffs at slightly newer money, found itself deeply divided about having this new species of businessman, this *Homo outrageicus*, as a resident.

"It seems to me there are two groups: There are those who like the celebrity and the high-tone kind of affair, and there are those who are more understated, and which Palm Beach has a longer history of," said Blades. "You could find some people very upset about Trump being here, and some who think it's just fine. He has his own way of doing things, and it's usually not based on trying to fit in."[36]

Donald's wives were integral to his peculiar and particular brand of celebrity, helping to define New York pop culture in the 1980s and '90s and assuring the Trumpster of safe passage, in perpetuity, aboard *The National Enquirer* and *People*. His first two marriages, to Ivana and Marla, were enveloped in the sort of *Peyton*

Place histrionics that would have left lesser mortals irretrievably shell-shocked. But for all of the embarrassing, louche turns that Donald's marriages and divorces took (including odd revelations like a book of Adolf Hitler's writings he kept by his bedside[37]), there was a large and needy part of him that thrived on the loopy, steamy attention his romances generated. Besides, Donald had bolted rather unique emotional Teflon to his psyche long before the tabloids began hurling scandal and gossip his way.

"You know, it really doesn't matter what they write as long as you've got a young and beautiful piece of ass," he told a reporter.[38]

And lo and behold, fifteen years after swishing and swashing through liaisons and high-end carping that made *The Honeymooners* seem like a field trip, Donald married Melania, an engaging, babe-alicious model twenty-seven years his junior. Melania and Donald considered each other soul mates and their wedding was the talk of Palm Beach and Manhattan, praised for its understated elegance. Yes, that's right, Donald's journey gets somewhat unpredictable, doesn't it?

Billionaire arm candy is as old as the Medicis, but by the time moguls began upping the ante in the 1980s in terms of how openly they prowled for young lovelies, a willingness to drop the pretense of marriage as anything more than a property transfer was a hallmark of how both men and women partook of the Fifth Avenue to Worth Avenue dating game.

People laid it all squarely on the line in an article penned at the height of Donald's divorce battle with Ivana and the revelation of his romance with Marla.

"Billionaires, or near-billionaires, are a dollar a dozen these days, and anyone—we mean anyone—who wants to marry one has a chance," *People* theorized. "Successful billionaire hunters share certain traits, such as statuesque presence, shameless charm, small-town or exotic backgrounds—and enough chutzpah to persist even if their prey is married. . . . For their part, the billionaires are attracted to their opposites. Bores want bewitchers. Shrimps fall for amazons. Fatties want beanpoles. And the haves frequently seek out the have-nots.

"Once captured, a billionaire must be nurtured. The traditional maintenance plan consists of building or renovating multimillion-dollar homes, throwing million-dollar parties, sending thoughtful gifts, keeping up spa-induced, couture-enhanced appearances and deflecting criticism by generously supporting charities," *People* continued. "In the end, even if the relationship does not work out—and many don't—a billionaire's ex has gained cash, prizes and entry into society."[39]

Among those the magazine identified as the most prominent practitioners of early 1990s billionaire snagging were Georgette Mosbacher, Gayfryd Steinberg, Carolyne Roehm, and Mercedes Bass—whose combined exploits drew nary a scintilla of the attention that swept up Donald's courtiers. For his part, Donald didn't give *People*'s how-to guide much weight.

"I happen to believe that unless a woman is a prostitute or close, you can't sleep with a guy's money," he told me. "You can usually tell a woman, 'There's a guy over there, he's an unattractive guy but he's very rich. Go out with him.' You know what? They go, they try, but ultimately it can't work. They still have to be attracted to him."[40]

Money, unfortunately, became the focal point of Donald's first two marriages, notably in the divorce mess with Ivana and a prenuptial tussle with Marla. Donald shared his toys, but when it came to cash—cold, hard cash—his purse strings tightened. He had never been an active or particularly generous philanthropist, and he circled his wives with a wariness of their *People*-perfect designs on his bank account.

Both he and Ivana said their fifteen-year marriage unwound in 1990 because they had drifted apart, their primary bond becoming business rather than pleasure. Ivana, capable of being just as steely as Donald, said the avalanche of publicity surrounding their marriage was something to which she adapted.

"Once you're in the public eye, unless you go to Australia with your head in the sand for months or years, maybe people will stop talking about you. But you come back and it's all over again," she told me, brandishing the world's most imitated Czech accent. "Once you are in that, you are in that. I don't enjoy it or I don't dislike it; it has both its advantages and its disadvantages.

"You don't have much of the privacy, but again you learn how to protect your privacy. I feel many of my friends which are in spotlight and they have a new boyfriend and they go for opening of the ballet season—I mean, what they thinking? Of course there will be reporters up there and they're going to catch them. You know, the husband is going to freak out. If you want to have the privacy, you just have the privacy, it's not that hard. It's common sense."[41]

Ivana reinvented herself as a novelist after her divorce and tapped her expertise to write a column for *Divorce* magazine. She is currently developing a small real estate project and producing her own reality TV show, titled *Ivana Young Man*. And she believes that her marriage to Donald will prove to be his most enduring.

"We had three children and we definitely had a relationship. We were very good business partners and maybe the business took over and it became, you know, just a business partnership," she said in early 2005. "But we were together for a long, long time. Donald was married to Marla for one year—whatever he calls it— and with Melania he's married for two months. We were together for fifteen years. Maybe after fifteen years the relationship is going to change in all of the day-to-day relationship rather than the hot, steaming sex life.

"I don't regret anything. For me, out of adversity emerged opportunity," she added. "Boy, oh boy do I have a ball now . . . Some women, they get so different and they go and they just dwell on the past. I never looking past. Past is done and over for everybody."[42]

Donald is equally philosophical.

"Sadly, you grow away from people," he said of Ivana. "And I just grew away from her. It wasn't her fault. I didn't leave her because of Marla. I didn't leave her for Marla. I probably should have left years earlier."[43]

The first time I interviewed Donald in his office, in 1996, he had a life-size, cardboard cutout of Marla Maples in a bikini standing against the windows behind his desk, overlooking Central Park. As I sat down across from him he gestured toward the cutout, grinned devilishly, and raised his eyebrows in a *hubba-hubba, can-you-believe-she's-mine, whoa-ho* sort of way.

Donald and Marla met in 1985 and became involved two years later, when he was forty-one and she was twenty-four. They churned through the gossip mill in 1990, were married at the Plaza Hotel in 1993 in front of a thousand guests including Howard Stern, Rosie O'Donnell, and O. J. Simpson, and they divorced in 1997.[44] Donald told me he hated the media's coverage of the wedding, which he said was overly cartoonish in its portrayal of the occasion.

Still, the couple gave the media ample reason to sometimes think in terms of the funny pages. When ABC television correspondent Nancy Collins interviewed them at Mar-a-Lago for a show that aired just a few months after they were married, the Trumps offered viewers an up-close-and-personal glimpse of the intimate ties that bound them:

Marla: "Everyone around Donald was, like, 'You've got to get a pre-nuptial!' And Donald knew how I felt about it, which was that, 'Please don't talk to me about it. I've stuck by you through everything. Don't even offend me by'—you know—you know, 'You know I love you.'"

Donald: "I hate the concept of a pre-nuptial agreement because it basically says, 'If and when you get divorced, this is what you're going to get.' And there's something very bad about that. But I think it's a modern-day necessity."

Marla: "I mean, I really felt that it was very offensive to both of us. And he'd say, 'You know, you're right, but what am I supposed to do?'"

Donald: "Well, Marla hates it, doesn't want to sign it. Ultimately, she has to sign it, just from my standpoint."

Marla: "So I said, 'Whatever you need for your bankers, for, for your associates, I'll sign that. Let's just not call it a pre-nuptial and

let's not put a dollar amount on what happens once we're divorced.'
Once we're divorced, right? I mean, that's the way you start thinking."

Collins [voice-over]: "In the end, they made a deal. Reports had
her asking for $25 million, but he negotiated her down to a mere
million dollars." [interviewing] "It looks a little . . ."

Donald: "Cheap?"

Collins: "Yeah. It looks cheap."

Donald: "Yeah, it's—you mean, the amount of money?"

Collins: "Well, the amount of money and the fact that you . . ."

Donald: "Not so bad. Somebody gets married and it doesn't
work out, you get a million bucks. I mean, you know . . ."

Marla: "You shouldn't be able to pay a price and be able to walk
away. You make a commitment between yourselves and God and,
and you should not be able to just, like, write a little check, 'See
you later.' "

Donald: "It's, it's a lousy thing. I hate the concept, but it's totally necessary. And I think a million dollars is a lot of money . . . I
guess I look at everything like a deal. I mean, you know, it's just
one of those things."

Marla: "Well, everything's a deal. We, we have to work on separating his business from his personal. You know, we both have to
sometimes stop and say, 'Is this business or is this us?' Because there
is a difference."

Donald: "I built this empire and I did it by myself. Nobody did
it for me—not Ivana, not Marla—nobody. And I think that because
somebody marries somebody that built something huge doesn't
necessarily mean that just because they get a divorce that they
should end up, you know, like the Queen of Sheba."[45]

Although Donald didn't have an "empire" or much money in
1994, he was already semi-aware that his marriage to Marla might
be doomed. Among other thoughts, the struggling debtor left Nancy
with a candid confession about the burdens of being a modern
Svengali.

"I create stars. I love creating stars. And, to a certain extent, I've done that with Ivana. To a certain extent, I've done that with Marla," Donald said. "And I like that. I mean, I've really given a lot of women great opportunity. Unfortunately, after they're a star, the fun is over for me. It's like a creation process. It's almost like creating a building. It's pretty sad."[46]

Though Donald frequently said he left Marla because he was bored (including on the day he married her), Marla had a different take.

"I can't believe he would say it was boring, because we were always differing on so many things," she told me. "I kept hoping we could have a little home in the country where we could raise our child. I was probably not the best wife I could have been because I was focused on being the best mother I could be."[47]

Donald may be many things, but a husband who settles down with the wife and kids in a country house he is not.

After the divorce, Marla eventually moved to California with the couple's young daughter and remained active as an actor and producer. She lost the pre-nup fracas, however, departing with $1 million and $8,333 a month in child support when her marriage ended.[48] Donald briefly refused to fork over some of the money after Marla told an interviewer, in the midst of his 2000 White House bid, that the developer was an "ego-driven attention addict unfit to run for president."[49]

Donald said that leaving Marla, and finding Melania in 1998, when he was fifty-two and she was twenty-five, gave him room to breathe. Melania, born in Slovenia, had made her way to New York via Milan and Paris before Donald hired her to work for his modeling agency.

"Marla used to use that expression, 'You have to work at a relationship.' And I used to hate that expression," he told me. "My parents were married sixty-three years and they didn't come home and work. I always felt that if you have to work at a relationship that the relationship is not going to work. Melania and I have the easiest relationship."[50]

Donald and Melania's chemistry became apparent during a radio interview with Howard Stern during the 2000 White House race. The couple, confiding to Stern and his audience that Melania was seated naked next to Donald in their Trump Tower triplex, waxed poetic about the parameters of their sex life. Donald also said that Melania had all the makings of a great first lady.[51]

"Howard, you look and you say, 'How can something be so beautiful?'" Donald said of Melania. "For a presidential candidate, I'll tell you this, for a presidential candidate, I have the best time."[52]

But the Reform Party found their candidate's radio appearance a bit discomfiting.

"The very first principle of the Reform Party is to set the highest ethical standards for the White House and Congress, not the most base, crass attempt to appeal to the lowest common denominator," said party chairman Russ Verney.[53]

Melania said she actually wasn't naked next to Donald during Stern's interview. "What else than to joke on the Howard Stern show!" she told me. "We were laughing the entire time but you can't see that in print. And it was Donald saying those things, not me."[54]

While Donald's presidential run soon fizzled, his relationship with Melania eventually led to 2005 nuptials in Palm Beach that easily eclipsed Prince Charles's marriage to Camilla Parker Bowles as the wedding of the year. Ever aware of layering another chapter onto his celebrity story, and making a quick buck in the process, Donald wanted to sell NBC exclusive rights to broadcast his wedding for $2.5 million. Melania talked him out of the idea. Instead, she went for class—and got it. *Vogue* featured Melania and her satin Dior wedding gown on its February cover. Guests at her Mar-a-Lago reception sat at long, lace-draped tables piled with gardenias, hydrangeas, peonies, and roses. Cristal flowed, and a five-foot Grand Marnier wedding cake covered in white roses was served.[55]

"I'm completely different personality from the first one and completely different personality from the second one," Melania said of her predecessors. "If you marry someone with as big a personality as Donald you have to make sure to always be yourself. I don't think he had that before and lots of people say he's the most happy and the most comfortable now."[56]

Donald later told me how proud he was to have the wedding in Palm Beach and at Mar-a-Lago. "It's considered the greatest or top two or three houses in America, in all of North America," he said. "This is a painting. This isn't a house. This isn't a real estate deal. This is really a painting; it's a piece of art."[57] (Author's note: Donald invokes his late-'80s deal language! It's not about money, it's all about art!)

Donald also took pleasure and comfort in the idea that regardless of how Palm Beach felt about him, his wife had arrived.

"She has a base, if she wants to, to be a great and prestigious woman," he said. "There are young women in Palm Beach that totally respect and admire Melania for her beauty, for her style, for her grace, for her elegance. And if she wanted to be, she could be a major force. If she wanted to do that—I'm not sure if she does and I couldn't care less. You know, my attitude on that stuff is sort of like: *Bullshit, who cares?*"

TrumpQuiz #9

This is the second of two essay exams in this chapter. Answer them artfully and you will master the craft of billionaire-dom. Remember to see how your responses match up with those of a famous New York real estate developer.[58] Penmanship and vocabulary still count:

1) *How would you describe the role of women in your life?*
"Vital and essential. Without women, there is nothing.

Vital. It's all about women, you know. It's all about women. Totally important."

2) *Do you believe in Viagra?* "I'll tell you what. I believe in it 100 percent. Fortunately, I have never used it. I don't need it. But I've always said to friends of mine, if you need Viagra, it's very possible that you are with the wrong woman."

3) *Why are pre-nuptial agreements important?* "Pre-nups are important for the obvious reason. Anybody of wealth or even modest wealth who doesn't have a prenuptial agreement is mentally retarded, okay?"

4) *What do children mean to you?* "A lot . . . You've got to have them, man. You know, it keeps you going. I have good kids, so it makes it a little easier. It keeps the whole wheel going."

5) *What's the definition of a good father?* "The ultimate definition is somebody whose children really love them . . . If the kids love the parents, that's on the way to being a good definition."

6) *What is America?* "I think America has changed a lot in the last four years. I think America went from a country of openness and somewhat complacent and free, to a country that sadly is perceived around the world as a bully. America is a lot different place today than it was four years ago . . . We could have been a country where the world embraced us. And instead, the world hates us. Is that making sense?"

7) *What is the American Dream?* "The American Dream is at least perceived as what I have . . . I think the real dream, whether it's the American dream or otherwise, is just happiness. You can create something where you are happy with yourself."

8) *What do you think of the recent wave of corporate scandals?* "To me the most interesting one of all, by far, is [for-

mer AIG chairman] Hank "The Scum" Greenberg. Hank Greenberg I've known, and he's scum. He's a bad guy . . . And now it turns out, shockingly, that he was a crook, perhaps."

9) *Did you get stoned in college?* "No, I have never had a drug in my life."

10) *Do you believe in God?* "Yes. There has to be a reason we are here. What are we doing? You know there is an expression: 'Life is what you do while you're waiting to die.' . . . There has to be a reason that we're going through this. There has to be a reason for everything. I do believe in God. I think there just has to be something that's far greater than us."

11) *Have you ever cried, as an adult?* "I don't believe in crying. For whatever reason, I'm just not a crier. The closest I came was when my mother and father died. It's just not my thing. I have nothing against it when someone cries, but when I see a man cry I view it as a weakness. I don't like seeing men cry. I'll give you an example. I never met John Gotti, I know nothing about John Gotti, but he went through years of trials. He sat with a stone face. He said fuck you. In other words, tough."

12) *Do you think Larry King sucks up to you too much?* "I hope so . . . I get his highest ratings."

13) *What's your favorite Bond movie?* "Goldfinger. I thought Goldfinger was just a great character. To me he was the best of all the characters. Semi-believable."

14) *Do you ever think of yourself as Bond-like?* "A lot of people do, I don't. Other people do."

15) *If Donald Trump didn't exist, would we have to invent him?* "No. The world will get along just fine . . . You see people that are very important—they go and the world continues to go along."

CHAPTER EIGHT

TRUMPSPIN

I see myself as a very honest guy stationed in a very corrupt world.[1]
—DONALD TRUMP

E VERY SPRING THOUSANDS OF INVESTORS TREK TO OMAHA TO PARTAKE IN the "Capitalist Woodstock," a sprawling, financial lovefest featuring Berkshire Hathaway Chairman Warren Buffett, a legendary investor who has spent decades beating stock market averages and making his long-term shareholders vastly wealthy (a $10,000 investment with Buffett in 1956 would, by 2005, be worth about $350 million).

As they have done for years, Buffett, who is seventy-four, and his longtime compadre, Berkshire Vice Chairman Charles Munger, eighty-one, sit for several hours with their shareholders during the company's annual meeting and patiently field questions from the worlds of finance (what about long-term bonds? what about housing prices? what about those nagging insurance investigations?); stocks (what about Coca-Cola? what about Gillette?); management (how do you motivate employees and managers? how do you select which companies to buy?); and public policy (what about education? what about nuclear war?).

In the spring of 2005, the meeting convenes in Omaha's Qwest Center, an indoor sports arena and concert venue on North Tenth Street that seats about seventeen thousand people. The stadium is packed to the rafters, and attendees have come for dollops of market wisdom and business advice that Buffett ladles with candor, humor, and unusual insight—his version of *The Apprentice*, live, unedited, and with a decidedly different philosophical bent than Donald's hit TV show.

Before Buffett and Munger take center stage each year, they screen a short, homemade film that typically spoofs Buffett and some of the previous year's events, while nakedly and good-naturedly promoting a panoply of Berkshire products. This year's main attraction is a send-up of *The Wizard of Oz* called *The Wizard of Omaha*. It features Buffett playing both Dorothy and the Tin Man, joined by Bill Gates as the Scarecrow and Arnold Schwarzenegger as the Cowardly Lion, as the group sets off to see the Wizard, Federal Reserve Chairman Alan Greenspan. Interspersed around the feature are shorter films, including one that begins with a cascade of 2004 newspaper headlines noting that Donald's casinos have filed, yet again, for bankruptcy.

After the ugly headlines fade away, the film cuts to an *Apprentice*-like boardroom where an actor, decked out in a tousled auburn wig and a trademark dark suit and bright tie, sits weeping. "Donald" has come to Omaha! To Omaha! "Donald" and Warren, the yin and yang of American business, are together! But why is "Donald" crying?

Buffett slips consolingly into a chair next to "Donald" and gently drapes his arm across the shoulders of *The Apprentice*'s sorcerer, asking him why he's so distressed.

My casinos are bankrupt, a sobbing "Donald" tells Buffett.

There, there, it happens to everybody, says Buffett.

Has it ever happened to you? asks "Donald."

No, Buffett replies bluntly.

Fade to black.

Donald, of course, has never shed a tear about his casino woes. In fact, in an unflinching and Orwellian maneuver of inimitable dexterity, he simply redefines bankruptcy as he wades single-handedly into the public relations battle surrounding his casino meltdown.

"I don't think it's a failure; it's a success," Donald tells the Associated Press when his casinos filed for bankruptcy protection in late 2004. "It's really just a technical thing."[2]

His thoughts on being the subject of a Buffett film, bankruptcy and all, are also upbeat.

"It's kind of an honor to be included in one of his movies," he tells me. "I'm glad he said [bankruptcy] happens to everybody. Because it does . . . It happens to everybody.

"The only thing bad about it is I get some unsophisticated press that says, 'Trump went into bankruptcy.' A lot of negative shit could have happened but we're saving $100 million a year now and we did it all by the laws of the land. Somehow the B-word [bankruptcy] never caught on very well in this country. But the smartest people in the country call me and say 'How the fuck did you pull that off?' "[3]

Donald also points out that condo sales in Manhattan are soaring and that he's been able to bank $1 billion (in equally good faith, his financial adviser has told me just two weeks earlier that they deposited only $500 million into Trump accounts). Delving into condo sales also gets us away from bankruptcy chatter.

"It's the hottest market in the history of New York," Donald confides. "The condo market is booming."[4]

But Donald, Buffett had $43 billion in cash on hand, all accounted for in publicly available financial statements, and a personal fortune of more than $40 billion, all accounted for in publicly traded stock.

"Yeah, well, he's running a public company and he's, like, a hundred years old," Donald responds. "You know, I'm a fucking smart guy."[5]

Although Donald's business career is marked by early successes overshadowed by later, repeated failures, flirtations with personal bankruptcy, sequential corporate bankruptcies, the squandering of billions of dollars, and the safety cushion of a multimillion-dollar inheritance from his wealthy father, he is prime-time TV's most sought-after and enchanting guru for aspiring entrepreneurs. Donald is the country's premier embodiment of the self-made man.

For more than two decades, Donald has weathered grueling personal and professional vicissitudes by combining an acute marketing sensibility with unvarnished schmaltz. As the P. T. Barnum of the business world, he is a master showman who deploys a shrewd mixture of personal confidence and promotional stunts to maintain his gilded reputation and snare a national following.

"There's something about him that's ever juvenile. It's hard to believe he's a grown-up person who went to college," says Liz Smith, matriarch of New York's gossip columnists and a longtime chronicler of Donald's ups and downs. "He's like a kid, and he's got that brash, narcissistic thing that works for him. He has enormous appeal to the masses because of that.

"He once threatened to buy the *Daily News* so he could have me fired. And yet I still go on liking him, no matter what you or I think about him taste-wise."[6]

By capitalizing on his appeal, Donald, while hardly a successful business operator, is a business promoter nonpareil. And however mixed his record as an entrepreneur, Donald retains center stage by deftly massaging the news media, distracting attention from his business setbacks and doing just about anything to keep himself in the spotlight.

"He's the greatest manipulator of the media there is—he's got a very fertile and creative imagination about how to spin issues, and he's brilliant at turning lemons into lemonade," says Alan Marcus, a business and political consultant who oversaw Donald's public relations activities from 1994 to 2000. "If I ever had a weak company that I wanted to make look strong, I'd hire Donald. Everything that fails he spins into a victory."[7]

IN THE FALL OF 2004 HOWARD RUBENSTEIN, ONE OF MANHATTAN'S MOST prolific and well-regarded public relations gurus, asked Donald to speak at the Public Relations Society of America's fall conference. Rubenstein, a courtly, soft-spoken, and deft information broker, had counseled Fred Trump and Donald, as well as a flock of mayors, senators, corporate titans, entertainers, athletes, financiers, and cultural institutions. And the dean of the public relations community regarded Donald as a master of self-promotion.

"Over the years, I've found Donald to be an absolutely brilliant image maker," Rubenstein told me. "He's been uniquely good in publicity, marketing, and promotion—especially as an individual. He never or rarely uses outside people such as me. I told him once that he better not go into my business or he would drive me out."[8]

So, addressing a crowd of more than four thousand PR specialists in the ballroom of the New York Hilton, Donald told the experts how to do their jobs.

"*Entertainment Tonight* asked me this question: 'Mr. Trump, you're totally brilliant. How brilliant are you?' Now who the hell would put that in an ad, no one would believe it. An ad on *Entertainment Tonight* would cost me like $150,000 for about 22 seconds. If I ever put something like that in an ad, I'd be run out of town," Donald advised. "I've always felt that public relations is much more important than advertising. You pay $100,000 for a full-page ad, and [the readers] don't even look at it. But if they read a story about the genius of Donald Trump, everybody reads every word of it. In one case it costs me nothing, in the other case it costs millions and millions of dollars. If you can do that, you go for it."[9]

Donald told the experts that good PR rescued his sagging business empire in the early 1990s. What was the insider's technique he used to manage this feat? Pay attention. This is important. "I said to the press: Fuck you!"[10] (Well, Donald's PR in the '90s may have salvaged pieces of his '80s image, but the Trump "empire" actually went down the tubes.)

Amid ample, expletive-strewn dishing on his marriages, dating, and pre-nuptial agreements, Donald indulged the PR legions with some of his rules for achieving success (while dispensing little in the way of actual tactical PR advice). A key Trump recommendation was to always anticipate the negative:

"Being a little bit paranoid isn't bad. Being a lot paranoid probably isn't so good, because you have a life to lead," Donald said. "Watch out for people who are even close to you, because in the end, if it's a choice between you and them, they're usually going to choose themselves."

And, he said, never expect anyone, even your own employees, to support you:

"Sad, isn't it? You really have to think of yourself as a one-man show. There are so many examples of men and women who go out and get taken advantage of by their own people. So don't expect anyone to be on your side."

And then Donald appeared to get very candid:

"I'll be honest with you: I think I get the worst press of any human being in the world. I think I get terrible public relations. I can read four pages of a story in *The New York Times* and if there's half of a sentence that says like, my hair is terrible, I look like [crap], I take it very personally. I've gotten tougher through the years. I used to go really crazy. I think I get terrible press—I really do."[11]

Terrible press? Donald, in the guise of frankness, was spinning his audience of spinners. For every one of his critics, Donald had many more acolytes in the media and the public at large during his long samba on the national stage. Even in his darkest days, slumped beneath a mountain of debt, he managed to generate publicity that often emphasized his wily survival skills rather than his pell-mell dissipation of bundles and bundles of money.

"I think his media coverage is great. The media covers him with lots of affection," said Donald's sister Maryanne Barry. "Given all the things he does, I think he gets great publicity. He *is* P. T. Barnum."[12]

Barnum, indeed.

Phineas Taylor Barnum, godfather of the modern age of hot press and self-promotion, was Donald's direct precursor, the man who anticipated the Trumpster more than a century before the Trumpster was born. Long before *The Art of the Deal* and the rest of Donald's extensive literary canon landed in bookstores, Barnum wrote a multivolume 1855 autobiography extolling his own virtues as a promoter and offering readers inside tips on how to polish their images and spread their words. *The Life of P. T. Barnum, Written by Himself* was a best seller by an early master of flim-flam, a book that brought readers inside the mind of the man who gave New Yorkers the American Museum—a freak show populated by the Bearded Lady, General Tom Thumb, the Fejee Mermaid (a mummified monkey's head attached to a dried fish), Siamese twins Eng and Chang, the 161-year-old woman, and singing sensation Jenny Lind (whose talents were peddled by about two dozen reporters whom Barnum paid off to feed stories to the newswires).[13]

Barnum built his riches on lucrative American Museum revenues, an early appreciation of the powers of advertising, and the gimlet-eyed certainty that "the people like to be humbugged" (Barnum, alas, never said suckers were born every minute).[14] Phineas's fortunes also followed an eerily Donald-like path.

"Barnum was everywhere regarded as being 'a made man' and at the head of his business. So he continued for a time, engaging in many new enterprises," *The New York Times* reported in an 1891 obituary. "But, as the years went on, trouble fell upon him, and by unwise speculation . . . he lost every penny he had in the world. Still he did not give up the fight, but by the help of friends, the increase in value of certain real estate owned by him, and the great energy which was ever one of his chief traits, he again commenced in a small way."[15]

Before starting the American Museum, Barnum had worked as a store clerk, newspaper editor, and lottery operator. After he went broke, he reinvented himself yet again, opening a traveling circus based in Brooklyn that bore his name and that he dubbed "The Greatest Show on Earth." Onward and upward.

"By this time it was clear to my mind that my proper position in this busy world was not yet reached," Barnum wrote, once again mystically channeling the arc of Donald's career a century later. "The business for which I was destined and, I believe, made had not yet come to me. I had not found that I was to cater for that insatiate want of human nature—the love of amusement; that I was to make a sensation in two continents, and that fame and fortune awaited me so soon as I should appear in the character of a showman."[16]

A decade after Barnum's circus debuted he merged with James Bailey's road show, and the Barnum & Bailey Circus took the nation by storm. Barnum, after completing his autobiography, penned three more books with very Trumpy titles: *Humbugs of the World*, *Struggles and Triumphs*, and the pièce de résistance, and with a title even more to the point than Donald's own *How to Get Rich*, a tome called *Money Getting*.

Students of the Barnum way all understood that Phineas knew his audience was largely in on his tricks and in on his hype. The audience actually liked being humbugged.[17] Being taken for a ride entertained them. And Barnum's flair for showmanship—he spent a third of his revenues on advertising, aggressively lobbied reporters, circulated a twenty-four-page, self-congratulatory "newspaper" to small towns about a week before his circus arrived there, and sponsored what may have been the first national beauty pageant[18]—provided an early road map of spin that newly forming corporations and the entertainment industry latched on to with zeal, pairing the machinery of modern public relations to the shine of celebrity worship. Public relations became a powerful, and often invisible, force in American life.

Formalized as a twin to the newspaper boom and mass communications, public relations found its epicenter in New York where John D. Rockefeller Sr., architect of the modern corporation, retained the services of the father of corporate PR, Ivy Lee, after the oil magnate was blindsided by an avalanche of critical and sometimes inaccurate articles.

Lee tried to repackage the industrialist as a humane philanthropist, convincing the old man to hand out dimes wherever he went, and in so doing became an important counsel to his son John D. Rockefeller Jr. as well.[19] Lee, whose career later foundered when it was revealed that he did promotional work for the Nazis, advised the Rockefellers to be frank and direct when discussing their business practices with the press—a relief to a family averse to the practice, then common, of bribing reporters for coverage.[20]

Like Barnum, and like Donald, Lee believed in the persuasive force of relentless, blanket media coverage.

"We shall give to the newspapers some kind of story practically every morning and every afternoon," he said of a PR campaign he mounted for the Red Cross in 1918. "We shall have speakers going all over the country giving our story by word of mouth, by lantern slides and pamphlets which will be placed in the seats of the people who attend the speeches."[21]

The game became more complex in the 1920s, when Edward Bernays, a relative of Sigmund Freud, led publicists into new waters by emphasizing psychological research and advocating the use of seemingly objective third-party authorities to sway public opinion. He professionalized PR while also introducing new forms of manipulation, such as establishing bogus front groups to promote the benefits of smoking.

Other seminal PR figures dismissed the idea of disingenuous spinning and positioned themselves as members of the anti-Bernays school. Arthur Page, an in-house public relations adviser to AT&T from the 1920s through the 1940s, embraced the concept of good corporate citizenship and pushed businessmen to be open and honest in their media dealings. But the tension between proponents of Bernays-like manipulation and Page-style transparency became PR's great divide, and where one decided to come down personally in that particular debate was usually determined by the most elusive of qualities: character and integrity.

By the time Donald came on the publicity scene in the 1980s, everyone from nouvelle Hollywood starlets to corporate chieftains was well schooled in the need for in-house PR, outside PR, personal PR, strategic PR—the entire burgeoning kaleidoscope of services available to visitors of PR country.

Donald, however, chose to avail himself of very little of this streamlined machinery. Like Barnum, he was a born huckster. The rhythms, directions, and metronomic requirements of spin existed in his bones. As Rubenstein pointed out, Donald really didn't need a handler because Donald was his very own greatest-show-on-earth.

This explains why, perhaps, Donald's speech that fall day in 2004 to thousands of PR specialists disappointed some of the more sophisticated members of the business. Any PR advisers who came to the Hilton gathering expecting to get new skills for their professional tool kits came away empty-handed. Instead, they were treated to Donald's raz-ma-taz about the nature of success and other bon mots about the magic of young girlfriends and the necessity of cold-blooded skepticism. Some PR folks even felt that Donald's ramblings denigrated their trade.

Paul Holmes, a veteran PR analyst, fully and accurately anticipated the parameters of Donald's performance at the Hilton before Donald even appeared there. Writing in *PR Week,* a trade publication, Holmes forecast how he thought Donald's speech would progress.

"It's possible, I suppose, that Trump's presentation discussed the great value of corporate reputation; the importance of building strong, mutually beneficial relationships with key corporate stakeholders; PR's role in 21st century corporate governance; how globalization will impact corporate PR; how word of mouth is now more credible than advertising and what that means for PR pros—or any one of a dozen important issues that could transform our profession over the next decade," wrote Holmes. "If Trump addressed these issues with a level of sophistication he hasn't previously demonstrated, I'll gladly eat my words in a future column.

"It's more likely, however, that he spent the allotted time talking about his favorite subject: himself. He will probably talk about his own experiences with PR, which—as far as one can tell—involve generating as much publicity for himself as possible, with little regard for whether the publicity is positive or negative," he added. "I'm not sure what the leadership of the [PR industry] saw in Trump that led them to believe that he could impart great wisdom and insight on the subject of strategic PR. But to me it looks as if [they] went for the sizzle rather than the steak—and, in so doing, simply perpetuated misconceptions about our business."[22]

Holmes was right. Holmes was also wrong. Donald, as Holmes astutely surmised, gave little practical assistance to the PR specialists at the Hilton. And Donald, as always, rambled on about himself. But all of this didn't mean Donald had nothing meaningful to say about spin, about straightforward public relations, or about how to efficiently stoke and stroke the media.

Donald, consciously or unconsciously, simply did not want to say anything of real value or consequence to his Hilton audience. Why should the wizard have pulled back the curtain cloaking the bells and whistles that make Oz hum? Why should Donald have told anyone anything about how he managed his image? It wasn't in his self-interest to let people in on his trade secrets.

Although Donald gave little of practical value to his PR audience, he has branded and promoted himself in ways more calculating and effective than his Hilton speech suggested. Donald's marketing talents are grounded in an actor's disciplined ability to always hit his mark, on cue, and an unwavering commitment to staying on message (the message being: Trump = Success, and Trump = Glamour).

Having traveled this far through TrumpNation, we owe it to
ourselves to dig a little deeper into how Donald hustles. So, forth-
with, a recipe for "Spin Soufflé à la Trump" from a survivor's cookbook as it might have been written by one of the world's premier
gourmands of hype.

Step One: Manage the Story

In early 2004 Donald's Atlantic City casino holdings, having already been miraculously resurrected once in the mid-1990s, were
again hemorrhaging cash and teetering on bankruptcy. As competitors in Atlantic City spruced up and expanded their properties,
Donald's casino group, Trump Hotels & Casino Resorts, withered.
Donald's casinos never earned a penny of profit in any year since going public in the mid-'90s, and the operations were smothered beneath about $1.8 billion in debt that made upgrading or expanding
them impossible.

Things had gotten so dicey that Donald, who routinely ex-
tracted millions of dollars in management fees and tolled his casinos to help pay the salaries of pilots who flew his personal jet, did
not take home a bonus in 2003.

Despite the sorry state of affairs in casinoland, Donald had renewed his standing as a business icon via his star turn on *The Apprentice,* which had catapulted up television's ratings ladder into
a full-fledged hit. Two days after his book *How to Get Rich* debuted, it rose to tenth place on Amazon.com's best-seller list by
offering Trump fans indispensable nuggets of advice such as Business Rule No. 1: "If you don't tell people about your success, they
probably won't know about it." Donald even herded his young
TV apprentices into what he described as "the number one hotel"
in Atlantic City, the Trump Taj Mahal, where they were given the
thankless job of luring gamblers into the fraying, warehouse-size
casino.

But Donald's investors were restless, and talk was in the air of forcing the developer's casinos into bankruptcy so bondholders could recoup some of their funds and find a new manager to replace him. In response, Donald distanced himself from any personal financial liability that might result from his casinos' demise—even though he was chairman and chief executive of a company that bore his name and used his initials, DJT, as its ticker symbol on the New York Stock Exchange.

"This has nothing to do with me," he told me and my colleague, Eric Dash, in an interview for *The New York Times*. "This has to do with a company in which I'm a major shareholder."[23]

Donald had serious financial skin in the game (though not billions, of course). His company had a market capitalization of about $102 million, making his 49 percent equity stake worth about $50 million. For the latter half of the 1990s and into the first couple of years of the new millennium, that stock represented the single largest pillar of his wealth. Donald, yet again, was toeing a financial high wire. If his casinos wound up bankrupt, his stock would be worth even less—perhaps nothing at all.

No doom and gloom for Donald, though. In February, as the parameters of the bankruptcy story took shape, he crafted a press release announcing that happy days were on their way. A financial bailout that he was hastily trying to arrange with a Wall Street investment bank was touted as a "recapitalization plan," and the release noted that even though bankers planned to remove him as chief executive, the casino was going global! Even though the casinos would remain firmly planted on the New Jersey shore, their proposed new moniker would be Trump International.

In July, as Trump Hotels reported even weaker quarterly financial results and the crisis brought his company closer to bankruptcy, Donald issued a tandem press release about an exciting new endeavor: a proposed sixty-four-story hotel and condo tower that he said would be "the tallest building in Las Vegas."[24] Not one to waste good names, Donald christened the Las Vegas project . . . Trump International.

The PR head fake worked. The following day, more newspaper articles focused on the upbeat prospects of the nebulous Las Vegas proposal rather than on the reality behind the Atlantic City casinos' financial problems. An enterprising reporter with *The Las Vegas Review-Journal* did point out to Donald that his proposed skyscraper would be about 500 feet shorter than the nearby Stratosphere Tower, a hollow concrete mass that housed a thrill ride, restaurant, and observation deck and rose to an impressive 1,149 feet.

How, the reporter wondered, could Donald lay claim to erecting the tallest building in Las Vegas? Come on! Donald was ready for that one. The Stratosphere, he said, was "not a building."[25]

When *The New York Times* asked Donald about the strategic value of issuing a release about new prospects in Las Vegas at the same time that his Atlantic City company posted poor results, Donald said he really didn't know he had done such a thing.

"I think I'm lots less aware of things like that," he said. "But people found that Las Vegas story great, that's true."[26]

But Donald continued to manage the developing bankruptcy story by deploying tandem press releases. A month later, in August, Donald's casino company announced that it was, indeed, going to file for bankruptcy. The same day that he announced the bankruptcy, Donald also disclosed that he had become a haberdasher, unveiling a line of men's suits cut like 1980s power wear and stitched with the Donald Trump logo.

Jeffrey Brody, co-president, with his brother, of Marcraft Apparel, Donald's partner in the suit venture, said looming bankruptcy didn't undo the aspirational pizzazz of the Trump brand. "With Donald Trump, you get one day of bad press and then 20 good days," said Brody. "People can identify with someone who has been through ups and downs."[27]

Brody was spot-on. Donald had been there before. A decade earlier he'd lost control of prized assets in New York like the Plaza Hotel and the West Side Yards because he had stuffed his real estate portfolio with choking amounts of debt. Donald sidestepped personal bankruptcy in the earlier period by tapping Fred's riches and by convincing banks that they needed his participation to spare themselves from getting more deeply ensnared in his real estate problems.

Donald came through the real estate debacle with greatly diminished holdings. The 1997 memoir he penned in the aftermath of his financial dislocation, *Trump: The Art of the Comeback,* offered an example of story management writ large: It portrayed his business meltdown as a rebirth, a reconsideration that the nation's media corps largely parroted in subsequent years.

The 2004 casino drama played out in a similar fashion. After a false start, Donald put the whole leaky mess into bankruptcy in November. By the spring of 2005 the casinos had been restructured in a deal that Donald's representatives negotiated with great savvy. Trump Hotels cut a third of its debt and lowered the interest rate it was paying. For his part, Donald lost control of his board of directors and the company's CEO slot. But he retained the chairman's title, a minority stake in Trump Hotels, and a cozy, $2 million salary. Donald's fat salary came with no strings attached—the welfare-state nature of executive compensation left him with a three-year contract stating, "Mr. Trump shall not be required to devote any fixed amount of time to the performance of his duties."[28]

Whatever Donald dug out of the investors remained tethered to an enterprise with an uncertain future. Trump Hotels also remained a business that had missed out on the upside of the gambling boom, undercut by years of neglect and surrounded by more nimble competitors. By most business standards, the bankruptcy symbolized failure and uncertainty. But the restructuring meant that Donald still had a hand in the game. That, he said, was the real story.

"It's a successful deal," Donald told me. "You'll never write that, but it's a great deal."[29]

Step Two: Control the Dialogue

Although Donald renovated the Wollman Skating Rink in Central Park nearly twenty years ago, and it was hardly the most significant project he oversaw, it remains one of his favorite things to talk about. He continues to take pride in jump-starting a venture that had become mired in a bureaucratic tangle. And by associating himself with the project he continues to give himself more polish as a can-do guy.

But ask Donald about the series of failed deals from the 1980s—the Trump Shuttle, the Plaza Hotel, the USFL, the casinos—and he'll offer single-sentence responses. Press a little farther and he'll just change the subject, often to the Wollman Rink, or to the handsome new golf courses he's opened.

True to form, Donald accentuates the positive. Eliminates the negative. Latches on to the affirmative. And he doesn't mess with Mr. In-Between.

This works. Flooding an interviewer with a torrent of colorful remarks, flattering press clippings, and various other huzzahs related to the projects that he does want to talk about inevitably steers the conversation, and hence the subject matter, in that direction.

On matters personal, Donald jests, expounds, and responds with amusing, disarming candor to almost any question, no matter how intimate. On matters of business and money, candor evaporates. Donald decides what he wants to talk about and then stays immovably on point.

"In his world he's not the most successful, he's not the richest, he doesn't have the most clout in the real estate world, but ever since he came out of Queens he successfully controlled the communications process," said John V. Allen, a senior partner at Lippincott Mercer, a brand management consultancy in New York, who admires Donald's marketing prowess. "He's very rarely defined by other people because he defines himself. He's out there talking so people have to respond to what he's saying."[30]

Going into most interviews, Donald maintains a small list of bullet points in his mind's eye, and he largely hews to those topics regardless of the questions he's asked. After *The New York Times* inquired in early 2004 about how his casino woes might affect his finances, Donald decided to tell anyone in the media who asked that question that his casinos represented only a small percentage of his overall wealth.

"I said it was less than 1 percent of my net worth. It started at less than 2 percent and then the stock went down," Donald told me. "People would say, 'Oh wow, that doesn't mean anything.' That was an important bullet point . . . When people saw that it was less than 2 percent of my net worth, it was like, no big deal . . . Bullet points are very important."[31]

Voilà. Donald said the casinos were a small percentage of his wealth and so it was reported in the press—with the occasional doubter arching an eyebrow.

"Actually, it's hard to know exactly what percent of Trump's net worth is tied to the casino business, because most of Trump's portfolio is in privately held companies that don't report earnings," wrote David Segal in *The Washington Post*. "He's described himself as 'a billionaire many times over,' but who knows? There are skeptics out there who believe Trump has $300 million, tops. And the guy has a reputation for, let's say, shading the news in a light that reflects his enthusiasms."[32]

One thing that went missing from the reporting of Donald's percentages was some quick math. Donald was in the midst of his *I-am-worth-$5-billion-to-$6-billion* phase, but by valuing his casino stake at 1 or 2 percent of his net worth he gave himself a personal treasure chest worth no more than $1.7 billion. Still, such is the hypnotic power of the Trumpster that his verbal billions convince people to stop doing multiplication and division.

"I've had times where I get good press. I've had times when I get bad press. Regardless, it only lasts for a certain period of time. More so for me than for others," Donald allows. "The press is very powerful but it lasts for, both good and bad, lasts for a finite period of time.

"The one thing about the press is that it's fleeting. It's Fleet Street. You know, that's why they called it Fleet Street. You know that, right? . . . I just actually made that up."[33]

Step Three: Be Everywhere, All at Once

From days with Oprah to nights with Larry King, from the pages of *People* to prized gossip column terrain on Page Six of *The New York Post*, from Don Imus's radio show to the cover of *Fortune*—the Trumpster is there.

Donald is also the Energizer Bunny of modern marketing, slapping his name on all that he sees and all that he sells. And however much Donald may spin the dialogue, his persona is reliably and reassuringly unmalleable. Amid Donald's verbal fictions ticks the heart and soul of our outrageous uncle who cheered us up when we were kids by saying the most unpredictable and inflammatory things at family cocktail parties.

"He could be the poster boy for proper brand management. He's consistent, he's simple to understand, and he's heavily marketed," said Allen, the branding consultant. "He's never had to reinvent himself. Who he was in 1986 is who he is in 2004."[34]

Two of Donald's passports to ubiquity are the interview (dispensed en masse and to all comers, especially if they have their own TV show) and the tender morsel of gossip (dispensed with great regularity and to a favored few).

"Despite what you may have heard, I don't love doing interviews," Donald told me. "What do you think when you are making big money? Only an idiot would love going through the whole thing."[35]

It's true. Donald doesn't love doing interviews. He revels and delights in interviews. He thrives on interviews. And one of the main reasons he adores them is that they are a bargain to anyone with an ounce of marketing mojo.

"If I buy the commercial, it costs me $300,000 to $400,000 and nobody watches it because they all go out and get a beer," Donald told me, echoing one of the real tips he shared with the PR folks back at the Hilton. "If I sit down and do the interview, I'm giving a commercial that cost me nothing and everybody is watching because they want to see it."[36]

While Donald has been skewered from time to time in Manhattan's gossip columns, for the most part he is a highly prized anchor of the genre, particularly on Page Six.

"I think Page Six definitely played a role in helping push Donald Trump to the first round of his never-ending whatever. It definitely helped create his first level of celebrity hell," former *Post* gossip columnist Susan Mulcahy told *Vanity Fair*. "I wrote about him a certain amount, but I actually would sit back and be amazed at how often people would write about him in a completely gullible way. He was a great character, but he was full of crap 90 percent of the time."[37]

Donald seconded Mulcahy's motion: "I agree with her 100 percent," he told *Vanity Fair*. In fact, working the rumor mill is so important to Donald that he'll even cut into his busy work schedule to make sure that he's helping turn the wheels.

"Donald will spend more time each day leaking items to Page Six than he will focusing on his business," said Alan Marcus, Donald's former PR adviser. "He likes to surround everybody with his ether."[38]

Richard Johnson, Page Six's resident potentate and an occasional judge in Donald's Miss Universe contests, said the Trumpster is a gossip mainstay because he's a hungry columnist's dream meal.

"He's outspoken, he's quotable, and people ask him about all sorts of unrelated subjects because he says whatever's on his mind," Johnson said. "What more could you ask for? I like Donald because he makes my job easier. He's a character. I don't think there's anyone else like Donald Trump, and it's kind of fun watching him operate."[39]

And Donald loves Page Six just as much as it loves him.

"Page Six is great," he told me. "It's also concise. It's not like you have to read ten thousand words to find out that somebody is having an affair. You read it in fifty words and then you go to another story and another story. It's sort of interesting."[40]

Step Four: Remember to Share

Donald may be the country's first round-the-clock "billionaire," accessible to the public twenty-four hours a day, seven days a week. Donald's fairy-tale world—defined by buildings limned in marble, logos embossed with gold, insignias sketched in brass, easy money, fast cars, and new girlfriends and wives always at the ready—is open to all of us. You just have to close your eyes, click your heels, and whisper: *There's no one like Trump, there's no one like Trump, there's no one like Trump.* Then turn on your TV or open your newspaper. Donald will be there.

"He's one of the greatest choreographers of business and image that the business world has ever seen," said Peter Arnell, an advertising and marketing consultant in Manhattan. Like others in the small, and relatively elite, group of business moguls who are fixtures in the popular imagination, Donald manages to "share his dreams in the public arena," Arnell said, which "allows for an infinite number of people to also revel in that dream."[41]

Donald sprinkles his stardust well beyond fans and followers. He also spreads it liberally among business acquaintances.

"I think the first time I remember seeing Donald was when he lived at Fifth Avenue and I think it was 61st Street—and he had his famous hairdo and my recollection is that he was wearing yellow shoes," said Harvey Miller, a Manhattan attorney who represented Citibank in its debt negotiations with Donald. "I couldn't believe it.

And he parlayed this image of being a great real estate entrepreneur. But I think if you scraped underneath in the '80s, it wasn't there.

"Based upon the image that he built, he capitalized on that to get deeper into the real estate business," Miller added. "Putting his name on things became very important to him. And it added to the legend of 'The Donald.' [Bankers] would write memos about 'The Donald.'"[42]

Donald, the Bling-Bling White Man, fully embraces his role as a dreamweaver. "I think sharing dreams is a positive thing," he said. "People really believe, and it's fact, that if I'm building it's going to be a great building. People, from Europe, from all over the world, will buy without even seeing it."[43]

Donald relishes sharing his worldly goods. Taking me on a tour of his Trump Tower triplex, he pulls me into a bathroom and fingers a blue-onyx wall. His eyes narrow in conspiratorial amazement. The stone sheath on the wall, he whispers, is from a remote mine in "deepest, darkest Africa." Or, I wonder, from a remote warehouse on Long Island.

But Donald shares more than his wares. He also shares his survival instincts, his determination to pull himself up from the mat each and every time he's flattened.

"He doesn't retreat. He doesn't beg. He is very aggressive and engages his adversaries," said Jeffrey Sonnenfeld, an associate dean of the Yale School of Management, who is a frequent critic of Donald's business dealings but respects the tycoon's durability. "He doesn't acknowledge defeat in what would normally be considered a defeat. . . . There is always a new quest that gets people excited about the future."[44]

Donald—courtesy of *The Apprentice,* his voyeuristic openness, and his audience's willing suspension of disbelief about his business life—has defied well-worn maxims about spectacular failures. He got to have a second act.

"The '80s were a great time for me, but the mid-'90s to present are a better time," he told me. "They used to try and put me into the '80s. Like at the beginning of the mid-1990s, they'd say, 'Oh, he was hot. So '80s.' . . . I'm much hotter now. My company is much bigger, stronger. Everything else, I'm on top of everything. I have the top show and all that shit. But it's interesting. I used to hear that a number of years ago. Sort of like: passé, '80s. And now I don't hear that anymore."[45]

But Donald still is the '80s. He dresses like it's the '80s. He chatters like it's the '80s. He plays like it's the '80s. He loves like it's the '80s. Authentically Trumpy, he never changes. Donald is our hot-blooded, walking, talking repository of *Apprentice* Era–Reagan Era–Coolidge Era–Gilded Age mojo. Donald is the once and future wheeler-dealer, reminding us of larger appetites, of the righteousness of chowing down on that fourth or fifth dessert. Spinning like a top, he invites us to hop on for the ride.

Whatever course Donald charts, he's unswerving. And he knows exactly why naysayers can't get with the Trump program.

"They're all jealous people," he says. "They don't have the number one show on television."[46]

TrumpQuiz #10

To spin like a famous billionaire, you should:

1) Pour on the Bernays sauce.
2) Be a Page Boy.
3) Make sure lots of good news hits the wires at the same time as bad news, but say you rarely do this.
4) Show lots of visitors your swank triplex high above Manhattan, but say you rarely do this.
5) Take lots of reporters on your jet, but say you rarely do this.
6) Give reporters inside details about private business deals, but say you rarely do this.
7) Share your innermost thoughts, but say you rarely do this.

8) Belittle Buffett's Billions By Becoming Barnum.
9) Host your own hit TV show.
10) Talk Wollman Skating Rink. Talk golf courses.
11) Stay hungry. Stay Trumpy.
12) Dream the impossible dream.

TRUMPEVERLASTING

Our guest is Donald Trump, who is an ongoing,
endless, forever story, right? You're a forever story.
—LARRY KING, 1990[1]

DONALD IS DRIVING ME SOUTH ALONG THE HUDSON RIVER. WE'RE IN his black Mercedes and we've spent a rainy, late-winter afternoon at a golf course he's building in Westchester. It's an attractive course, but not nearly as spectacular as the new golf club he has under way on the old DeLorean estate in New Jersey horse country.

Donald tells me he's pondering some new career moves.

He says that he's exhausted all of his possibilities for writing nonfiction fiction about getting rich, and he's considering becoming a novelist. His editor at Random House, Jon Karp, suggested the idea. Donald would like to write an updated version of *The Carpetbaggers*, Harold Robbins's soft-core porn take on the life of Howard Hughes. I've never read the book but an online study guide informs me, "Robbins re-creates an adolescent view of the adult world, defining the parameters of power in the imagery of sexuality that is the only arena of power the adolescent mentality can understand."[2] That's heavy. Donald is pondering some heavy stuff.

Earlier in the day he also told me about his plans for making the Miss Universe Pageant, a portion of which he owns, into the world's most dominant beauty show.

"Miss Universe is one of the largest audience in the world because it's all over the world. And Miss America is dead," he tells me. "Because they don't know what they are doing. They have a lot of basic, inherent problems. Number one, they have a talent contest. Nobody cares about the talent. There's only one talent you care about, and that's the look talent. You don't give a shit if a girl can play a violin like the greatest violinist in the world. You want to know what does she look like."[3]

When Donald later finds out that ABC is planning a TV movie about his life, tentatively titled *Ambition*, he threatens to sue the network if its portrayal gets too cheeky. Donald is the star of his own show, nobody else. He even weighs appearing for a brief Broadway run as the rich, WASPy senator in the comedy *La Cage aux Folles*.

As we cruise along in his Mercedes, the windshield wipers thump thumping in the rain, Donald glances over at me from the driver's seat.

"I have one asset that I think nobody else has. And that's that if somebody writes about me badly, I sort of own my own newspaper in a way. Like I went after you on the *Today* show," he tells me. "I do have the ability to fight back in the media. I can say that, 'You, Tim, is not smart. Is a terrible guy.'"

"A total whack job," I suggest, since he's used that one before on the *Today* show.

"Is a fuckin' . . . He loves men. He loves boys."

"I fully anticipate that," I say.

"Oh fuck, I can say that. Nobody else can," Donald continues. "In other words, I'm the only guy who can fight back on an almost even plane. I mean, I'm not saying it's an even plane because you may have an advantage. But I have an advantage, too. Because I'm on television every day."

Donald lists the reasons he decided to cooperate with me.

"Number one, it's going to be an experience for me. Number two, I do enjoy your company. Number three, I want to see if you get it right," he says. "It's almost like a competitive thing with me. I almost wanna see if you can get Trump."

"Why not just blow me off entirely?" I ask.

"Because I'm sort of curious," he says. "And I think you are starting to get me much better than you started to get me when you first came up to my office. And I think you believed some of my competitors who are jealous as shit.

"They have to call me to get a reservation in a restaurant and kiss my ass. And then they'll say bad [things] behind my back."

That explains it.

"I'm not saying this to try to convince you to try to do a good book or bad book," Donald says. "I think people are tired of seeing the negative shit. You know one of the reasons my books sell is because they're positive. People don't want to read about a negative Trump. I really believe that. I think they'll say, 'Fuck that.' And I'm going to attack the shit out of it."[4]

If Donald doesn't like *TrumpNation,* does that mean my pen pal won't send me any more press clippings about himself? I'd miss those. Donald usually annotated the clips in the margins with black ink and exclamation points ("Interesting!" or "See!"). My *New York Times* mailbox was full of letters from Donald, containing everything from news about *The Apprentice*'s ratings and his book sales to copies of advertisements (one for All detergent, with Donald's image superimposed behind the product, bore a helpful note at the top: "Big Bucks!") and magazines containing photos of a buxom, scantily clad Melania. (Donald attached bright yellow Post-Its to the pages featuring Melania; in some shots, Trump Tower's dove has an unusually stern, tough, Trumpy look on her face. She and Donald are doing the Trumpy look together! Joint marketing!)

Donald also sent me copies of his correspondence with enter-tainment bigwigs (an invitation from DreamWorks co-founder Jef-frey Katzenberg to an Oscars party at the Beverly Hills Hotel), and even correspondence with his old political nemesis Ed Koch (thank-ing Donald for offering to contribute to an anthology of stories by "role models such as yourself"; Donald underlines this sentence and scribbles in the margin that it is "Two-faced honesty!").

All this mail will end, I suppose, but Donald will go on.

He's excited about returning to Las Vegas, and another former nemesis, Steve Wynn, can hardly wait to have him.

"I've been encouraging Donald to come to Las Vegas since 2000," Wynn tells me. "He's a value-added person here, who adds to Las Vegas because he's a kinetic promoter and showman. He's a fit here more than anywhere else I think, much better than in New York. All that theatrical promotion and razzmatazz is perfect for Las Vegas. This is a place where we take ourselves less seriously than in New York. It's institutionalized frivolity."[5]

He's building a mammoth skyscraper in Chicago that he says will eventually net him bounteous amounts of dollars, though he is not the primary person financing the project. He would like the building to be the tallest in Chicago, but the city wants something less overbearing, more manageable.

"It's great for Chicago. People don't get it. It's great for Chicago," Donald says, bewildered by a Midwestern insistence that he also honestly account for the actual height of the building —and not add phantom stories as he can in New York when he wants to boost a building's profile. "You know, in Chicago, if you have a floor, it's called, *a floor.*"[6] But he is also philosophical and sensitive, telling me that "when you see pictures of people on fire jumping off the build-ing when the World Trade Center was hit, you think: *This may be hard to rent.*"[7]

In the spirit of Barnum, Donald keeps barnstorming. He partic-ipates in joint appearances in 2005 with motivational guru Tony Robbins and hip-hop honcho Russell Simmons as part of national seminars sponsored by the Learning Annex ("One weekend can make you a millionaire," the Annex promises in ads for the Los Angeles event).

"It's a mega-event," Learning Annex founder Bill Zanker tells *Los Angeles Times* reporter Martin Miller when Donald appears there. "L.A. is responding like wild. Everybody in L.A. is talking about real estate. It's the new aphrodisiac."[8]

Among the courses the Learning Annex offers participants in Donald's event are "The Lazy Way to Create Real Estate Wealth," and "How to 'Quick Turn' Real Estate in Los Angeles with No Money, Credit or Risk." The *Times*'s Miller inquires about Donald's casino bankruptcy.

"It's a very, very strong company," Donald tells the reporter. "Remember, too, it's less than one percent of my net worth."[9]

Donald, a decade after hawking stuffed-crust pizzas on TV with Ivana, returns to his roots. He agrees to be a spokesman for Domino's Pizza when a "cheeseburger pie" cooked up by contestants on *The Apprentice* proves to be popular. "It takes my two favorite foods—pizza and cheeseburgers—and blends them together," Donald attests. "I've tried this product and it's fabulous."[10]

The Art of the Deal, having sold five million hardcover and paperback copies since its publication in 1987, is reissued after *The Apprentice* becomes a hit. Donald's autobiography makes the best-seller lists again.[11] The book is a memento of sorts, a reminder of the halcyon years in the 1980s when Donald was hot for being something he really wasn't: a great businessman. In the new century, *The Apprentice* makes him hot for something he's been his entire life: a character.

And there's nothing wrong with being a character, Donald.

"I'm not just some fifteen-minute guy. I've been around a long time," Donald tells me in the lobby of Trump Tower during one of our last interviews. "Have you heard about my suits? Have you? They're through the roof. Through. The. Roof."[12]

ACKNOWLEDGMENTS

I owe heartfelt thanks to a wide variety of colleagues and friends who, in various and important ways, made it possible for this book to come together. I also want to thank the dozens of people cited in the text and footnotes who provided me with interviews or information, as well as several others who spoke with me on background and asked not to be identified.

The New York Times is a gratifying, challenging place to work, and it's a privilege to write for what has always been, and will continue to be, the finest newspaper in the world. Interest in *TrumpNation* grew out of a number of stories I wrote in 2004 for the *Times* about Donald Trump's casino woes, most of which I reported with a dedicated, sharp-minded young journalist at the paper, Eric Dash. Our first piece landed on the cover of the *Times*'s Sunday business section thanks to the good graces of Jim Impoco, the Sunday pages' dazzling editor. Jim's enthusiasm, story sense, and commitment are rare gifts. Jim and the *Times*'s business editor, Larry Ingrassia, have given me the freedom to rummage around in a wide variety of stories of my own choosing, and I'm deeply grateful to both of them. Gretchen Morgenson, *Times* reporter nonpareil, is an incredibly generous friend and standard-bearer, as is Mike Siconolfi at *The Wall Street Journal*. Bill Keller, the *Times*'s executive editor, has been a stalwart for years, personally and professionally. Andy Rosenthal, the *Times*'s deputy editorial page editor, and Chris Drew, a fellow *Times* reporter, fit the same bill. Tina Brown, Manhattan's magazine goddess, gave astute advice when I was considering this book.

Others at the *Times* with whom I have had the fortune of intersecting on Trump news and other topics include Jill Abramson, Donna Anderson, Jenny Anderson, Charlie Bagli, Lowell Bergman, Walt Bogdanich, Jeff Cane, Diane Ceribelli, Dan Cooreman, John Geddes, Jeff Gerth, Marty Gottlieb, Ken Jaworowski, Joe Kahn, Steve Labaton, Jon Landman, Danielle Mattoon, David McCraw, Steve Myers, Dan Niemi, Fred Norgaard, Cass Peterson, Julia Preston, Matt Purdy, Tom Redburn, Larry Rohter, Jim Schachter, Don Van Natta, and Scott Veale. Glenn Kramon brought me aboard years ago and has been a gentleman, and the *Times*'s resident good soul, ever since. Al Siegal, the *Times*'s style guru, kindly greenlighted this book—but wouldn't approve of how I used the word *greenlight* in this sentence.

Joseph Plambeck, jack-of-all-trades at the *Times,* was my research assistant, and he conducted more than a dozen interviews with insight and wit. The final product would have been lessened without Joe's involvement, instincts, and steady hand.

Andrew Blauner is my agent, and consigliere, extraordinaire. Every writer should be as lucky as I have been to have an agent of Andrew's caliber and character on their side. My editor at Warner Books, Rick Wolff, is a model of support, patience, and good humor. Both Rick and Jamie Raab, the publisher of Warner Books, came after *TrumpNation* with loads of energy and interest, and I can't thank them enough. Emi Battaglia, Bob Castillo, and Jason Pinter at Warner Books were equally gracious. Brent Bowers, one of the most dexterous editors at the *Times,* took time to read my chapters piecemeal. Brent is a gem in every way imaginable, and his fine-tuning, and friendship, are much appreciated.

Dan Heneghan at New Jersey's Casino Control Commission allowed me to try his patience on more than one occasion. At the Trump Organization, Rhona Graff went out of her way repeatedly, always with grace and enviable efficiency. Norma Foerderer, Donald Trump's taskmaster, also helped arrange interviews and appointments. Phyllis Colazzo and Lioudmilla Koudinova in the *Times* photo department patiently walked me through the archives.

Mark and Amy Alexander (heroes), Lynne and Phil Beauregard, John Betterman, Jim Burke, Sonia Cole, Devon Corneal, Lisa Dallos, Paolo Diflorio, Roberta Diflorio, Dave Dillon, Kelley Holland, Ed and Isabelle Latimer, Michelle Madden, Mark McAuliffe, Margaret Mikol, Alex Prud'homme, Amy Goldman Putman, Marion Schwartz, and Michael "The One" White—as well as my brothers and sisters—went out of their way to be exceptional friends over the last year. No surprise, because they're all exceptional people.

My late parents, Arthur and Barbara O'Brien, made everything possible and traveled through their lives with imagination, wit, and honor. Most of all, I would like to thank my two children, Greta and Jeffrey, for being the magic in the whole mix and giving me a sense of purpose. They are remarkable, lovely pals, and I'm fortunate to have both of them in my life. (Greta and Jeffrey: All of the swear words in this book are Donald Trump's.)

REFERENCES

I first covered the Trump businesses in 1990 as a research assistant to Wayne Barrett, when he was writing a Trump biography; from 1996 to 1997 I reported on Donald's casino dealings for my book *Bad Bet*, a social history of gambling in America.

Books

Barrett, Wayne. *Trump*. New York: HarperCollins, 1992.

Blair, Gwenda. *The Trumps*. New York: Touchstone, 2000.

Boorstin, Daniel J. *The Image*. New York: Vintage, 1961.

Browne, Arthur, Dan Collins, and Michael Goodwin. *I Koch*. New York: Dodd, Mead, 1985.

Caro, Robert A. *The Power Broker: Robert Moses and the Fall of New York*. New York: Vintage, 1974.

Chernow, Ron. *Titan: The Life of John D. Rockefeller, Sr*. New York: Random House, 1998.

Cutlip, Scott M. *The Unseen Power: Public Relations*. Hillsdale, NJ: Lawrence Earlbaum Associates, 1994.

Fainstein, Susan S. *The City Builders: Property Development in New York and London, 1980–2000*. Lawrence: University of Kansas Press, 2001.

Gamson, Joshua. *Claims to Fame: Celebrity in Contemporary America*. Berkeley and Los Angeles: University of California Press, 1994.

Griffin, Merv, and David Bender. *Merv*. New York: Simon & Schuster, 2003.

Holt, Douglas B. *How Brands Become Icons*. Cambridge, MA: Harvard Business School Publishing, 2004.

Hurt, Harry. *Lost Tycoon*. New York: W. W. Norton, 1993.

Iacocca, Lee. *Iacocca*. New York: Bantam Books, 1984.

Johnston, David. *Temples of Chance*. New York: Doubleday, 1992.

Koch, Edward I. *Mayor*. New York: Warner Books, 1984.

Kushner, Tony. *Angels in America*. New York: Theater Communications Group, 1995.

Mahon, Gigi. *The Company That Bought the Boardwalk*. New York: Random House, 1980.

Marshall, P. David. *Celebrity and Power*. Minneapolis: University of Minnesota Press, 2004.

Morehouse, Ward. *Inside the Plaza*. New York: Applause Books, 2001.

Newfield, Jack, and Wayne Barrett. *City for Sale*. New York: Harper & Row, 1988.

O'Brien, Timothy L. *Bad Bet*. New York: Times Business/Random House, 1998.

O'Donnell, John R. *Trumped!* New York: Simon & Schuster, 1995.

Patterson, Jerry E. *Fifth Avenue: The Best Address*. New York: Rizzoli, 1998.

Rein, Irving, Philip Kotler, and Martin Stoller. *High Visibility: The Making and Marketing of Professionals into Celebrities*. Lincolnwood, IL: NTC/Contemporary Publishing, 1997.

Shachtman, Tom. *Skyscraper Dreams: The Great Real Estate Dynasties of New York*. Boston: Little, Brown, 1991.

Sternlieb, George, and James W. Hughes. *The Atlantic City Gamble*. Cambridge, MA: Harvard University Press, 1983.

Trump, Donald J. *The Way to the Top*. New York: Crown Business, 2004.

Trump, Donald J., and Kate Bohner. *The Art of the Comeback*. New York: Times Books/Random House, 1997.

Trump, Donald J., and Charles Leerhsen. *Surviving at the Top*. New York: Random House, 1990.

Trump, Donald J., and Meredith McIver. *How to Get Rich*. New York: Random House, 2004.

Trump, Donald J., and Meredith McIver. *Think Like a Billionaire*. New York: Random House, 2004.

Trump Donald J., and Tony Schwartz. *The Art of the Deal*. New York: Warner Books, 1987.

Trump, Donald J., and Dave Shiflett. *The America We Deserve*. Los Angeles: Renaissance Books, 2000.

Documents

Report of the Division of Gaming Enforcement to the Casino Control Commission. *In the Matter of the Joint Petition of Trump Taj Mahal*

Associates Limited Partnership and Trump Hotel Management Corporation for Renewal of Their Casino Licenses. Trenton, NJ, April 5, 1991.
State of New Jersey Casino Control Commission. *Report on the Financial Position of Donald J. Trump.* April 11, 1991.
State of New Jersey, Department of Law, Division of Gaming Enforcement. *Preliminary Report on the Financial Condition of the Donald J. Trump Organization, Post-Restructuring.* Trenton, NJ, 1990.
United States District Court, Southern District of New York. *Mirage Resorts Inc. against Donald J. Trump, et al.* 97 Civ. 6693.

DVD

Universal. *The Apprentice: The Complete First Season.* A Mark Burnett Production in association with Trump Productions LLC, 2004.

Prologue: Smooth Operator

1. CNNMoney, September 23, 2004.
2. Interview, December 1, 2004.
3. Interview, December 1, 2004.
4. Interview, December 1, 2004.
5. Trump, *The Art of the Comeback*, page 176.
6. Interview, December 20, 2004.
7. Interview, January 12, 2005.
8. PR Newswire, January 21, 2005.
9. Associated Press, January 23, 2005.
10. *The New York Times*, September 8, 2004.

One: TrumpTV

1. *The Apprentice: The Complete First Season*, DVD production notes.
2. www.tvtome.com; www.timvp.com/candid.html.
3. *The New York Times Magazine*, January 28, 2001.
4. *Sports Illustrated*, May 12, 2003.
5. *The Apprentice: The Complete First Season*, DVD production notes.
6. *Sports Illustrated*, May 12, 2003.
7. *The Apprentice: The Complete First Season*, DVD production notes.
8. Interview, January 12, 2005.
9. Interview, January 6, 2005.
10. Interview, January 6, 2005.
11. *USA Today*, April 15, 2004.
12. *The Apprentice: The Complete First Season*, Episode One.
13. Interview, January 12, 2005.
14. Interview, December 22, 2004.

15. Interview, December 21, 2004.
16. Ibid.
17. Ibid.
18. *The Apprentice: The Complete First Season,* Episode Three.
19. *The Apprentice: The Complete First Season,* DVD production notes.
20. Ibid.
21. *Today,* September 30, 2004.
22. *The New York Times,* January 2, 2005.
23. *PR Week,* November 1, 2004.
24. Interview, December 21, 2004.
25. Interview, December 22, 2004.
26. Interview, January 12, 2005.
27. Interview, April 22, 2005.
28. *Fortune,* August 23, 2004.
29. *Bloomberg,* January 20, 2005.
30. Interview, August 26, 2004; *The New York Times,* September 8, 2004.
31. *USA Today,* April 15, 2004.
32. www.richmond.com.
33. Interview, December 22, 2004.
34. NBC videotape of pre-season interview.
35. Interview, December 22, 2004.
36. *The New York Times,* September 8, 2004.
37. *The Independent,* December 11, 2004.
38. Associated Press, February 3, 2000; *Esquire,* April 1, 2000; CNN, February 9, 2001; *Time,* April 22, 2002.
39. *Los Angeles Times,* September 6, 2004.
40. www.blogmaverick.com.
41. Ibid.
42. Interview, January 12, 2005.
43. Associated Press, January 18, 2005.
44. *The New York Times,* March 28, 2004.
45. *The Wall Street Journal,* July 27, 2004.
46. Interview, May 11, 2005.
47. www.trump.com/main.htm.
48. www.thesmokinggun/archive/0826041_donald_trump_1.html.
49. Associated Press, December 7, 2004.
50. Interview, January 12, 2005.
51. *Crain's New York Business,* Book of Lists 2005.

52. Interview, December 29, 2004.
53. Interview, December 22, 2004.
54. *The Apprentice: The Complete First Season,* DVD production notes.

Two: TrumpRoots

1. Trump, *Art of the Deal,* pages 69–71.
2. Caro, pages 843, 921.
3. *The New York Times,* August 26, 1980.
4. *Smithsonian Magazine,* October 1999.
5. Interview, January 12, 2005.
6. *The New York Times,* June 26, 1999.
7. Interview, January 12, 2005.
8. Interview, December 28, 2004.
9. Blair, pages 81–93, 116–118.
10. *The New York Times,* June 26, 1999.
11. Trump, *The Art of the Deal,* pages 79–80.
12. Fred Trump biographical information is from the dedication of the Fred C. Trump/William O. Walter Music Center, Congregational Church of Manhasset, April 28, 2002; *The New York Times,* January 2, 2000; Barrett, page 48.
13. Barrett, pages 51–52; Blair, pages 171–172.
14. Barrett, pages 54–58; Blair, pages 175–193.
15. *The New York Times,* September 30, 1961.
16. *The New York Times,* July 5, 1980; Barrett, page 63.
17. Barrett, pages 67–70.
18. Interview, January 12, 2005.
19. Interview, with Maryanne Trump Barry, May 6, 2005.
20. Interview, January 25, 2005.
21. *The New York Times,* August 7, 1983.
22. Ibid.
23. *The Chicago Tribune,* March 12, 1989.
24. Interview, May 6, 2005.
25. *Playboy,* October 1, 2004.
26. Interview, April 24, 2005.
27. Interview, March 21, 2005.
28. Interview, April 18, 2005.
29. Interview, January 12, 2005.
30. *Playboy,* October 1, 2004.

31. Trump, *The Art of the Deal*, page 94.
32. Interview, January 19, 2005.
33. Interview, January 12, 2005.

Three: TrumpCity

1. *The Washington Post*, November 15, 1984.
2. Interview, January 4, 2005.
3. *Time*, September 15, 1975; Felix Rohatyn, speech at Columbia University, February 26, 2003.
4. Interview, January 4, 2005.
5. Trump, *The Art of the Deal*, page 102.
6. *Business Week*, May 26, 1975.
7. Barrett, page 94.
8. Interview, January 14, 2005.
9. Hurt, pages 84–85.
10. *The New York Times*, August 26, 1980.
11. Interview, January 21, 2005.
12. Interview, January 24, 2005.
13. Interview, January 18, 2005.
14. Interview, January 24, 2005.
15. Barrett, page 159.
16. Blair, page 305.
17. *The New York Times*, December 15, 1984.
18. Interview, January 12, 2005.
19. Ibid.
20. *The New York Times*, June 24, 1986.
21. Interview, December 23, 1997.
22. *The New York Times*, June 10, 1990.
23. Interview, January 12, 2005.
24. *The New York Times*, October 16, 1973; July 29, 1973.
25. Barrett, page 88.
26. Trump, *The Art of the Deal*, page 181.
27. Interview, January 12, 2005.
28. Ibid.
29. Interview, January 5, 2005.
30. Interview, March 2, 2005.
31. *The Washington Post*, August 3, 1981.
32. Interview, February 24, 2005.

33. *The New York Times*, October 15, 1982; *Business Week*, July 22, 1985.

34. Interview, January 5, 2005.

35. Interview, December 28, 2004.

36. Interview, January 4, 2005.

37. Interview, January 12, 2005.

38. Interview, February 16, 2005.

39. Interview, January 18, 2005.

Four: TrumpLand

1. www.rockefellergroup.com; *Manhattan Inc.*, January 1990.

2. *Manhattan Inc.*, January 1990.

3. Interview, January 18, 2005.

4. *The Wall Street Journal*, November 15, 1985 (1975 figure adjusted for inflation).

5. *The New York Times*, December 12, 2000.

6. *The New York Times*, July 21, 2004; www.tishmanspeyer.com.

7. Shachtman, page 231.

8. *The New York Times*, April 8, 1984.

9. Interview, January 6, 2005.

10. *The New York Times*, April 8, 1984.

11. *The Washington Post*, November 8, 1983.

12. UPI, November 20, 1983.

13. Associated Press, February 24, 1985.

14. From an interview with Greg Garber, www.thisistheusfl.com/ESPN_20th_Anniversary_USFL.htm.

15. Interview, February 16, 2005.

16. Interview, February 18, 2005.

17. *Bridge News*, June 8, 2000.

18. From an interview with Greg Garber, www.thisistheusfl.com/ESPN_20th_Anniversary_USFL.htm.

19. *Forbes*, November 5, 1984.

20. Interview, February 16, 2005.

21. *The Washington Post*, February, 1985; *The New York Times*, July 1, 1984.

22. *The Toronto Star*, July 31, 1986.

23. Barrett, page 373.

24. Interview, February 16, 2005.

25. UPI, July 18, 1986.

26. Trump, *The Art of the Deal,* page 295.

27. *The Los Angeles Times,* July 30, 1986.

28. Associated Press, May 10, 1987.

29. Letter from Donald J. Trump to Edward I. Koch, May 26, 1987.

30. Interview, January 4, 2005.

31. Letter from Edward I. Koch to Donald J. Trump, May 28, 1987.

32. Interview, January 12, 2005.

33. Ibid.

34. *The Chicago Tribune,* June 28, 1987; UPI, June 3, 1987.

35. *Newsday,* September 11, 1987; *The Seattle Times,* September 19, 1987.

36. *New York Newsday,* November 13, 1988.

37. Trump, *The Art of the Deal,* pages 353–354.

38. *Business Week,* July 20, 1987; *The Wall Street Journal,* June 4, 1990.

39. *The Wall Street Journal,* November 30, 1987.

40. *The Los Angeles Times,* December 20, 1987.

41. Associated Press, October 11, 1990; *The Washington Post,* August 2, 1990.

42. *The Nation,* March 17, 1997; interview with Donald Trump, March 2, 2005.

43. State of New Jersey, *Preliminary Report on the Financial Condition of the Donald J. Trump Organization,* August 13, 1990, pages 98–99.

44. Author interview with confidential source, March 31, 2005.

45. www.fairmont.com.

46. Morehouse, pages 12–13, 24.

47. *The New York Times,* September 25, 1988; *The Washington Post,* April 23, 1991.

48. Trump, *Surviving at the Top,* page 113.

49. *The New York Times,* September 25, 1988.

50. *New York Newsday,* May 6, 1990.

51. Interviews in 2005 with two former Trump Organization executives who requested anonymity.

52. Trump, *Surviving at the Top,* page 130.

53. Interview, January 5, 2004.

54. State of New Jersey, *Preliminary Report on the Financial Condition of the Donald J. Trump Organization,* August 13, 1990, page 95.

55. Associated Press, September 30, 1987; *The Washington Post,* October 1, 1987; www.superyacht.org.

56. *The New York Times,* April 12, 1995; *New York Newsday,* March 29, 1994.

57. *Newsweek,* July 18, 1988; Associated Press, September 30, 1987.

58. *The Washington Post,* October 23, 1988; State of New Jersey, *Preliminary Report on the Financial Condition of the Donald J. Trump Organization,* August 13, 1990, page 101.

59. *The Washington Post,* October 23, 1988.

60. *Fortune,* November 21, 1988.

61. Ibid.

62. Barrett, page 426.

63. *The Boston Globe,* October 23, 1988.

Five: TrumpChips

1. *The New York Times,* June 7, 1990.

2. *Time,* January 16, 1989.

3. Associated Press, August 10, 1989.

4. *New York Newsday,* March 18, 1990.

5. Interview, February 25, 2005.

6. Interview with Steve Wynn, February 25, 2005; interview with Donald Trump, March 1, 2005.

7. O'Brien, pages 84–89.

8. Interview, August 23, 1996.

9. *Fortune,* May 27, 1985.

10. Interview, January 21, 2005.

11. Trump, *The Art of the Deal,* page 197.

12. O'Brien, pages 65–66.

13. American Gaming Association.

14. Interview, April 15, 1996.

15. O'Brien, page 72.

16. Interview, May 1, 1996.

17. Barrett, pages 217, 229–231.

18. Ibid., page 229.

19. FBI memorandum, September 22, 1981, New York (137-19967).

20. Interview, March 4, 2005.

21. *The New York Times,* March 28, 1984; *The Las Vegas Review-Journal,* August 21, 1994.

22. Barrett, page 235; author interview with Trump, May 18, 2005.

23. Author interviews with New Jersey law enforcement officials, 1996, 2004, 2005.

24. Author interviews with confidential sources, 2004, 2005.

25. *The Wall Street Journal,* November 11, 1985.

26. *The Los Angeles Times,* July 28, 1985.

27. State of New Jersey, *Preliminary Report on the Financial Condition of the Donald J. Trump Organization,* August 13, 1990, pages 17, 73.

28. Interview, February 25, 2005.

29. Interview, March 4, 2005.

30. O'Brien, page 83.

31. *Fortune,* July 22, 1996.

32. *New York,* February 16, 1998.

33. *Mirage Resorts Inc. v. Donald Trump, et al.;* 97Civ6693, U.S. District Court, Southern District of New York.

34. *The Las Vegas Review-Journal,* May 30, 1997.

35. O'Brien, page 47.

36. Interview, March 4, 2005.

37. *Forbes,* June 11, 1990; Griffin, page 155.

38. *Life,* August 1988.

39. *People,* December 26, 1988.

40. Griffin, pages 155, 164.

41. *The Los Angeles Times,* July 24, 1988.

42. Interview, March 4, 2005.

43. Ibid.

44. *New York Newsday,* April 12, 1990.

45. O'Donnell, pages 43, 80–82.

46. Ibid., pages 115–117, 152.

47. Ibid., page 124.

48. Interview, April 22, 2005.

49. ABC, *Primetime Live,* March 10, 1994.

50. Hurt, page 149.

51. Interview, April 12, 1996.

52. Interview with Donald Trump, April 23, 2005; the incident was also confirmed by former Trump employees. Tyson's manager, Shelley Finkel, said in a May 17, 2005, interview that he had heard about the incident but could not recall details. Tyson did not respond to an interview request.

53. State of New Jersey, *Preliminary Report on the Financial Condition of the Donald J. Trump Organization,* August 13, 1990, page 39.

54. Interview, March 2, 2005.
55. *The Herald Sun* [Melbourne], May 4, 1991.
56. *New York Newsday,* March 24, 1991.
57. ABC, *Primetime Live,* March 10, 1994.
58. *USA Today,* March 20, 1990; *New York Newsday,* March 24, 1991.
59. *New York Newsday,* March 18, 1990; *CBS News,* April 6, 1990.
60. CNN, July 27, 1990.
61. *The Wall Street Journal,* April 27, 1990; June 4, 1990.
62. *New York Newsday,* April 28, 1990.
63. State of New Jersey, *Preliminary Report on the Financial Condition of the Donald J. Trump Organization,* August 13, 1990, page 107.
64. State of New Jersey, *Report on the Financial Position of Donald J. Trump,* April 11, 1991, page 14.
65. Ibid., page 5.
66. *The Wall Street Journal,* June 27, 1990.
67. State of New Jersey, *Preliminary Report on the Financial Condition of the Donald J. Trump Organization,* August 13, 1990, pages 15–16, 105; State of New Jersey, *Report on the Financial Position of Donald J. Trump,* April 11, 1991, page 6.
68. *New York Newsday,* June 17, 1990.
69. State of New Jersey, *Preliminary Report on the Financial Condition of the Donald J. Trump Organization,* August 13, 1990, page 109.
70. *The New York Times,* April 8, 1990.
71. *The New York Times,* June 7, 1990.
72. *Forbes,* May 14, 1990.

Six: *TrumpBroke*

1. Interview, April 1, 2005; Barry is deceased; Maryanne Trump Barry, Donald's sister and Barry's widow, said she could not recollect the incident. Robert Trump did not respond to interview requests.
2. Author interview with confidential source, March 1, 2005.
3. Interview, August 11, 2004.
4. Interview, February 16, 2005.
5. Interview, March 5, 2005.
6. UPI, August 24, 1983.
7. *The New York Times,* September 28, 1983.
8. *The Washington Post,* August 28, 1982.
9. *The New York Times,* October 11, 1984.
10. Johnston, page 83.

11. Interview, April 1, 2005.

12. Interview, March 28, 2005.

13. *The New York Times,* March 28, 2004.

14. Interview, March 5, 2005.

15. Interview, April 21, 2005.

16. Interview, April 25, 2005.

17. Interview, February 28, 2005.

18. State of New Jersey, *Preliminary Report on the Financial Condition of the Donald J. Trump Organization,* August 13, 1990, page 110.

19. *Playboy,* March 1990.

20. *State of New Jersey, Casino Control Commission, Report on the Financial Position of Donald J. Trump,* April 11, 1991, page 5.

21. New Jersey Division of Gaming Enforcement, *In the Matter of the Joint Petition of Trump Taj Mahal Associates,* April 5, 1991, pages 38, 52.

22. Ibid., pages 58–59.

23. Ibid., page 36.

24. Interview, February 10, 2005.

25. Interview, March 5, 2005.

26. Interview, February 10, 2005.

27. *Playboy,* November 1990.

28. *Playboy,* March 1990.

29. *Playboy,* November 1990.

30. *South China Morning Post,* November 8, 1998.

31. Trump, *Surviving at the Top,* page 149.

32. Ibid., page 30.

33. *The New York Times,* February 1, 1993; Associated Press, October 11, 1990.

34. Interview, March 23, 2005.

35. Interview, March 28, 2005.

36. *The Washington Post,* November 29, 1992.

37. Interview, March 18, 2005.

38. Interview, March 18, 2005.

39. *The Washington Post,* November 29, 1992; Trump, *The Art of the Comeback,* page 24.

40. O'Brien, page 88; *Business Week,* July 31, 1995.

41. Trump, *The Art of the Comeback,* page 13.

42. State of New Jersey, *Preliminary Report on the Financial Condition of the Donald J. Trump Organization,* August 13, 1990, pages 97–98; *The Wall Street Journal,* June 8, 1994.

43. CNN, July 27, 1990.

44. U.S. Department of Housing and Urban Development, Applicant Recipient Information, Hudson Waterfront Associates LP, March 24, 1995; New York State Department of Finance, Assignment of Mortgage, June 30, 1994; *The New York Post,* April 18, 1999; *Fortune,* July 22, 1996.

45. Interviews with former Trump Organization executives; *The New York Times,* June 3, 1998.

46. Interview with former Trump Organization executive, March 31, 2005; Barrett, page 403.

47. State of New Jersey, *Preliminary Report on the Financial Condition of the Donald J. Trump Organization,* August 13, 1990, pages 98–99; *The New York Times,* April 12, 1995.

48. O'Brien, page 280.

49. Ibid.

50. Trump, *Surviving at the Top,* page 101.

51. *The New York Times,* July 26, 1996.

52. *Fortune,* July 22, 1996.

53. Author interview with confidential source, February 28, 2005.

54. *Newsweek,* February 10, 1997.

55. O'Brien, page 88.

56. Ibid., page 82.

57. TheStreet.com, April 4, 1997.

58. *Fortune,* April 3, 2000.

59. *The New York Times,* March 28, 2004.

60. Trump, *The America We Deserve,* acknowledgments.

61. Ibid., page 261.

62. Ibid., pages 36, 286.

63. Interview with Allen Weisselberg, April 21, 2005.

64. Ibid.

65. Interview, April 21, 2005.

66. Ibid.

67. Interview, March 4, 2005.

68. *The Boise Weekly,* January 12, 2005.

Seven: TrumpStyle

1. *Playboy,* March 1990.

2. Trump, *Surviving at the Top,* page 55

3. Interview, March 5, 2005.

4. Ibid.

5. *Interview with Donald Trump,* March 6, 2005; *Time,* April 27, 1998: Combs did not respond to an interview request.

6. Interview, March 5, 2005.

7. Ibid.

8. Boorstin, page 58.

9. Boorstin, page 65.

10. *The New York Times,* December 4, 1983.

11. Iacocca, pages xvi–xvii.

12. *Business Week,* June 23, 1986.

13. *Business Month,* July 1990; *Fortune,* November 16, 1992.

14. *Business Week,* June 23, 1986.

15. *The Wall Street Journal,* April 11, 1996.

16. *The Wall Street Journal,* March 28, 1988.

17. Interview, April 8, 2005.

18. *Fortune,* April 3, 2000.

19. Interview, March 5, 2005.

20. All data from Marketing Evaluations interview, March 28, 2005.

21. Interview, March 28, 2005.

22. Interview, February 24, 2005.

23. Interview, February 25, 2005.

24. ABC, *Barbara Walters Special,* December 8, 2004.

25. *WWD,* February 25, 2005.

26. Interview, March 16, 2005.

27. Interview, February 16, 2005.

28. Interview, February 16, 2005.

29. Interview, March 5, 2005.

30. Interview, March 29, 2005.

31. http://errolmorris.com/content/projects_donald.html.

32. Ibid.

33. Ibid.

34. Interview, March 14, 2005.

35. O'Brien, page 287; Chernow, pages 106–107.

36. Interview, March 28, 2005.

37. UPI, August 9, 1990.

38. *New York Newsday,* July 2, 1991.

39. *People,* May 7, 1990.

40. Interview, March 28, 2005.

41. Interview, April 22, 2005.

42. Ibid.
43. Interview, April 23, 2005.
46. *The New York Times,* May 3, 1997.
45. ABC, *Primetime Live,* March 10, 1994.
46. Ibid.
47. Interview, April 29, 2005.
48. Details from a person who has seen the agreement.
49. Ibid.
50. Interview, April 23, 2005.
51. *The New York Daily News,* January 11, 2000.
52. *The New York Post,* November 10, 1999.
53. *The New York Post,* November 10, 1999.
54. Interview, April 27, 2005.
55. *The Washington Post,* January 30, 2005.
56. Interview, April 27, 2005.
57. Interview, March 6, 2005.
58. Interviews, March 6, 2005; April 26, 2005.

Eight: TrumpSpin

1. *The Washington Times,* April 18, 1995.
2. Associated Press, November 22, 2004.
3. Interview, May 5, 2005.
4. Ibid.
5. Ibid.
6. Interview, August 26, 2004.
7. Interview, August 23, 2004.
8. Interview, September 2, 2004.
9. PRSA press release, October 24, 2004.
10. *Fast Company,* January 2005.
11. PRSA press release, October 24, 2004.
12. Interview, May 6, 2005.
13. Gamson, page 21; *Direct Marketing,* September 1, 2000.
14. *The Independent,* February 15, 1990.
15. *The New York Times,* April 8, 1891.
16. Ibid.
17. See Boorstein's explication in *The Image.*
18. *Direct Marketing,* March 1, 2000.
19. Cutlip, page 58.

20. Chernow, pages 525–526.
21. Cutlip, page 69.
22. *PR Week,* October 25, 2004.
23. *The New York Times,* March 28, 2004.
24. Associated Press, July 29, 2004.
25. *The Las Vegas Review-Journal,* July 30, 2004.
26. *The New York Times,* September 8, 2004.
27. Ibid.
28. *The Atlantic City Press,* May 15, 2005.
29. Interview, May 5, 2005.
30. Interview, August 24, 2004.
31. Interview, March 28, 2005.
32. *The Washington Post,* September 9, 2004.
33. Interview, March 28, 2005.
34. Interview, August 24, 2004.
35. Interview, March 28, 2005.
36. Ibid.
37. *Vanity Fair,* December 2004.
38. Interview, August 23, 2004.
39. Interview, April 22, 2005.
40. Interview, March 28, 2004.
41. Interview, August 24, 2004; *The New York Times,* September 8, 2004.
42. Interview, March 23, 2005.
43. Interview, September 2, 2004.
44. *The New York Times,* September 8, 2004.
45. Interview, February 16, 2005.
46. *The New York Times,* September 8, 2004.

Epilogue: TrumpEverlasting

1. CNN, July 27, 1990.
2. http://www.bookrags.com/shortguide-carpetbaggers.
3. Interview, February 16, 2005.
4. Ibid.
5. Interview, February 25, 2005.
6. Interview, February 16, 2005.
7. Interview, May 11, 2005.

8. *The Los Angeles Times,* April 25, 2005.
9. Ibid.
10. CNN, April 1, 2005.
11. Interview with Random House editor Jonathan Karp, March 2, 2005.
12. Interview, April 23, 2005.